Can Families Survive In Pagan America?

by Samuel H. Dresner

Huntington House Publishers

Huntington House Publishers
P.O. Box 53788
Lafayette, Louisiana 70505

Library of Congress Card Catalog Number 94-72828
ISBN 1-56384-080-4

Contents

Introduction

The debate that underlies the tensions in American society today has been festering all along. It is between those who saw America as a "city upon a hill," as John Winthrop put it, striving for nobility and exaltation, and those who saw it as a place where the layers of civilization would be peeled off, revealing the natural man beneath, the "noble savage." It is between the liberty to live according to God's covenant and the liberty to pursue the self-destruction of anarchy. That keen observer, Tocqueville, in noting that moral discipline in America was administered less by the state than by religious conscience, wrote that "religion is much more necessary in the republic than in the monarchy." Thus, the "Protestant" work ethic of thrift, integrity, and pride in one's labor kept capitalist entrepreneurial avarice within bounds. For, he continued, "How is it possible that society should escape destruction if the moral tie is not strengthened in proportion as the political tie is relaxed? And what can be done with the people who are their own masters, if they are not submissive to the deity?"

Precisely our dilemma.

Since Tocqueville, the moral bonds of American religion have turned slack. Without the soil of faith to nourish it, the culture of virtue fades. The man-beast shakes himself loose from the man-angel and strides before us on screen and in print in all the arrogance of his terror and of his perversity. Though the new paganism has disguised its pantheon of deities with novel names and garbs, the same old demons of pleasure and power lurk beneath. The therapeutic, individual hedonism that the new paganism preaches has become an insidious voice in American society, trumpeting its wares in the halls of culture as in the council chambers. Some claim paganism has run its course, with the scourge of drugs and the plague of AIDS returning us to sanity. Alas, evidence for this is meager. Ironically, at the same time America indulges the new paganism, it holds aloft to a grateful mankind the precious flag of freedom and strives to teach democracy to those emerging from the darkness of tyranny. But, the troubling question persists: will inner decay sap America's strength? And, what would the post-Soviet world look like without its present model?

The old paganism was conquered by Judaism and its daughter faiths, Christianity and Islam, all religions of restraint. They understood that beneath normal human behavior boils a network of underground impulses which each age described in its own fashion—the Dionysian frenzies of the Hellenistic world, the Manacean rumblings of Rome, the holiness of sin of the Sabbatian and Frankist heresies of the Jews—and that these subterranean forces continue to beat against the mighty walls of religious restraint. Daniel Bell points out that with the substitution of culture—by which he means the expressive arts—for religion, modern man not only abandoned restraint, but these demonic impulses, once sublimated by religion, gradually embraced and pervaded all aspects of modern culture. The consequence is that nothing is now unutterable or untouchable. There is no longer any sacred grove which cannot be trespassed.

It is the thesis of this book that the biblical teachings and the life of the people-Israel can contribute to the moral renewal of America.

ONE

A Coalition for the Family

To support and strengthen American democracy is a Jewish imperative. One way to fulfill that imperative is by identifying and defining common causes that Jews and Gentiles can pursue together. Though currently less than 3 percent of the population, Jews, by virtue of their ancient heritage, have exerted an influence beyond their numbers in forming, joining, and furthering such common causes.

The most memorable recent effort was the civil rights coalition of the 1950s and 1960s, which included labor, academia, Christians, blacks, and Jews. All of these groups joined in the struggle against discrimination and prejudice and succeeded in introducing major legislative changes, as well as transforming the attitudes and practices of millions of Americans. Within several decades the main objectives of the original civil rights movement—the removal of legal discrimination and the creation of a climate in which racial bigotry was no longer respectable—had been largely accomplished.

Jews considered the civil rights battle to be a mandate which found its roots in the call of the prophets. Black preachers saw the agony of Israel's slave ancestors in the pain of black suffering. By the 1970s, however, the coalition of blacks and Jews, which had worked so effectively during the earlier civil rights struggle, had broken down. Issues such as black antisemitism, "quotas," and the Middle East, among others, served to widen the gap which was dividing the two groups. The black-Jewish civil-rights coalition had come to an end.

The New Coalition

Is there another cause for the common good that has the power to bring together a meaningful, broad-based coalition for the 1990s? I believe there is—the family. I believe Jew and Gentile must unite *in defense of the family*, the most fundamental of America's democratic institutions in jeopardy today, for the traditional family in America is under siege. There are those in our society who are now stating openly that the family is the source of social evil and must be destroyed, or else reconstituted. Such opinions, once regarded as barbaric, are now highly fashionable among the cultural elite. In a few years they may become the norm—unless good people from all segments of society come together to defend the family as an indispensable and nurturing institution. Now is the time when we should call forth concern for the health of the family, the most vital part of the common heritage of America.

This attack on the family is nothing new in America. It has a history that dates back at least to the 1950s, a time many people regard as stable and conventional. But, those trained to analyze society saw problems even then. Thus the great sociologist Pitrim Sorokin—deploring what he called even then "the sex revolution in America"—wrote in 1957:

> The family as a sacred union of husband and wife, of parents and children will continue to disintegrate. Divorces and separations will increase until any profound difference between socially sanctioned marriage and illicit sex-relationship disappears. Children will be separated earlier and earlier from parents. The main sociocultural functions of the family will further decrease until the family becomes a mere incidental parking place mainly for sex-relationships.[1]

In 1965, Pat Moynihan, in a statement that put the nation on notice, issued a warning against precisely the kind of society that Sorokin predicted eight years earlier:

> From the wild Irish slums of the 19th century Eastern seaboard to the riot-torn suburbs of Los Angeles, there is one unmistakable lesson in American history: A community that allows a large number of young men to grow up in broken families, dominated by women, never acquiring any stable relationship to male authority, never acquiring any rational expectations about the future—that community asks for and gets chaos.[2]

We now have ample evidence that such a society is at hand, that we have come to the edge and are staring into chaos. Consider the following data as some indication of the dangers we face.

Social Upheaval and the Decline of the Family: The Statistical Evidence

The late 1960s and early 1970s were characterized by a social upheaval unprecedented in the history of the nation. Students rioted in the streets, burned down university buildings, and began using dangerous drugs and engaging in casual sexual adventures. Parents and families became symbols of decadence, objects of ridicule. The new music, the new films, the new poetry reflected a contempt for the three great "pieties" that had commonly held civilization together–love of God, love of community, love of family.

Indeed, contempt for family became an ideology–a chic new way of looking at the world. Among the in crowd, it was "cool" to reject your parents and everything they believed in–to make up your own morals, your own ethics, your own religion. Parents, hurt and bewildered by their children, found it increasingly difficult to defend their traditional moral and social beliefs, particularly when Hollywood was praising rebellion, self-fulfillment, and promiscuity.

No institution can bear this kind of prolonged attack without severe damage. By the 1980s, the grim prophecy of Sorokin was beginning to come true. On 8 March 1982, a *New York Times Book Review* article surveyed a dozen books on the family and concluded (in a masterpiece of understatement) that the trend was "away from family living."

The review, by Andrew Hacker, began with statistics based on the 1980 census–figures that showed the remarkable degree to which the family had declined. The survey used two definitions of households–"non-family" and "family." About 55 percent of the new households established from 1970 to 1980 were of the "non-family" type. The largest increases were found in the number of unmarried couples living together, the number of separated or divorced men (up 128 percent), and those living alone (up 100 percent).

The "family" household was defined as two or more people living together by marriage or birth. In this category, the largest rise was that of single-parent households, which made up more than 50 percent of the group. And, the single-parent household was almost always headed by a woman.

Most astonishing of all, in the ten years of the survey, only 22 percent of the households were established by married couples. Dr. William Catton, Jr., of Washington State University, said of this trend, "We are now living in a society that seems to be undergoing a transformation from one that defines permanent and monogamous pairing to one that accepts ephemeral pairing as its norm."[3]

By the 1990s, the statistical picture of the family clearly defined the problem for all to see. What follows is grim quantitative proof that the decline has continued apace, with catastrophic consequences to society as a whole.

Where to begin? One catastrophe breeds another. The breakdown of the traditional family has led to more one-parent families, which has led to increased social unrest, which has led to a higher incidence of divorce and fewer marriages, which has led to greater teen-age sexual activity, which has led to increased out-of-wedlock births, which in turn has led to the further breakdown of the traditional family. The cycle is self-perpetuating—and it worsens with every generation.

Perhaps we should begin with the growing number of one-parent families in America, since most studies seem to indicate that the absence of a father in the life of a child can be highly influential in such important areas as academic achievement, school deportment, adolescent crime, and premature sexual activity.

- In 1960, the number of children who lived with the mother only, *was 5.1 million*—a disturbing figure to anyone who knows the potential problems of such a living arrangement.[4]
- By 1990, that number *had risen to 13.7 million*—an increase of 170 percent, and a social problem of major dimensions.[5]

- Today, slightly more than 27 percent of all American children are *born* into single-parent households.[6]
- Among blacks, 68 percent are *born* into single-parent households.[7]

Those who want to argue that rearing a child in a single-parent family entails no extraordinary risks should consider the evidence to the contrary, which is overwhelming and conclusive. The single mother faces enormous problems in contemporary society and runs terrible risks–Murphy Brown and the National Organization of Women notwithstanding.

- Deborah Dawson of the National Center for Health Statistics reports that in a study of more than 17,000 representative children, those who did not live with two natural parents were (1) 20 to 30 percent more prone to accidents, (2) 40 to 75 percent more likely to repeat a grade in school, and (3) 70 percent more likely to be expelled from school.[8]
- William Bennett reports that "children from single-parent families are two to three times as likely as children in two-parent families to have emotional and behavioral problems. In addition, they are more likely to drop out of high school, become pregnant as teenagers, abuse drugs, and become entangled with the law."[9]
- Bennett also reports that "eighteen- to twenty-two-year-olds from disrupted families are more likely to have poor relationships with their fathers and mothers, to show high levels of emotional and behavior problems, to have received psychological help, and to have dropped out of high school. Disruption-related problems are more apparent in young adulthood than they were in adolescence, especially among females.

Young women from disrupted families are more likely to have disturbed mother-child relationships and to receive psychological help, while males show more school dropout and problem behavior. Youth experiencing early disruption (prior to age six) are particularly at risk. And overall, marriage does not have a protective effect."[10]

- Girls reared in single-parent homes are much more likely to become pregnant than those reared by two natural parents, and this pattern is true of white families as well as black. In a study of white families, girls living with single parents were 164 percent more likely to have a premarital birth and 92 percent more likely to enter into marriages that end in divorce.[11]

The two most obvious reasons why more and more children are growing up in single-parent families are divorce and out-of-wedlock birth. Both have been on the rise in the past three decades. Indeed, the bare statistics provide us with a discouraging chronicle of our nation's decline. First, consider the increased rate of divorce, which greatly disturbed Sorokin in the mid-1950s.

- In 1950, the number of children affected by divorce was around three hundred thousand. By the 1990s, the figure had risen to more than 1 million.[12]
- To put this phenomenon in a slightly different perspective, in 1960, the rate of divorce per one thousand for married women was 9.2. By 1991, it stood at 20.9. (National Center for Health Statistics, quoted in Bennett)[13]

Given these figures, it is no surprise that the United States has the highest divorce rate in the world.[14]

The figures on divorce are all the more significant because marriage in America has declined precipitously over the same period of time. Opponents of traditional moral codes once argued that the high incidence of divorce was directly related to the pressure to marry in our culture. Yet, studies reveal that the fewer marriages we have, the higher the divorce rate.

- In 1960, the number of marriages per one thousand unmarried women was seventy-four and the number of divorces was nine per one thousand. In 1991, the figure for marriages had declined to fifty-four per one thousand unmarried women and divorces had risen to twenty-one per one thousand.[15]
- Even during the 1980s, when there was a slight improvement in many areas touching on the family (e.g., teen-age pregnancy, the divorce rate), marriage as an institution continued to decline. By 1992, married couples constituted the smallest percentage of American households in two hundred years–55 percent of 91.9 million households in 1992 as opposed to 60 percent in 1980.[16]

Of the growing incidence of divorce, social critic James Q. Wilson has written:

> The contemporary legal system views people as autonomous individuals endowed with rights and entering into real or implied contracts. The liberalization of laws pertaining to marriage and divorce arose out of just such a view. Marriage, once a sacrament, has become in the eyes of the law a contract that is easily negotiated, renegotiated, or rescinded. Within a few years, no-fault divorce on demand became possible, after millennia in which such an idea would have been

> unthinkable. It is now easier to renounce a marriage than a mortgage, at least the former occurs much more frequently than the latter. Half of all divorced fathers rarely see their children, and most pay no child support.[17]

The institution of marriage is the precondition of a traditional family. For one thing, marriage controls and dignifies the sexual impulse—a primitive drive that can contribute to social disorder, disease, and violence. Sex outside of marriage is a dangerous threat to the stability of society.

Yet, in today's society, more and more people are engaging in sex without either love *or* marriage. This is particularly true of teen-agers—the group least capable of dealing with the emotional trauma involved and the possibility of disease or pregnancy. According to studies from many quarters, sexual activity among teenagers has soared since the 1960s.

- According to surveys, a majority of America's young women now have sex before they turn twenty.[18]
- While many of these young people have had no more than one sexual experience, many are promiscuous. According to one report, eighteen-year-olds who are sexually active have more sexual partners on average than the current group of forty-year-olds have had in their entire lives.[19]
- More than a fourth of sexually active fifteen- to seventeen-year-olds say they've had at least four partners; and, if they've been sexually active for two years or more, almost 60 percent say they've had at least four partners.[20]
- According to the same study, 54 percent of fifteen- to seventeen-year-olds and 63 percent of

eighteen- to nineteen-year-olds say they've had at least two partners.[21]

This rampant disregard of ancient moral codes has resulted in social catastrophe. Among the most obvious are the following, as noted in *The Index of Leading Cultural Indicators*:

- In 1960, out-of-wedlock births constituted 5 percent of all births. By 1991, out-of-wedlock births had risen to 30 percent. During this period, out-of-wedlock births increased from 2 percent in 1960 to 22 percent in 1991. Among blacks, out-of-wedlock births increased from 23 percent in 1960 to 68 percent in 1991.[22]
- Some experts now predict that 40 percent of all births by the year 2000 will be out-of-wedlock, and 80 percent of all minority births.[23]
- William Bennett puts it this way: "In 1961 and 1991, roughly the same number of babies were born (about 4 million)–but in 1991, five times as many of them were born out of wedlock."[24]
- Over the past ten years, the illegitimacy rate has increased by nearly 60 percent. Almost 25 percent of single women in America have children out-of-wedlock.[25]

Those who don't regard out-of-wedlock birth as prima facie evidence that families are in decline will ask: "What evidence do we have that families are suffering because of these new social arrangements? Can't single parents rear children in the warmth and security of a conventional home? Must we say that just because families in the 1980s and 1990s are different, they are by definition worse?"

Well, for people who raise such questions, here are some statistics. First, consider juvenile crime, as reported by William Bennett in *The Index of Leading Cultural Indicators.*

- Children constitute the fastest growing segment of the criminal population.[26]
- In the years 1982 to 1991, the arrest rate for juveniles accused of murder rose by 93 percent, the arrest rate for aggravated assault rose by 72 percent, the rate rose for forcible rape by 24 percent, and for car theft 97 percent.[27]
- Since 1986, the Children's National Medical Center at Washington has reported a 1,740 percent increase of children and teen-agers being treated for knife and gunshot wounds.[28]
- According to the U.S. Department of Education, around 3 million thefts and violent crimes occur annually on or near a school campus. That's almost sixteen thousand incidents per day.[29]
- According to one estimate, 20 percent of high-school students now carry "a firearm, razor, club, or some other weapon on a regular basis."[30]
- In 1991 alone, a thousand acts of aggravated assault and eighty-one acts of forcible rape *were committed by children under ten*![31]

One of the reasons for this rising crime rate among juveniles is surely parental neglect.

- According to the Family Research Council, "Parents today spend roughly 40 percent less time with their children than did parents a generation ago. . . . In 1965, parents on average spent approximately 30 hours a week with their children; by 1985, parent-child interaction had dropped to just 17 hours a week."[32]

- In the same report, the Family Research Council makes a shocking comparison: "Parents in the United States today spend less time with their children than [do] parents in any other country in the world."[33]
- Harvard psychiatrist Armand Nicholi says of this phenomenon: "If one factor influences the character development and emotional stability of a person, it is the quality of the relationship he experiences as a child with both of his parents. Conversely, if people suffering from severe non-organic emotional illness have one experience in common, it is the absence of a parent through death, divorce, time-demanding job, or absence for other reasons."[34]

I could go on for many pages without exhausting the wealth of statistical evidence to support the claim that the American family is in deep trouble. If you want more up-to-date illustrations, then pick up your morning newspaper or watch the nightly news. Everyone knows what's happening in our small towns as well as our major cities. But, everyone does not share my concern. There are forces in society that either regard these developments as "necessary and desirable change," or else see them as irrelevant in the larger scheme of things, an unpleasant interlude necessary to usher in a new social utopia. If the family has its supporters, its also has its enemies–those who, because of hostility or indifference, pursue policies and agendas that damage family life in America.

The Destroyers of the Family

And, the forces promoting this downward spiral at the moment are operating without significant challenge. Indeed, they seem to be gaining strength with each passing day. They now speak with a unified voice, telling the American people in general, and our young people in particular, that the American family must either be redefined or abolished in the interest of sexual freedom and social permissiveness. Who constitutes this coalition against the traditional family? Here are some of the chief participants.

The Media and the Arts

If you are over fifty, you remember a time when there was no obscenity on television or in films—no nudity; no explicit sex scenes; no glorification of fornication and adultery; no gratuitous violence; no close-ups of decapitations, limbs torn off, women disemboweled. The slasher film—the combination of sex and brutal violence found in such movies as *Halloween* and *Friday the 13th*—hadn't even been invented. (Now, according to one survey, the average thirteen-year-old sees forty-eight such films a year.) MTV had not yet begun to produce erotic videos glorifying sex and drugs. Rap music, with its denigration of women and its praise of rape and cop-killing, was not yet an "art form." The National Endowment for the Arts had not yet funded performances that glorified homosexuality and sadomasochism. Television dramas and sitcoms were not routinely depicting clergy as bigots and sexual deviates as good-hearted victims of religious persecution. People for the American Way had not yet begun to charge that anyone who objected to such materials on the air or in the schools was attempting to violate the First Amendment rights of the sex industry.

Unfortunately, too many younger Americans have come to believe that current practice in the television and film industries is both normal and normative. Such an attitude is, in part, the consequence of our loss of a sense of history. But, it is also proof that as a people we are losing a sense of the divine. None of the great religions of the world–and certainly not Judaism–accepts the debased view of the human body and spirit promoted by the Hollywood crowd. It's as if, in the past two or three decades, a large number of Americans have forgotten who they are and what they believe in.

We don't need to argue in favor of higher standards of decency on religious grounds alone. As noted above, the practical consequences of our loss of commitment to "family values" have been degenerative and costly. Yet, the purveyors of the "new morality" and the "new esthetics" argue that this kind of cultural garbage has no ill effect on our young people.

In a Sunday *New York Times* feature, David Leavit–Jewish, homosexual, and artist–attacks the NEA's attempt to curtail grants for indecent art:

> Put yourself . . . inside the mind of Jesse Helms. Imagine a scrubbed, manicured neighborhood, a pocket of decency in the heart of our sinful land. The music is by Wayne Newton, the paintings are by Norman Rockwell, and sex takes place only between married men and women in bed at night. Then one day a church-reared boy or girl goes to a museum and sees a Robert Mapplethorpe photograph; or goes to a library and checks out a novel by Rita Mae Brown. . . . What does Jesse Helms thinks happens? Does the photograph or book emit something between a magic fragrance and a sales pitch, luring this high-minded but fallible child into the back alley of decadence and sin?[35]

In the first place, Mr. Leavit misses the point of Jesse Helms's objection to the Mapplethorpe photograph. The only reason the senator was involved in the first place is because Mapplethorpe was being funded by taxpayers' dollars. And, the same with the library he mentions, unless it is one of those rare public libraries owned by a private individual. Mr. Leavit and others like him seem to believe that the people who foot the bills have no right to say how their money is spent, that Senator Helms (who has the proxy of a lot more people than Mr. Leavit does) must allow Mr. Leavit, and a few of his friends, to determine what is and isn't good art–and apparently to do so without criticism from those elected to control the nation's purse strings.

But, assuming Mr. Leavit, and those who chose to inflict Mapplethorpe on the general public, have the absolute right to spend taxpayers' money the way they please, is it really true, as he seems to be saying, that what his hypothetical boy or girl reads and views doesn't really affect his or her values and behavior? That seems to be a common argument today, particularly in the pornography industry and among the Hollywood elite. On the one hand, art is so terribly serious and so terribly important to society that the U.S. government must fund it–and without challenge from the people or their tribunes. On the other hand, any suggestion that art might affect the values or behavior of society is greeted with screeches of scornful laughter.

Michael Medved, film critic and author of *Hollywood vs. America,* has made a convincing case that popular art has had a profound impact on American family life. He argues that the phenomenal rise in out-of-wedlock births and arrests of fourteen to seventeen year-olds (thirty times more in 1990 than in 1950) is related to the fact that films and television shows today are often filled with sex and violence. He points out that network executives deny there is any connection between such behavior and television programming.

> This same industry then turns around and asks advertisers to pay hundreds of thousands of dollars for thirty seconds of air time in the hope

> that this fleeting exposure will directly alter the public's buying behavior. Don't they grasp the contradiction here? On the one hand, we're told that an hour of television programming has no real-world consequences, and on the other we're led to believe that sixty-second spots that occasionally interrupt this program are powerful enough to change public perceptions of everything from canned goods to candidates.[36]

Who are these people we collectively call "the media"? What do they believe in? How do they think? How do they feel about traditional family values?

We can make educated guesses from the films and television shows and music they generate. But, why take the indirect approach? Lichter and Rothman, of the Center for Media and Public Affairs, have asked upper management in Hollywood to say precisely what they believe. The published results are shocking–but hardly a surprise:

- 93 percent say they seldom or never attend religious services;
- 82 percent voted for Democratic presidential candidate George McGovern in 1973, when Nixon won reelection by 63 percent of the votes cast;
- 97 percent believe that a woman has the right to decide for herself whether or not to have an abortion;
- 80 percent do not regard homosexual relations as wrong;
- 51 percent do not regard adultery as wrong.[37]

These are the elders of the "Prime Time Church" where America worships four hours a day, absorbing Hollywood's secular sermonizing. According to this religion, blacks and women have at present the least influence in American life among the ten key groups identified, but *should*, apart from consumer groups, have the most. (Religion was ranked next to last.) In the gospel of television–where adultery is cherished, where rich people and businessmen commit most of the murders, where blacks are killers only ten percent of the time, where military officers are sinister or pompous fools, where normative politicians are all liberal, where family values are regularly savaged–bestiality seems to be what ordinary Americans turn to when they tire of infidelity, incest, sadomasochism, transvestism, and idyllic homosexual trysts. Thus, in a 1985 episode of "Hill Street Blues," the only eyewitness to a murder was the dead man's lover–a pet sheep.[38]

Having read the opinions and moral convictions of those responsible for producing these entertainments, how can anyone expect other than what we are now being offered–a steady assault on our sensibilities and values?

The Pornography Industry

About the same time Mr. Leavit was telling readers of the *New York Times* that anyone who believed art could provoke misbehavior was a yahoo, a news item (unreported in the *Times*) told the rest of the nation that a thirteen-year-old child was charged with sodomizing a five-year-old child after his passions were aroused by viewing an X-rated film. It was an ugly story–and by no means an isolated incident.

A recent study shows that 57 percent of sex offenders said they experimented with sexual acts they first saw depicted in pornographic material, and 97 percent of all child molesters said they were aroused and encouraged by pornography. A 1988 FBI study found that 81 percent of violent sexual offenders regularly read or viewed violent pornography, and the Michigan State Police testified that 41 percent of forty-eight thousand sex offenders viewed pornography *just before committing their crimes*. Further, a five-year crackdown on pornography and sex-oriented businesses in one Oklahoma county resulted in a 24.4 percent drop in rape cases.

While words of a convicted killer must be taken with a grain of salt, Ted Bundy, serial sex killer, said the following to Dr. James Dobson on the subject of pornography–said it just hours before his execution:

> Once you become addicted to pornography, and I look at this as a kind of addiction like other kinds of addiction, I would keep looking for more potent, more explicit, more graphic kinds of material.
>
> You keep craving something that is harder, harder, something that gives you greater excitement. Until you reach a point where pornography only goes so far. You reach that jumping-off point where you begin to wonder if maybe actually doing it would give you that which is beyond just reading or looking at it.
>
> I don't know why I was vulnerable to it. All I know is that it had an impact on me that was just so central to the development of the violent behavior I had reached. Those of us who are or who have been influenced by violence in the media, in particular pornographic violence, are not some kind of inherent monsters. We are your sons, and we are your husbands, and we grew up in regular families. And pornography can reach out and snatch a kid out of any house today. It snatched me out of the home 20, 30 years ago, and as dedicated as my parents were,

> and they were diligent in protecting their children and as good a Christian home as we had, and we had a wonderful Christian home, there is no protection against the kind of influences that are loose in society.
>
> I have lived in prison for a long time now, and I've met a lot of men who were motivated by violence, just like me. And without exception, every one of them was deeply involved in pornography, without question, without exception, deeply influenced and consumed by an addiction.[39]

Whether or not Bundy's interpretation of his own life is accurate, his observations about the prevalence of pornography in today's society are beyond dispute: "And what scares me, Dr. Dobson," he concluded, "[is] when I see what's on cable TV, some of the movies that come into homes today, the stuff they wouldn't show in X-rated theaters 30 years ago."[40]

Of course, pornography doesn't merely feed the abnormal urges of potential perverts and sex criminals. It also distorts the nature of sexuality in the eyes of normal people–those who have normal desires and expect to establish normal relationships. These extravagant erotic images and narratives depict sex in an abnormal light. They invite self-gratifying fantasies and promote the idea of sexual variety. Normative sex–that is, sex between man and wife within the institution of marriage–is both selfless and monogamous. Each partner accepts the responsibility of giving pleasure to the other. Both seek intimate joy in the infinite variety of a single relationship. Such a sacred bond is the very antithesis of the relationship between the user of pornography and the pornographic image.

Pornography provides "sexual miseducation," says Dr. Balin McGlaughlin, a psychiatric consultant to the

U.S. Justice Department. And, other experts agree. Dr. Victor Cline, a clinical psychologist, tells of a case in which a husband "preferred to see these [pornographic] films rather than to make love to his wife, an attractive, affectionate woman who became profoundly rejected and chronically depressed." Sex counsellors are increasingly asked to deal with this problem. Indeed, it has become so widespread that Dr. James Dobson has produced special materials to combat the ravaging effects of pornography among a constituency *largely composed of decent, religious people.*

Yet, in Los Angeles–where 80 percent of all pornography is produced–movie studios and producers have funneled huge sums of money into "front organizations" whose purpose is to protect the film industry, as well as the producers of hard-core materials, against the legitimate complaints of decent Americans. These organizations–with names containing phrases like "Freedom" and "First Amendment"–were established at the suggestion of a Washington PR firm to disarm the critics of such degenerate material and to put them on the defensive. Thus far, these efforts have been enormously successful–in large measure because those who oppose the corruption of society in this manner are poorly organized.

The Gay Rights Movement

Another force allied against the family in America is the gay rights movement–which has launched the most successful public relations campaign in the history of the nation. In little more than a decade, homosexuals have moved from pariahs to cultural heroes. During this period, Americans have not only come to accept homosexuality as an inevitable phenomenon in our society, but also as a legitimate "lifestyle" deserving of affirmation as well as tolerance.

By no means all Americans have adopted this highly fashionable attitude, but those who harbor reservations are too often cowed by the aggressive and accusatory rhetoric of gay rights activists. As a consequence, those who advocate the overthrow of traditional society and those who are too timid to protest its overthrow, have allowed the homosexual agenda to dominate virtually every phase of our communal life.

- In a nation where all fifty states outlawed sodomy as recently as the 1960s, homosexual activists have won repeal of such statutes in a majority of states and special legal protection in the two largest states in the Union–New York and California.
- Where Jews and Christians alike once taught that homosexual behavior was contrary to the order of God's creation, "liberal" scholars are now saying that Scriptures have been misinterpreted or are outdated. Reform temples now have lesbian rabbis and mainline Christian churches are ordaining avowedly homosexual ministers.
- Our schools once offered solid support for a traditional sexual morality. Many now teach that homosexuality is "normal" and "natural" and that any opinion to the contrary is "homophobic" and "bigoted."
- The media, and particularly films and television, consistently present homosexual characters as moral and likeable people and those characters who disapprove of homosexual behavior as ignorant or mean-spirited. In the first six months of the 1994 television season, no fewer than thirty-four shows presented homosexuals in a favorable light.[41]

- Major corporations like AT&T and Levi-Strauss have not only promoted the affirmation of homosexuality among their employees but have also funded the political and social agenda of the gay rights movement in society at large.[42]

As for the family, gay rights activists have adopted one of two attitudes in the pursuit of their own goals: They have either called for the destruction of the family or else demanded to have their own liaisons accepted as "family" and treated equally under the law and in society's eyes—with the right to become Boy Scout and Girl Scout leaders, Big Sisters and Big Brothers, and to adopt children.

Thus Michael Swift, writing in Boston's *Gay Community News*, a homosexual publication, says of a future time, when the homosexuals have triumphed:

> The family unit—spawning ground of lies, betrayals, mediocrity, hypocrisy and violence will be abolished. The family unit which only dampens imagination and curbs free will must be eliminated. Perfect boys will be conceived and grown in the genetic laboratory. They will be bonded together in communal setting, under the control and instruction of homosexual savants.[43]

In Swift's orgiastic future, religion—at least, as we now understand it—will also be abolished:

> All churches who condemn us will be closed. Our only gods are handsome young men. We adhere to a cult of beauty, moral and esthetic. All that is ugly and banal will be annihilated. Since we are alienated from middle-class heterosexual convention, we are free to live our lives according to the dictates of the pure imagination. For us too much is not enough.[44]

To be sure, this is an extreme (and somewhat childish) cry of arrested adolescence. But substantively, it is no different from what many gay rights leaders are saying in more moderate language. The family is where all "prejudices" are taught, all moral strictures learned. Until the influence of normal and traditional families is countered, the gay rights movement will never win the ultimate victory it desires–which is total affirmation by the American people of everything they do. Thus, the family must be bypassed, undermined, and finally eliminated as a way of organizing society. It is a theme that recurs throughout homosexual literature and is voiced by some of the movement's most responsible leaders.

An alternative to this view is expressed by a leader of the National Gay and Lesbian Task Force, speaking before the National Press Club on the eve of the homosexual "March on Washington":

> [W]e are no longer seeking just a right to privacy and a right to protection from wrong. We also have a right–as heterosexual Americans have already–to see government and society affirm our lives. Now that is a statement that may make some of our liberal friends queasy. But the truth is, until our relationships are recognized in the law–through domestic partner legislation or the definition of beneficiary, for example–until we are provided by the same incentives in tax law and government programs to affirm our family relationships, we will not have achieved equality in American society.[45]

This extraordinary goal, defined in a public statement made in 1987, has been all but achieved in the year 1994. Domestic partner laws have been passed in several states. Big Brothers and the Girl Scouts no longer prohibit admitted homosexuals from using the structure of their organizations to come in contact with small children. The Boy Scouts of America has lost public funding in some parts of the country for refusing to adopt such an "open-minded" policy.

In some states, homosexuals are allowed to adopt children. In Virginia, an appeals judge ruled that local authorities have no right to take a child away from a lesbian mother who is living with a female lover in a situation deemed detrimental to the child. And, in California, a judge took a boy in his early teens away from an "overly religious" mother and awarded him to the father and his homosexual lover. When the father died, the court awarded custody to the homosexual lover.

The Feminists

In her book, *Who Stole Feminism?* (New York: Simon & Schuster, 1994), Christina Sommers, who describes herself as a feminist, distinguishes between the "equity-feminist" and the "gender-feminist." By the former she means the legitimate search for equal opportunity, and by the latter she refers to those self-declared leaders of the movement they have "stolen," who argue that "our society is best described as a patriarchy, a 'male hegemony,' in which the dominant gender works to keep women cowering and submissive . . . in which all institutions, particularly the family, perpetuate male dominance."

Feminism, like many successful social movements in recent years, has received its initial impetus from genuine injustice. Many women have been treated badly by brutal and insensitive husbands. In the past, unequal pay for equal work has been the policy of too many employers. Some professions and vocations have posed barriers for women highly qualified to enter them. The role of women in society has sometimes been unnecessarily restrictive. Most of these injustices have been corrected by federal law, though laws can never completely correct the flaws of human society.

However, like the homosexuals, the feminists want more than justice and fair play. They want to argue that the traditional role of woman as wife and mother is not only limiting, but demeaning. Many have come to insist that bearing children is a curse only to be remedied by contraception, abortion, or lesbianism. For them, the family is a trap, a masculine invention to keep women from entering into the "important" arenas of life–business, politics, sexual adventure.

In the distorted world of the quintessential feminist, men are wicked and predatory enemies who bully women, beat them, and structure a society in which even language insults and denigrates femininity. Thus, we have such linguistic barbarisms as "wymyn" and "personhole cover." The feminists have even re-created God in their own image and demanded that scriptural language be altered to make God a woman.

For such people, a household without children is a luxury, but a household without men is a necessity. Consequently, like the gay rights activists, with whom they've made common cause, they too would like the family eliminated or else redefined to include living arrangements that bar the masculine influence.

If a single individual were to exhibit these characteristics–a belief that half the population constitutes an enemy committed to enslave them, a conviction that societies throughout the world have been structured to keep them from fulfilling their own potential, a demand that God must be reinvented to look just like them–psychiatrists would diagnose such a person as "paranoid-schizophrenic," and perhaps hopelessly so. Yet, among a cultural elite that sees psychiatry as its priesthood, feminists are regarded today as purveyors of a new wisdom, seers with a better, higher vision of society. Meanwhile, we see politicians, regardless of whether they buy into the new "wisdom," increasingly willing to endorse and promote at every level a feminist, antifamily agenda that includes taxpayer-funded abortion-on-demand, tax penalties for traditional families, single-parent adoption, tax-supported day-care centers, and public-school indoctrination in the feminist ideology.

What ultimately underlies extreme or radical feminism is a disturbed misunderstanding of human nature, a self-centered confusion of priorities. What goes on in the marketplace has traditionally been subordinate to what goes on in the home. Men have been breadwinners so that women could perform the all-important work of raising the family. No calling is higher, no goal so revered. That is what religious people of all faiths have perennially believed.

And, if men, caught up in the business world, sometimes confused their priorities, women were less likely to—until the rise of the feminist movement and the subsequent subordination of love and family to money-grubbing and sexual politics. Some women have adopted the worst habits of men and suffered their consequences—for example, drug addiction, alcoholism, lung cancer, and imprisonment. The greatest victim of this change in attitude has been the American family.

Sex Educators

The sexual revolution, the highly erotic content of films and television shows, and the general breakdown in the traditional structure of the family have led to a moral crisis among our young people. Most have tried drugs and/or are engaging in sexual intercourse; even more are confused about basic questions of right and wrong. If their parents bother to tell them that sex outside of marriage is a sin, society at large is voicing a much more permissive message: Sex is O.K. if you and your partner mutually agree and if you take precautions to avoid pregnancy and sexually transmitted disease.

Indeed, this was the burden of a brochure prepared by the U.S. Department of Health and Human Resources sent to every household in America during the "conservative" Reagan administration. It is the wisdom we hear on thirty-second prime-time spots prepared by the Clinton administration and paid for with tax dollars. And, more and more it is what children hear in their schools from "sex educators."

Sex education is what the Band-aid society offers after it has slit the throat of public morality. Now that teen-age pregnancy, syphilis, and AIDS are major problems among adolescents, the educational establishment, steeped in moral relativism, wants to step in and teach our young people how to avoid the unpleasant consequences of fornication. Teachers, assuming the responsibilities and prerogatives of parents, are now telling our young people in classrooms all over the country that they needn't obey old religious prohibitions against premarital sex, that they have a "right" to engage in sex with willing partners–but that they must use a condom. (Some school systems even distribute condoms to children, thereby further encouraging the young to take physical as well as moral risks, since condoms are by no means infallible.)

Most parents don't realize the content of these sex education programs. Indeed, some curricula actually warn teachers against allowing students to take material outside of classroom, lest it fall in the hands of parents. One such program is *About Your Sexuality*, created by Deryk Calderwood and published by the

Unitarian-Universalist Association, sometimes called the Unitarian Church. This multimedia program–which includes slides, audiocassettes, and printed materials–is designed to be presented to students in junior high school and middle school. It is as explicit as any X-rated movie and as contemptuous of conventional morality as any issue of *Playboy*. Among other items, it contains:

- The following warning to teachers: "*Caution*: Participants should not be given extra copies of the form to show to their parents or friends. Many of the materials of this program, shown to people outside the content of the program itself, can evoke misunderstanding and difficulty." (If you have any doubts as to why this warning was necessary, read on.)
- Color slides of heterosexual and homosexual couples engaging in a variety of sex acts, including oral and anal intercourse. In these slides, nothing is left to the imagination. Sex organs and penetration are explicit.
- Instructions to the teacher, suggesting what to do if youngsters are repelled by color slides of homosexual acts: "You might compare any negative responses concerning the difficulty of accepting same sex lovemaking with the difficulty some people experience in watching a birth film for the first time. It is a natural part of life, but we aren't used to seeing it. It may take some time to appreciate and enjoy the beauty of the experience."
- Testimonials from homosexuals indicating their satisfaction with the life they lead and the perversions they practice.
- The argument that homosexual experiences in youth actually help heterosexuals to adjust to

sexual relations with members of the opposite sex in later life.

- Two slide segments which in turn depict a naked boy and a naked girl, while the audio portion tells the audience how each subject masturbates. In the film sequence, the boy tastes his own semen, and male viewers are subtly urged to do likewise.

About Your Sexuality has been in the marketplace for twenty-five years now and is apparently doing quite well. In its own advertising flyer, the Religious Education Committee of the Unitarian Universalist District of Metropolitan New York boasts:

> *About Your Sexuality* has been used extensively across the continent by religious organizations: Protestant, Catholic, Jewish and others; public and private schools; junior high, senior high, and colleges; and by community organizations including: YMCA, YWCA, Planned Parenthood affiliates, youth agencies, adolescent shelters, public and private health care agencies, etc.

Public school officials claim they are obeying the Constitution by refusing to teach traditional sexual morality in school, though they are perfectly willing to teach other moral values, such as tolerance. They claim that the idea of confining sex to marriage is peculiar to Judaism and Christianity and hence a "religious" notion rather than one of those beliefs that are virtually universal. In point of fact, while Judaism invested in marriage a new dignity and meaning as a divine gift, all great societies, ancient as well as modern, have grounded their civilizations in the family. In fact, the Ancient Greeks, Romans, Muslims, Hindus, Buddhists, Jainists, and Shintoists all have beliefs that include the sanctity of the family and the exercise of sexuality within the confines of marriage. Had they not held these beliefs, they would never have created coherent and successful societies. Indeed, no great society has ever risen that failed to honor the family, and no great society that has ceased to respect the institution has survived for long.

Yet, secular school officials, and even some civil libertarians, are arguing that somehow family, marriage, and sexual restraint are blatantly religious ideas that cannot be tolerated in the public school system. Thus, in California the ACLU challenged the right of the state to teach that sex within marriage was a norm of our society. In Louisiana, a judge ruled that a sex education course advocating abstinence was by definition "religious" in nature. By and large, our public schools have been successful in resisting attempts on the part of parents or level-headed educators to teach young people the virtue of self-control.

Liberal Religious Leaders

In the wake of such attacks on the twin ideas of family and chastity, you would think that religious leaders and institutions would step forward to aid parents in rearing their children to practice restraint until marriage—a commonly accepted code of conduct until the 1960s. Yet, Jews and Gentiles alike have failed to meet the challenge of the new secular society. Instead of banding together to take on the burden of combatting unrestricted abortion, antifamily legislation, and promiscuity, religious groups have been fighting among themselves, or else surrendering outright to the forces of nihilism and chaos.

Take, for example, the Episcopal church. In addition to sponsoring an official committee that recommended *About Your Sexuality*, this branch of Christianity also issued AIDS education materials that encourage homosexual behavior among its youth. For example, the church published a booklet described as "an educational project of the Youth Ministries Office." This booklet, entitled "What Young People Should Know About AIDS," contains an "AIDS Crisisline." When a caller dials the 800 number, instead of receiving "counselling" on AIDS, as billed, he is connected to a recorded male voice, who says: "You've dialed Manfinder-800–America's wildest, hottest phone sex service. For only $1.98 per minute, you'll hear explicit messages, one on one service, and enjoy hot, uncensored gay phone sex."

One wonders if the Episcopal church, in any of its programs, ever tells young people to abstain from sexual behavior prior to marriage, as both the Old Testament and the New Testament prescribe. Like many of the mainline Protestant denominations, this shrinking but still influential religious body seems perfectly willing to accommodate itself to the new morality and to teach its young people to do likewise.

The Episcopal church's response to the threat of AIDS is to recommend "gay phone sex," not chastity or abstinence–not even as the best and only certain means of avoiding HIV infection. It's as if the Episcopal hierarchy were afraid to preach the ancient doctrine of self-denial, one of the important ways we show our obedience to God.

But, "mainline Jews" haven't done much better. Some Reform Jews employ lesbian and gay rabbis who marry homosexuals in public ceremonies. There are gay temples whose membership is virtually 100 percent homosexual–and quite open about their sexual practices. And, many liberal rabbis are in the forefront of the proabortion movement. In fact, surveys indicate that Jewish women are among the most likely of all groups to support "abortion on demand." Few conservative rabbis have taken a strong stand against the kind of sex education promoted by our public school system. As a group, only orthodox Jewish leaders have been unanimous in insisting that young people follow the Torah in refraining from sexual intercourse outside of marriage. Indeed, Jews have played just as strong a role in the promotion of the sexual revolution as have mainline Protestants.

The U.S. Government

Most Americans were surprised to see the Reagan administration do so little to strengthen the family and discourage promiscuity in American society. During the Reagan years, little was done to correct the tax burdens on American families or to roll back the red tide of abortion. When the AIDS epidemic emerged, President Reagan himself argued that morality and medicine sent essentially the same message—practice abstinence and avoid HIV infection. Yet, during his term in office, weak, ill-informed, and arrogant officials launched the federal response to AIDS, which emphasized condoms and called for a nonjudgmental attitude toward sexual behavior outside of marriage. Thus, Dr. C. Everett Koop, in his Surgeon General's report, said that the answer to the AIDS epidemic was condoms, not abstinence, and he called for more explicit sex education, including segments on homosexuality. Otis Bowen, secretary of Health and Human Services, allowed government-funded attacks on the family under the guise of scholarly reviews of such topics as youth suicide. Only William Bennett, who called for abstinence and a sex education acceptable to parents, carried the banner for family values and traditional morality as Reagan's secretary of education. His publication *AIDS and the Education of Our Children* presented sobering statistics on condom failure rates and gave examples of abstinence-based sex education programs that actually worked to reduce disease and teen-age pregnancy.

During the Bush administration, there was little, if any, federal effort to strengthen the family. President Bush paid lip service to "family values," but none of the agencies of the executive branch brought forth bold profamily initiatives or tax reforms. As a matter of fact, several federal agencies took steps to strengthen antifamily forces or to weaken further the structure of the family in our rapidly deteriorating society.

- The Bush administration funded Planned Parenthood of Northern New England to the tune of $479,510 in fiscal year 1990. Among other things, this organization is responsible for publishing *The Comprehensive Family Life Curriculum*, which contains the following statement in a chapter entitled "Same Sex Relationships": "Relationships with members of the same sex are not only rewarding, but contribute to development of our sense of who we are. . . . In general, our society does not consider homosexuality acceptable, although the medical psychiatric communities do not find any indication that this is abnormal. . . . By indices social researchers, physicians, and psychiatrists use, it is as normal as heterosexuality."[46]

- The Bush Justice Department pushed for legislation that would, for the first time, mandate that department officials collect reports of crimes against homosexuals, which homosexual activists said they needed to build a case for a national "gay rights" bill. When this legislation passed, gay rights activists for the first time were invited to the White House to participate in the signing ceremony.[47]

- In the "Report of the Secretary's Task Force on Human Sexuality," published in 1989 and widely disseminated by the Bush administration, one segment states: "Parents should know that homosexuality is a natural and healthy form of sexual expression. They do not need to feel bad about something that is good." In order to combat homophobia, the report states that "religions need to reassess homosexuality in a positive context within their belief systems." The report goes on to say that "public and private schools need to take responsibility for providing all students at the junior high and high school level with positive information about homosexuality. . . . Family life classes should present homosexuality as a natural and healthy form of sexual expression."[47]

The Clinton administration has been even more aggressive in its promotion of antifamily initiatives. During the first two years of his term, President Clinton appointed a number of people to high positions who were known as antifamily activists.

- Joycelyn Elders, surgeon general of the United States, in an interview published by *The Advocate*, a homosexual publication, said "Society wants to keep all sexuality in the closet. . . . We need to speak out to tell people that sex is good, sex is wonderful" and "a normal . . . and healthy part of our being, whether it is homosexual or heterosexual." She came out in favor of homosexual adoption and condemned the Boy Scout ban on homosexual leaders as "unfair." She ridiculed religious opposition to abortion by saying: "Look who's fighting the prochoice movement . . . a celibate, male-dominated church."[49]

- Roberta Achtenberg, as a lesbian activist and elected official in San Francisco, fought to have the Boy Scouts defunded by United Way for refusing to allow homosexuals to become Scoutmasters. Now an assistant secretary at the Department of Housing and Urban Development, Achtenberg has established policies that would require middle-management employees to join activist groups in their off-hours in order to be considered for substantial raises and promotion.

- Kristine Gebbie, appointed by President Clinton as the first AIDS czar, barged around the country, urging explicit sex education and condom distribution in order to prevent the spread of AIDS. Gebbie represented the administration at a New York conference sponsored by the federally funded Gay Men's Health Crisis, a gathering restricted to young people in their adolescence and early twenties. At this meeting, the Gay Men's Health Crisis offered obscene homoerotic materials to the assembled young people.
- The Clinton administration, at the urging of Secretary of Health and Human Services Donna Shalala, increased the funds for abortion and contraception under Title X and abolished Title XX, the only program in the federal government that provided a small amount of money for abstinence education.

So, the difference between Republican and Democratic Washington regimes seems to be one of degree, and the same kind of antifamily programs and policies are being funded at the state and local levels as well. Literally billions of dollars are being poured into initiatives that cater to such advocacy groups as gender-feminists and gay rights advocates and are designed to undermine or replace the family. If you had only the programs and their effects by which to judge, you would have to conclude that the American family can regard government as one of its most powerful and destructive adversaries.

What We Must Do

These, then, are the chief adversaries of the family in our society, and combined they appear almost invincible. Who, after all, can hope to prevail against an army composed of government, the media, the sex industry, the educational establishment, the feminists, and the homosexual lobby? Certainly the "megatrends" seem to be against survival of the American family in any recognizable form and that, in turn, bodes ill for the survival of our nation–our civilization. If all these forces are out to destroy the idea of the traditional family, then what can anyone hope to accomplish by opposing them? And, why at this late hour should we presume to begin? There are a few hopeful signs.

In the first place, the sexual and cultural revolution that has taken place over the past three decades may have run its course. Some of the most prominent revolutionaries have begun to question the wisdom of tearing down an orderly society on the lean prospect of building a better one.

Jerry Rubin is now a stock broker. Jane Fonda says that as a parent she has an entirely different view of pornography than she once did. Novelist Erica Jong, whose *Fear of Flying* is a feminist cult book, has recently written a recantation in *Ms.* magazine, saying that the marriages of her parents and grandparents, with all the moral strictures they implied, were much better for women than the transient arrangements they have endured in the past few years. And, Lenore Weiztman, in *The Divorce Revolution*, has put into words what many "liberated" women have learned the hard way: "Divorced men experience an average 42 percent rise in their standard of living in the first year after divorce, while divorced women (and their children) experience a 73 percent decline."[49]

Perhaps the most dramatic statement of disillusionment came from Barbara Dafoe Whitehead, writing in the April 1993 issue of *Atlantic Monthly*, a magazine that has for many years been politely liberal and intensely supportive of the sexual and social revolution. In a lengthy and well-documented article entitled "Dan Quayle Was Right," she surveys a mountain of existing evidence and comes to the conclusion that "family diversity in the form of increasing numbers of single-parent and step-parent families does not strengthen the social fabric but, rather, dramatically weakens and undermines society."

She goes on to say,

> If we fail to come to terms with the relationship between family structure and declining child well-being, then it will be increasingly difficult to improve children's life prospects, no matter how many new programs the federal government funds. Nor will we be able to make progress in bettering school performance or reducing crime or improving the quality of the nation's future work force–all domestic problems closely connected to family breakup. Worse, we may contribute to the problem by pursuing policies that actually increase family instability and breakup.

She concludes by saying:

> Over the past two and a half decades Americans have been conducting what is tantamount to a vast natural experiment in family life. Many would argue that this experiment was necessary, worthwhile, and long overdue. The results of the experiment are coming in, and they are clear. Adults have benefited from the change in

> family life in important ways, but the same cannot be said for children. Indeed, this is the first generation in the nation's history to do worse psychologically, socially, and economically than its parents. . . . Whether Americans will act to overcome the legacy of family disruption is a crucial but as yet unanswered question.

So many of those who have advocated changes destructive to the family are beginning to see the error of their ways. The dawning of the Age of Aquarius has not tinged the fields of Eden with a rosy glow; instead it has illuminated the ugliest side of human nature. Some still turn away from the light, but others are willing for the first time to face the awful truth: that "old-fashioned family values" are essential for the survival of a society–any society, including one that is affluent, blessed with advanced technology, and led by well-meaning politicians.

A second reason why the nation may be ready for a counterrevolution is because good, traditional-minded people–long complacent about the changes in society–have recognized for the first time that the social tinkering of the past decades threatens the very survival of the American community *and they have begun to speak out.* When Sorokin first published his sharp warnings in the 1950s, few people believed his prophecy that American society was in danger of rapid and catastrophic decline. In the middle 1990s, they have awakened to the truth. Some of these include major figures in the arts, sciences, and in public life. Here are just a few examples of sensible cultural and political leaders who have recognized the true nature of the crisis.

Karl Zinmeister of the American Enterprise Institute has written:

> There is a mountain of scientific evidence show-

ing that when families disintegrate, children often end up with intellectual, physical and emotional scars that last for life. . . . We talk about the drug crisis, the education crisis, and the problems of teenage pregnancy and juvenile crime. But all these ills trace back predominantly to one source: broken families.[50]

Daniel Yankelovich, pollster of the Public Agenda Foundation, has demonstrated a widespread belief that the social and economic problems we face as a nation are the result of a breakdown of the family:

> Americans suspect that the nation's economic difficulties are rooted not in technical economic forces (for example, exchange rates or capital formation) but in fundamental moral causes. There exists a deep intuitive sense that the success of a market-based economy depends on a highly developed social morality—trustworthiness, honesty, concern for future generations, an ethic of service to others, a humane society that takes care of those in need, frugality instead of greed, high standards of quality and concern for community. These economically desirable social values, in turn, are seen as rooted in family values. Thus the link in public thinking between a healthy family and a robust economy, though indirect, is clear and firm.[51]

Walter Williams, a syndicated columnist who is black, has written of the problems in the black community:

> The fact that Washington and Harlem have 80 percent illegitimacy has nothing to do with racism in America. It has to do with 13-, 14-, and 15-year-old girls having sexual intercourse without the benefit of marriage. In 1925, 85 percent

> of black kids lived in two-parent families. Surely in Harlem in 1925, blacks were far poorer and there was more discrimination.[52]

Concerning the rise of the single-parent family, Professor David Popenoe of Rutgers University writes:

> I know of few other bodies of data in which the weight of evidence is so decisively on one side of the issue. . . . If our prevailing views on family structure hinged solely on scholarly evidence, the current debate would never have arisen in the first place.[53]

Professor Christopher Jencks of Northwestern University comments on the degree to which acceptance of single-parent families has affected the ability of the underclass to maintain traditional family values. He has written:

> Now that the mass media, the schools, and even the churches have begun to treat single parenthood as a regrettable but inescapable part of modern life, we can hardly expect respectable poor to carry on the struggle against illegitimacy and desertion with their old fervor. They still deplore such behavior, but they cannot make it morally taboo. Once the two-parent norm loses its moral sanctity, the selfish considerations that always pulled poor parents apart often become overwhelming.[54]

One of the most eloquent pleas for action comes from Samuel Lipman, music critic and editor of *The New Criterion*. Lipman laments the Left's capturing of modern culture, which has been accomplished, he shrewdly observes, through the destruction of traditional family values. Then, he calls for a positive response on the part of those who complain about the current ills of society without attempting to counter these disturbing trends. He writes:

The sexual revolution that the Left has made is the true cultural revolution; it has invaded every family, split children from parents, and put all parents in terror of losing their children's love. As a matter of ordinary prudence, parents avoid discussing these questions with their children.

But culture begins at home. We cannot demand from either government or society a higher standard of culture than we demand from ourselves. We cannot demand that schools be made places of learning rather than leftist indoctrination unless we back up our demands with new curriculums, oversight of administrators and boards, refusal to fund what offends us, willingness to fund what we advocate, and withdrawal of our children from schools that do not meet our standards, even at some financial sacrifice. We cannot mock government, foundations', and corporations' support of culture if we do not privately support what we find good. We cannot expect government or society to assist in making moral beings of our children if we do not start by demanding moral behavior in our own families. We cannot complain about the tidal wave of malign popular culture if we are not willing to give up most television programs, most popular music, and most movies, and to demand something better in their place. . . .

The myriad things we do are either better or worse, higher or lower, more desirable or less desirable, more beautiful or less beautiful, more on the side of life or less on the side of life. This idea of cultural hierarchy stands in direct opposition to cultural relativism, the notion that everything is equally valid, nothing better than

> anything else and nothing worse. There will be those who call this elitist; I think it only describes the way one chooses a physician.
>
> Just as cultural relativism is unacceptable, so is moral relativism, the idea that what people do cannot be judged, only empathized with. Morality here means examining what people do in terms of a higher value; in our society this value can only be the carrying on of a civilized life. Art, learning, liberty, and even the market are not suicide pacts. All these components of human action are important, not just in themselves, but because they serve the purpose of life. . . .
>
> It is not enough to say what government or society should *not* do. Our larger task is to say what *should* be done, first for us, then, if we can make our case well enough, for others. What we want for ourselves, we should want for others; what we want for our children, we should want for everyone's children.[55]

Like Lipman, some people have already responded to the growing call for counterrevolution. In addition to the writings of social and cultural critics, many groups have been organized to preserve and defend the family. Focus on the Family, headed by Dr. James Dobson, produces a highly popular radio program, books, newsletters, and videos that are supportive of the traditional family. The American Family Association is primarily concerned with the prevalence of pornography and obscenity in contemporary society, though it addresses other issues as well. The Family Research Council is an organization of writers and researchers who publish studies, surveys, and analyses that touch on American family life. The Rockford Institute also publishes profamily materials, including *The Family in America*, a publication that surveys new research in the field and evaluates its significance.

Clearly such groups are making a difference in the current debate. They are primarily effective as purveyors of knowledge and information. They alert their millions of followers to the growing problems in our society generated by the collapse of family values, and on occasion they urge their constituencies to take action in the political arena, though, because of their tax status, they do so only tentatively and indirectly.

Merely transmitting information is not enough, however essential it may be. Sorokin and Moynihan understood thirty or forty years ago what most people now recognize–American society is in a state of rapid decline and at the heart of that decline is the collapse of the family; by the same token, if this evident decline is to be reversed, it must be accomplished through the reconstitution of our families–the strengthening of society's building blocks. This is a task that must be undertaken by a new coalition, a union of Jews and Gentiles with a common commitment to civilization and a common abhorrence of social and moral chaos.

What the current crisis requires is grassroots activity in every part of the country–a movement designed to restore American families to the position of health and authority they once enjoyed. This new coalition need not be modeled precisely on the old coalition, but it should contain some of the same elements: (1) the same moral fervor, which gave the civil rights movement its greatest impetus; (2) the same generosity, which prompted people of various faiths and backgrounds to give willingly of their time, energy, and substance to the cause; and (3) the same unselfishness, which allowed people to work together without the distraction of competing demands for public recognition or private gain.

A preliminary proposal for such a coalition might include the following:

CONSENSUS: to create the broadest possible agreement on family issues within policy guidelines;

IMAGE: to reestablish the image of the family as the normative social unit;

RELIGION: to restore the central role of religion in the family and explore its insights into present dilemmas;

EDUCATION: to involve the family more closely in the education of the child, to restore "right and wrong" to the curriculum, to direct schools to respect parental opinion in areas such as sex education or the selection of textbooks;

PARENTS: to communicate their rights, responsibilities, skills, and attitudes necessary for raising children;

SEXUALITY: to formulate a public code of sexual ethics;

MEDIA: the acceptance of such a code by the media, either through persuasion or imposition; to regularly recommend individual films, programs, and works of literature for family consumption;

AIDS: to focus attention on behavior–homosexuality and drug use–as the central issue in understanding the AIDS epidemic, and to advocate celibacy before marriage and fidelity after marriage as preventative measures;

WELFARE: to reduce radically and to reform the welfare system, stressing individual responsibility;

SINGLE PARENTS: to discourage such families by treating their moral causes;

PORNOGRAPHY: to curb its production and punish those who trade in it;

ABORTION: to implement a policy to hinder illegitimate pregnancy and to safeguard the child and mother.

Cicero called the family the "first society," the oldest and most universal human institution. Every culture prescribes a moral relationship between parents, children, husband, and wife. No alternative to the family has worked for long: not open marriages, which have inevitably led to divorce; not the communes of the 1960s; not the present-day, epidemic disaster of single-parent homes; not even the *kibbutz*, where families are reverting to traditional patterns; not any variation concocted by prior and present generations. Failed experiments in forming an alternative/egalitarian society are once again giving way to classical patterns. All of this confusion points to the fact that the traditional family has stood the test of history. It is, according to Michael Novak, "the only department of health, education and welfare that works."

What could the Jewish contribution be to a coalition for the family? That is the subject of the next chapter.

Endnotes

1. Cited in *The Family in America* (December 1988).

2. Daniel Moynahan, cited by William Bennett, *The Index of Leading Cultural Indicators* (New York, 1994), 53.

3. Andrew Hacker, *New York Times Book Review*, 8 May 1982.

4. U. S. Bureau of the Census, *Current Population Reports*, Series p-20.

5. Ibid.

6. U. S. Bureau of the Census, *Statistical Abstract of the United States*, 110th ed., 1990, 67.

7. Ibid.

8. Deborah Dawson, National Center for Health Statistics, 1990, cited by Family Research Council, *Free to Be Family*, Washington, 1992, 16–17.

9. William Bennett, *The Index of Leading Cultural Indicators* (New York, 1994), 52.

10. Ibid.

11. Ibid.

12. Family Research Council, *Free to Be Family*, Washington, 1992, 25.

13. National Center for Health Statistics, cited by Bennett.

14. National Commission on Children, *Just the Facts*, Washington, 1993.

15. *Statistical Abstract of the United States*, 1992.

16. Ibid.

17. James Q. Wilson, *The Moral Sense* (New York: The Free Press, 1993), 26.

18. U.S. Department of Health and Human Services, *National Survey of Family Growth*, cited by Family Research Council, 75.

19. Ibid.

20. Ibid.

21. Ibid.

22. U. S. Department of Health and Human Services, *Vital Statistics of the United States*, 1991; *Natality*, 1993.

23. Lee Rainwater, cited by George Will, "The Tragedy of Illegitimacy," *The Washington Post*, 13 October 1993.

24. Bennett, 47.

25. Ibid., 48.

26. U. S. Department of Justice, *Combating Violent Crime*, 1992.

27. U. S. Department of Justice, *A Sourcebook of Criminal Justice Statistics*, 1992.

28. Daniel Goleman, "Hope Seen for Curbing Youth Violence," *New York Times*, 13 August 1993.

29. U. S. Department of Education, cited by Bennett, 31.

30. Ibid.

31. *A Sourcebook of Criminal Justice Statistics*, 1992.

32. Family Research Council, 21.

33. Ibid.

34. Ibid.

35. David Leavit, *New York Times*, 19 August 1990.

36. Michael Medved, *Imprimus*, Hillsdale College, 1992.

37. Robert Lichter, Stanley Rothman, and Linda Lichter of the Center for Media and Public Affairs.

38. See Don Kowet, "Prime Time Watchers See Society Through a Distorted Screen," *Insight* (1 July 1991): 36–40.

39. Ted Bundy, in interview with Dr. James Dobson.

40. Ibid.

41. *American Family Association Journal* (September 1994): 1920.

42. Paul Cameron, *The Gay Nineties: What the Empirical Evidence Reveals About Homosexuality* (Franklin, Tennessee), 77–115.

43. Michael Swift, *Gay Community News*, 15–21 February 1987.

44. Ibid.

45. Quoted by Paul Cameron, *Exposing the AIDS Scandal* (Lafayette, Louisiana: Huntington House Publishers, 1988), 34.

46. Family Research Council, p. 62.

47. Ibid.

48. Ibid.

49. *Washington Times*, 23 March 1994, A-1, A-9; 27 March 1994, B-2.

50. Lenore Weitzman, *The Divorce Revolution: The Unexplained Consequences for Women and Children America* (New York: Free Press, 1985).

51. Karl Zinmeister, "Raising Hiroko," *The American Enterprise* (March/April 1990).

52. Daniel Yankelovich, "Foreign Policy After the Election," *Foreign Affairs* (Fall 1992).

53. Walter Williams, quoted by Bennett, 49.

54. David Popenoe, "The Controversial Truth," *New York Times*, 26 December 1992.

55. Christopher Jencks, "Review–The Truly Disadvantaged," *New Republic*, 13 July 1988.

56. Samuel Lipman, "Can We Save Culture?" *National Review* (26 August 1991).

TWO

The Jewish Family

The decline of the family in our time represents a perennial conflict between utopians and the Hebrew Bible, where, in the story of the creation, the family as society's fundamental unit is already established at the beginning of Genesis.

Bryce Christensen, in *Utopia Against the Family*, points out that utopian philosophers have always considered the family a threat to the ideal state. Thus, in classical Greece, Plato sought to advance his Republic by destroying the family through selective breeding, communal marriage, and collectivized child care, to the end that "no parent is to know his own child, nor any child his parent."

In the seventeenth and eighteenth centuries utopias were back in style. Thomas Hobbes saw the family, the church, and the guild as obstacles to the individual's identification with leviathan–the state. Jean Jacques Rousseau believed that in rearing children, the state might take the place of the father and his "prejudices." In the nineteenth and early twentieth centuries, the utopias of William Morris and Edward Bellamy promoted a society in which the role of the family is curtailed and its centrality diminished. While Morris is little read by twentieth-century thinkers, Bellamy's *Looking Backward* was enormously influential during the 1930s and 1940s.

In *Walden Two* (1948), described by its author, psychologist B. F. Skinner, as an "improvement on Genesis,"(!) we are told that since the family is "no longer an efficient economic or social unit or transmitter of culture," it should be replaced. The child is to be taken from the parent and turned over to full-time group care, which is said to be superior to "parental care" with its "abrupt changes of the home-and-school system" and its "Freudian problems which arise from asymmetrical relations to the female parent." Parental care, says Skinner, was acceptable in the "old pre-scientific days" before behavioral psychology, but certainly not in his utopian society where adults are to accept all children as their own, where children accept all adults as their parents, and where "blood relationships can be happily forgotten." Once the family is sufficiently weakened, Skinner continues, "experimental breeding" will commence.

Skinner's perspective is that of the behavioral psychologist, the man who has run enough rats and people through mazes to know how to structure society. But, Marxism, the most persistent ideology of the past century, has produced its own utopias. American Communist philosopher Herbert Marcuse, in his assault on Genesis, *Eros and Civilization* (1955), agrees that human liberation from repression will only come with the "disintegration . . . of the family."

The twentieth century has produced its "distopias" –dark visions of planned societies gone awry–as well as utopias. Yevgeny Zamyatin's *We* (1924), Aldous Huxley's *Brave New World* (1932), and George Orwell's *1984* (1948) portray the dread of a society regimented into submission by crushing the family. Mothers turn over their infants to the One State, which raises them in the notorious Child-Rearing Factory. Indeed, the words *mother* and *family* are regarded as obscene or else linguistic fossils from another age. Each novel features a rebellion against such state-mandated anonymity in the form of an isolated and illegal attempt to recapture family life, mother-child bonding, or simply love. "If I only had a mother like the ancients," one hero despairs, "mine–yes *my* mother, to whom I would not be number D503, not a molecule of the One State, but a simple human being, a part of her!"

These fictional depictions of controlled societies that attempt to eliminate the very notion of family are not without their counterparts in the modern ideological state. Not only were the policies of Nazi Germany and Communist Russia based on antifamily utopian schemes, but the same kind of thinking has influenced the collectivist nations of Scandinavia. In Sweden, for example, the word *family* seldom if ever appeared in social legislation until recently, when the voters–watching their society deteriorate in the wake of such a policy–threw out the social planners and elected a more traditional-minded regime.

Yet, we need not look toward Europe to find examples of utopian thinking. The literature and political discourse of our own nation are full of such concepts. Echoes of Soviet "initiatives" such as "easy divorce, abolition of the distinction between legitimate and illegitimate birth, collectivized child rearing, and broad definitions of family" ring loud and clear in America today. "The clash between utopia and Genesis is not merely a theoretical concern," Christensen concludes. "The real effect of utopian thinking upon the family must be recognized at a time of high divorce and illegitimacy rates and low birth and marriage rates. Writing a new introduction for *Brave New World* in 1946, Huxley marveled that 'it looks as though Utopia were far closer to us than anyone, only fifteen years ago, could have predicted.' "[1]

The utopians were correct in believing that Genesis was their avowed enemy. It is there one finds the authority for the concept of family that they repudiate. While other creatures–beasts, birds, fish–are fashioned by fiat *en masse*, the human creature is unique in receiving the divine breath of life and in being created as a couple. *Male and female He created them and called their name adam* (i.e., "man" or "human"). In noting that the word *adam* is applied here collectively to both, the Talmudic rabbis add that only when there are male and female (husband and wife) is their humanity (*adam*) complete. To drive the point home, the blessing–"Praised art thou O Lord, Our God, Creator of 'adam'"–is recited not, as one might expect, over the birth of a male child, but at the marriage ceremony that joins male and female. Further, Genesis tells us that the bond between Adam and Eve, between husband and wife, transcends all other attachments, even the relationship between parent and child.

This paradigm of the couple, Adam and Eve, is repeated in the twosomes of the later patriarchs and matriarchs. The telling of the stories of their lives is the primary substance of the first book of the Bible–not the giving of commandments and dogmas, nor a recitation of miracle tales, nor the offering of syllogisms and ethical pronouncements. Both the successes and the failures of these families are faithfully recounted with little or no whitewashing: bearing and raising children, finding suitable mates for them, and insuring that the covenant with God be handed down from generation to generation.

These stories—whether in their concise original form or as expanded and embellished by later hands into a rich, imaginative literature—became a primary vehicle of Jewish morality for the simple and learned alike. Held up as edifying lessons to children (who were themselves called after the characters), these family stories early occupied a central place in the Jewish psyche. Furthermore, in the exiled people's long trek through history, the integrating power of the family—along with devotion to the teachings of the Torah—served as the portable baggage that enabled them to accomplish the singular task of enduring for two millennia without a land of their own.

While secular, futuristic utopias discarded the family as "outmoded" and "retrogressive," the retrospective Jewish utopia of the Garden of Eden placed the family at the very center of life itself. And, when a sinful world was to be destroyed, and a second Adam named Noah was to father mankind again, he was told to bring into the ark for the new world *only families*. Even the animals are referred to in these terms.

Others who have come to the Jewish community seeking the secret of survival need look no further than this concept. Consider one example.

When the Dalai Lama, exiled leader of Tibetan Buddhists, wanted to learn about Judaism, he arranged a meeting with a number of Jewish leaders in order to be instructed in the wisdom of Israel. These leaders talked among themselves about how to carry out their mission and finally decided to bring to the gathering certain artifacts in order to teach the truths of Judaism in the most concrete way possible. In the end, they achieved their purpose, though not in the way they had expected.

The Dalai Lama opened the meeting by observing that his land had been occupied, his priests and people slaughtered, their houses of worship destroyed, their holy books confiscated, he and his retinue exiled. He wondered if his culture would survive another generation.

He told them he had heard that the Jews had suffered similar persecution and exile, not merely for a generation or two but for two thousand years. "Perhaps we can learn a lesson from you," he concluded. "Tell me, what is your secret?"

"It is prayer," replied one of his guests, an expert in Jewish mysticism, who showed him a "Shiviti," the handwritten Hebrew diagram containing the verse from Psalms which begins with the word *shiviti*–"*I have set* the Lord before me at all times"–which is placed in front of the prayer leader, reminding the worshipers that they are to stand in awe before His presence and pour out their heart until they are drawn by love into His embrace.

"It is Torah," suggested another, holding up a small Torah scroll, which he opened to display script on parchment, describing it as the most precious of Jewish possessions, still written by hand, just as the scribes had done centuries ago, and publicly read at worship services, a record of the covenant made at Sinai–revered, studied, and obeyed to this day.

"It is the Talmud," said a third, displaying a small folio volume that he had brought with him on the trip, pointing to its composition of text and commentaries and explaining that it was the living law, the portable homeland, the lifeblood of the people, adapting to their changing needs, evolving commentary after commentary through the centuries, the chief source of study in the Jewish academies.

"It is Tzedakah, or charity," said another, displaying a tzedakah box found in every Jewish home. He went on to explain the Hebrew word *tzedakah*, which more correctly means righteousness rather than charity, describing how the practice of sharing was central to Jewish life, because Judaism taught that the world belonged to God who lent its wealth to humankind in trust that they might share it with others less fortunate, for which act of justice no special praise was deserved.

The last participant, a woman, brought nothing to display–no concrete example of what she believed to be the secret of Jewish survival. Instead, she spoke of the family and home, where, she claimed, all the other elements mentioned by her predecessors–prayer, learning, good deeds–were expressed. She described how the Sabbath day and the Passover seder, among the most precious Jewish religious rites, were observed more by the individual family at home than in the communal hall. She explained why, with the destruction of the temple in Jerusalem, the sages called the home "the sanctuary in miniature."

She went on to point out that the family has always been the very heart of the Jewish people, that the holy bond of male and female together was called "adam," a bond marked by fidelity, respect, and love. In this understanding, she continued, the bearing and the raising of children was paramount, with the parent rather than the teacher given the primary responsibility of teaching the child Torah and mitzvot, thereby making the home a school. I believe, she concluded, that the family is the secret of our survival. The Dalai Lama, after listening to everyone, agreed with the last speaker that the family has been the secret of Jewish survival.[2]

Of course, in this respect the Jews are not unique. Every great civilization has maintained the sanctity of family life, not merely as an institution for social control, but also as the chief means to transmit the essential elements of culture from one generation to the next. Edward Gibbon, in *The Decline and Fall of the Roman Empire*, argued that the deterioration of family life in Rome led to a malignant moral corruption that ultimately rendered the empire helpless when faced by Teutonic warriors, who had only to lean on the gates of the Eternal City to see them collapse.

The parallel to our own time is forboding. With the weakening of the family as a crucible for molding character, community life is falling to pieces before our very eyes. Dreaded diseases spread among us, despite the advances of modern medicine. Drugs ravage entire communities. The fear of crime follows every citizen into the streets, despite the doubling of courts, prisons, and police. Schools have become centers of violence and conflict. So have many homes. The vast bureaucracies of welfare, immigration, and health care are collapsing under the weight of pervasive fraud. Presidential campaigns exhaust more than they enlighten. Widespread scandal contributes to public disillusionment with politicians in particular and democratic institutions in general. Art and entertainment appeal to ever-lower tastes and appetites. In such a society, the enemies of American democracy might also find the gates ready to topple.

When asked shortly before his death for his predictions about the next great epoch of man, the preeminent historian Arnold Toynbee expressed grave concern for the future–and based this concern on the status of the family. "Nations rise and fall," he wrote, "with the health of its families." He went on to say, "The Jewish family particularly seems to have maintained itself well."

Toynbee's two propositions are clear: The family is essential to the survival of society, and the Jewish family is essential to the very notion of family. Despite an unwillingness to accord Jews a role in the continuity of Western humanity–for he held that Judaism was nothing more than a "fossil of Syriac civilization" and the source of Christian and Islamic fanaticism–Toynbee can only support the Jewish and biblical perspective on life and appears to find hope there for the modern family.

During the civil rights struggle, some believed that the future of America depended on extending true equality to blacks. Today, when the social fabric of our country seems about to come unraveled, the survival of this same society depends on the health and coherence of its families.

What is it about the Jewish family that qualifies it to play a special role in the revitalization of American society? The answer to that question is complicated, but clear. The Jewish family offers all of the following:

Home

The frailty of the contemporary family is related to the shallowness of the home, for it is there that we first learn to distinguish between right and wrong, good and evil. The home is where we reveal our true selves, where we learn to love and hope and cherish. So exalted was the Jewish concept of home that, with the destruction of the temple in Jerusalem, the Jews looked upon the home as a *mikdash m'at*–a sanctuary in miniature.

The home was to become a sanctuary, a place of retreat and renewal where the coldness of society gives way to the hearth of intimacy and concern. Jewish daily worship begins with the exclamation of the Gentile prophet, Balaam: *How fair are your tents, O Jacob, your dwelling places, O Israel.* The Talmud says, "Balaam was inspired by the fact that he saw the doors of the Israelites' houses were not open to those of their neighbors." As Abraham Heschel observed, "This is the spirit of privacy. It is a quality that is easily lost, particularly in our civilization." Private homes threatened with the invasion of alien values require constant vigilance.

The home is also a sanctuary of celebration. Eric Fromm writes about family religious practices as the "forgotten ritual," a bond that joins us to heaven as well as to our fellow human beings: building and decorating the fragile hut, the sukkah, into which the Jewish family moves for its meals during the days of the holiday (Lev. 23:42); feeling the sweet-peace, the holiness and family union at the weekly Sabbath table; changing the kitchen utensils for the special Passover foods used to celebrate the ancient story of the seder, surrounded by the enlarged family (Exod. 12:15); kindling the soft lights of the Hanukkah candles for eight nights; reciting the daily blessings for food at the table-become-altar; and learning lessons of Torah at the same table.

In performing such acts of celebration–or in being a part of those performing them–precious moments of exaltation are stored in memory to kindle sparks of recognition in darker moods. One who partakes in the "highs" of such events has, according to Heschel, little need for drugs. One reason for the spread of the drug culture, he has suggested, may be the decline of religious exaltation: young people who have never experienced the fervor of "forgotten ritual" seek to fill the terrible void.

Hope

In biblical times, Judaism waged a battle against sexual excess not unlike the struggle now in progress–and in those earlier times, Mosaic law was victorious. Unbridled sexuality lay at the heart of ancient pagan religion. The myths of fecundity, passion, and divine marriage flourished. The rites of coupling were thought, through sympathetic magic, to bring about the fertility of land, beast, and human. Homosexuality, adultery, incest, and even bestiality were common to these pagan peoples.

Such a world was a strange setting for the origins of the Jewish family. Yet, it was here that the battle was fought, and much of the Bible is its record. *According to the ways of the land of Egypt in which you dwelt, you shall not follow. And according to the ways of the land of Canaan, whither I bring you, you shall not go. You must not go in their ways. . . . For I am the Lord your God. You shall keep my laws and statutes and live by them* (Lev. 18:3-5).

The Genesis stories and the later rabbinic commentaries on the sin of Adam, the Flood, the sons of Noah, Sodom and the daughters of Lot—these were meant as a repudiation of homosexuality, adultery, and incest. In order to create a moral family life, the divine had to be demythologized. God is the one supreme, eternal spirit of Whom images are forbidden, Who created the world and demands righteousness from His creatures.

Further, the Israelites desexualized the cult by eliminating the priestess and placing religious worship in the hands of a single sex, the male priest. God, though referred to in male terms, is without sex.

The Bible also sanctified sexuality through circumcision for males and by establishing the laws of family purity for females. One of the central concerns of the Bible is the family, for whose legal and spiritual development it lays down several principles, among which are sexual purity, the home, the Sabbath, the honoring of parents by children, and the obligations of parents to children. Further, biblical morality is not communicated through abstract thought but through family stories as paradigms of life. Thus, the tales of Abraham finding a proper wife for Isaac, the jealousy and reconciliation of Joseph and his brothers, or the love of Jacob for Rachel posed lessons for all mankind.

Over the centuries, whatever was supportive of the family, Judaism favored; whatever was harmful, it opposed. It held the family to be the basic unit of society, the central agency of civilization, and the most successful institution to contain the sexual impulse and invest it with higher meaning. By thus placing the family at the center of its concern, Judaism could overcome the challenge of a hostile and corrupting environment. The past record of Judaism and the family is an encouraging sign in our present time of trouble.

Moderation

In sharp contrast to the beliefs of earlier times (as well as our own), Judaism taught moderation. Between the extremes of exploitation (hedonism, which sees sex as no more than the satisfaction of lust) and escapism (asceticism, which teaches the renunciation of pleasure), Judaism advocates the control of sexuality within marriage–a socially recognized and enduring male-female cohabitation.

Judaism affirms heterosexuality as the order of creation. *Male and female, He created them,* ordained them to be joined *as one flesh,* and called His creation *good.* The Bible's view is echoed by the rabbis: "No man should be without a wife, and no woman without a husband."[3] In the Talmud, the body is neither disparaged nor worshipped. All aspects of family life are examined quite frankly in this compendium of teachings, and the notion of sexuality within the confines of marriage and the family is fully explicated.

On another family issue, that of abortion, Judaism's approach is again one of moderation, advocating neither of the popular positions that dominate the present bitter debate. On the one hand, the Judaic tradition repudiates the prochoice position (though agreeing that under certain circumstances abortions can be performed) because "abortion on demand" could and does justify destroying the embryo for frivolous reasons—financial considerations, convenience, gender—even beyond the first trimester. On the other hand, Judaism (though agreeing that life is sacred and must not be destroyed) rejects the absolute prolife position, which prohibits abortion altogether, even when the mother's life is endangered. In short, Judaism affirms that human life is a divine possession and that the embryo is "potential life." Abortion must be forbidden except when the life of the mother is jeopardized, either physically or emotionally. (That decision, incidentally, cannot be hers alone.)

Moderation is likewise the key to the unique record of Jews and alcohol, in which both alcoholism and prohibition are rejected. Jews tend to drink moderately—that is, without getting drunk.

Sanctification

Kiddushin, or sanctification, is a focal word in understanding the Jewish view of the family. In itself, the sexual impulse is neither holy nor sinful, but neutral, awaiting direction. If that direction is for a noble purpose, ordered within marriage, then it is sanctified. Of course, a variety of other options have always been readily available. The sexual impulse may be magnified and exploited by those who view the human only as an animal, or deplored and constrained by those who measure the human against the angel. Taking the part for the whole, both lead to distortion and disaster. Judaism considers the entire person, both the angelic and the animal, and meets the sexual impulse with the mitzvah of marriage, which, by giving order to sexuality in the permanent bond of family and home, sanctifies it.

The Hebrew word *kaddosh* means to separate as well as to sanctify, which explains why the name given to the wedding service is a derivative–*kiddushin*. It is the commitment of each partner only to the other, and the restriction of sexual intimacy to the married couple. Thus, a biological fact of nature is sanctified. The Jewish way of sanctification must be recognized as representing a watershed in the history of civilization. It accepts corporeal man, but ties that acceptance to his spiritual nature.

Permanence

Divorce is possible, but it is not granted lightly. The Ketuvah, or marriage agreement, is more than just a piece of paper. It represents both a personal pledge between two people and a public commitment before a community that values the marital status and discourages its dissolution through social rewards and punishments, laws and regulations.

The current 50 percent divorce rate is unacceptable to Jewish tradition and destructive of any society. Marriage is the normative state: When death or divorce breaks the family unit, a second marriage to mend the fracture should be actively sought. While divorce is occasionally the only solution to the problems posed by an incompatible union, marriage should never be viewed as a temporary arrangement from the outset, a form of "vertical polygamy"–a view that is encouraged by our readily available "no-fault divorce" and prenuptial agreements that anticipate it.

"Whoever divorces the wife of his youth," observes the Talmud, in disapproval of easy separation, "even the altar sheds tears for her."[4] Selecting a marriage partner should be regarded as the most significant decision a person makes in life. It should be undertaken seriously and soberly as a lifelong commitment, for it is this commitment that lends marriage its stability and strength. Marriage–and remarriage in the event of death–is a socially recognized and lasting male-female cohabitation.

Responsibility

Responsibility is another characteristic of the Jewish family that stands as a reproof of the extramarital living arrangements common today. Sharing one's space, one's time, one's body with another requires special permission, special conditions, a special decision made with special considerations. Human society, over millennia of experience, has fashioned out of these "specials" the institution called marriage, requiring a public act of confession and entered into with the expectation of growing into a family, whose very essence is loving responsibility. Indeed, marriage could be described as the institution of responsible love.

Mutuality

In the story of creation, the idea of two equal genders side by side is implicit. The human couple emerges out of the very beginnings of biblical history, with Adam and Eve and Abraham and Sarah, as we have pointed out. But, equality does not mean interchangeability. For all his sympathy, the father does not carry, bear, and suckle the child. Nor should being the breadwinner or prime provider imply superiority. True sharing is surely not a matter of an exact division of hours or responsibilities, but the understanding that husband and wife stand as equals before God, that sharing is the very essence of their commitment. As the wife's devotion is toward her husband, the ancient rabbis called upon the husband "to love his wife as himself and to honor her more than himself."[5] There must be a measure of fidelity, each toward the other.

Civilizing

The family is the most civilizing of all institutions in society. In submitting to the discipline of marriage, men and women immediately begin to transform each other. Man is domesticated, and woman is raised to the level of "beloved companion." The male learns to live in the intimate company of a woman. The female learns to live in the intimate company of a man. And, as a consequence, both are better prepared to take their place in society at large, which is, by definition, both male and female.

Children are likewise civilized by the family. There one learns morals, manners, respect for proper authority. The family loves its members unconditionally and therefore can discipline them without rancor. However, once the son or daughter leaves the family and enters society, in that context love must be earned, and misconduct is often punished with anger and rejection. Thus, the family best prepares its children to earn respect and approval in society as a whole by civilizing them through good example and loving discipline.

Nurturing

A chief characteristic of the family is its natural tendency to nurture. This is true not only of the human family, but of mature animals and their offspring throughout nature. Among some species in the animal kingdom, both male and female nurture their young, while among others, it is the female or (more rarely) the male. Among animals, the nurturing usually takes place for only a short time; but, during that period, many species will die for their young in a manner that seems both mysterious and ennobling.

These natural examples point to a higher capacity among human families to nurture members from birth to death, the parents caring for the children into adulthood, and then the children caring for their parents into old age. The sacrifices parents willingly make for their children are often extraordinary, and most mothers and fathers would risk their lives to protect a son or daughter in danger.

This role is clearly embodied in the biblical accounts of early Jewish families, stories that, for thousands of years, have served as paradigms to be studied and emulated by succeeding generations. It is through such nurturing that human beings survive and learn to move about in the larger community.

And, just as instinctive nurturing among animals tells us something about nurturing among human beings, so does our relationship to God–the Father of all families, the nurturer of all children–tell us something about our relationships with other family members. Like God, who gains nothing for Himself by nurturing His children, we are to nurture one another through love and self-sacrifice. That imperative is best carried out within the warm and loving confines of family.

Sabbath

As truly as the Sabbath is a day for renewal of the individual, it is equally and uniquely a day for the family. No matter how exhausting and frantic the workaday week has been–often pulling family members into different and distant directions–with the setting sun, the arrival of the Sabbath bride/queen sweeps all before it, closing the mind to workday worries, collecting the scattered family into the home, around the table, and introducing them once again into the warm embrace of the family.

The Sabbath queen presides over a regimen of behavior, requiring withdrawal from commerce and travel, ordaining instead an order of prayer and fellowship from sunset to sunset. The Sabbath princess brings warmth and joy to family intimacy; and, as the shadows of the evening descend, marking its close, the family bids a bittersweet farewell to the lovely guest who has bestowed such an outpouring of love and laughter upon all their doings. Though the synagogue is the locus for communal Sabbath worship, it does not supersede the home, where the queen reigns and the bride smiles, as mother kindles Sabbath lights and father favors her by chanting the Book of Proverbs' "Woman of Valor"; where children receive the parental blessing; where father recites the Kiddush over a cup of wine to sanctify the day; where children review their lessons on the biblical portion for the week, punctuated by Sabbath songs sung to old family melodies. It is no accident that in the Ten Commandments the Sabbath commandment should follow the commandment to "honor thy father and thy mother."

Parents

The Jewish view of parents is implied in the commandment to honor–or revere–*your father and your mother.* Speaking at the White House Conference on Youth, Heschel said that when he grew up in Warsaw, there were a number of persons on whom he could look with a sense of reverence. Then he posed a question that made his audience wince: "Do we parents today deserve to be so treated by our children?" *Revere your father and your mother*, he went on, is not merely one of the Ten Commandments, but the essence of them all. The ability to keep the other nine, he said, may be hopelessly impaired by an unwillingness or inability to observe this all-important one. Reverence for parents is the essence of all reverence, because the parent represents the mystery of human birth. Rejection of the parent is rejection of the mystery.

Which parent is deserving of that reverence? Only the one who strives "to live in a way that is compatible with the mystery of human existence." To evoke reverence, the parent must have a character deserving of reverence–"the ability to delay satisfactions, to overcome prejudices, to sense the holy, to strive for the noble." The responsibility lies not with the child but with the parent.

The miracle of life is the chief glory of parents, since husband and wife join with God in the creation of a new human being. One from two, the child is both the fruit and the fulfillment of the promise of man and woman to become "one flesh." Since God is the giver of all life, parents are enjoined to remember His creative role in the miracle of birth and to treat their offspring as a child of the Father as well as of their own union. Thus, reverence for human life, as it proceeds from its divine source, becomes a primary tenet of the Jewish religion, and each new birth is the reaffirmation of an abiding faith in God, the Creator of all mankind.

The duties and tasks of the parent in raising the child are primary, from providing purely physical needs to training and nurture in matters intellectual, moral, and spiritual. These duties are spelled out in meticulous detail in the classic works of the Jewish religion. The greatest lesson of these works is to teach both by precept and example. The formal instructor only acts as a temporary stand-in for the parent, who is the first and last teacher.

You shall love the Lord your God with all your heart, and with all your soul, and with all your might. And these words which I command you this day shall be on your heart.

You shall teach them diligently to your children, and shall talk of them when you sit in your house, and when you walk by the way (Deut. 6:5–7). *You shall teach them diligently,* Heschel observed, "not vicariously."

Shalom Bayit

Finally, there is the notion of *shalom bayit,* or domestic tranquility and harmony (the translation fails to capture the full meaning of the Hebrew words). Shalom Bayit means that one strives to suppress strife, anger, jealousy, or selfishness and chooses instead the ways of understanding, patience, and love.

Hurtful words are not to be spoken within the sanctuary of the family, and hurtful deeds are even less appropriate. Shalom bayit means that mercy overcomes justice, that hurt feelings give way to forgiveness, that patience controls temper, that sacrifice is practiced daily, that one gives before being asked, that one sympathizes without being told to.

If the normal tension between the sexes often interferes with the achievement of such lofty levels of shalom bayit, the role of the child is pivotal. How is this so? In the language of Genesis, male and female are admonished to leave their mothers and fathers, to cleave to one another, to become "one flesh," in all likelihood a purposely ambiguous expression that invites multiple interpretations, three of which are particularly important. Obviously one meaning is the sexual union of man and wife. Since such encounters are comparatively fleeting in nature, however, the phrase would seem to have, as well, a second and larger meaning. The single home they now live in, the single family they now comprise, the singleness of their affection for one another–all are manifestations of two who have chosen to be one. Such unity, however, quite naturally waxes and wanes in accordance with the frailty of human nature.

But, in addition to sexual intimacy and familial harmony, there is a third way in which husband and wife become "one flesh," a way that, by its very being, serves as the permanent and visible evidence of their marital affection and physical joining. I refer, of course, to the child. Parents truly become "one flesh" with the birth of an offspring. For the child, composed of the flesh and the spirit of father and mother, rouses from each of them that natural rejoicing in one's progeny, a loving commitment to care for the well-being and character of this joint product of love. Such mutual nurturing diminishes discord, enhances harmony, and draws all nearer to the lofty goal of shalom bayit.

Conclusion

The founding fathers of America, taking the biblical record as their model, knew that political democracy could only flourish if established on the dual foundations of faith and family. Our contemporary malaise is the consequence of abandoning that ideal in favor of a society that is largely secular, hedonistic, and atomistic. Judaism–by advocating a God-centered, family-based society, established by the covenant and governed by the Torah–can play a key role in recalling America to its origins.[6]

In preparing to participate in a family coalition, however, Jews need to put their own house in order. Like other Americans, too often they have rejected the example that has been established for them and which they have followed over the centuries. Indeed, Jews are more likely to live in urban areas in the forefront of social change, affected by innovations that do not always strengthen traditional values.

However, instead of seeking ways to restore beliefs and practices that have nourished the Jewish community since ancient times, much of the limited energies of their leaders have regrettably been focused on debating and even accepting the aberrant behavior of unruly social rebels. Consequently, far from being defenders of the family, some Jews may well have become contributors to its decline.

Consider the following random statistics:

- According to a recent Gallup poll and a suppressed B'nai B'rith survey, fewer Jews are married than are Americans in general–48 percent to 63 percent.
- A greater percentage are divorced–7 percent, as against six percent in the population as a whole.
- A shocking 91 percent of Jewish women agree that every woman who wants an abortion should be able to have one, as against only 56 percent of their Gentile counterparts.
- Fully 50 percent of Jewish women signalled a high degree of affinity for feminism, compared to only 16 percent among non-Jews.
- It seems that 69 percent of Jewish women wanted their daughters to be "independent, self-reliant, ambitious, self-supportive, etc." as against 22 percent who had family-oriented goals for their daughters (e.g., to "have a good family, husband, marriage, children" or to be "loving, caring, and good parents."[7]
- While 55 percent of all Americans say religion is "very important" in their lives, only 30 percent of Jews make this statement, which explains why the percentage of those who reported attending synagogue the week before the survey was only half the national rate for church attendance–21 percent to 40 percent.[8]

One is reminded of Heschel's haunting words:

We are God's stake in human history.

We are the dawn and the dusk,

The challenge and the test.

How strange to be a Jew and go astray on God's perilous errands.

As seen in the history of Judaism, the family is divinely ordained in the very order of creation, and the acceptance of the responsibilities and obligations of family is the indelible mark of civilization. The family is a school and the home a sanctuary–a place of concern and love, mutuality and permanence. The family can replace an ethic of everyone-against-everyone with an ethic of cooperation and mutual concern.

Our individual incompleteness and our instinctive need for companionship are not necessarily defects in human nature but can be a source of a dignity and love that lie at the very essence of our being. It is our nature to be with others. The family is the institution that enshrines that need. It is the microcosm of mankind, and that is why the Bible uses the image of husband and wife and children for God, Israel, and humanity. It is possible to speak of a society without family, but then one is no longer talking about Judaism–or civilization.

The treasury of family values embedded in their tradition, which Jews are free to draw upon, may yet enable them to make one of their noblest contributions to a distraught American public–if they are wise enough to do so. Following the example of their ancestors millennia ago, they can demonstrate through their actions as well as their lips that the chaos of modern society can be overcome by exemplifying the kind of moderation, sanctification, mutuality, and child rearing that have characterized the traditional Jewish family.

In helping to form a coalition for the family, they can share the needs of society at large and join the search for answers to its most urgent questions. But, above all they can place before others–and themselves–the teachings and practices of Judaism regarding the family. In sharing their views, Jews will perform a long-needed act of self-renewal, for Jews are as much in need of a new coalition as is the rest of our troubled society.

Endnotes

1. B. Christensen, vii-18. Sources cited by Christensen are Plato, *The Republic*, V, trans. B. Jowett; B.F. Skinner, *Walden Two* (1948; reprint, New York: Macmillan, 1976), 279–281, 128, 291, 107, 131, 134, 126, 132-4; Yevgeny Zamyatin, *We*, trans. Mirra Ginsburg (New York: Viking Press, 1972), 189; David Popenoe, *Disturbing the Nest: Family Change and Decline in Modern Society* (New York: Aldine de Gruyter, 1988), 213.

2. Nathan Katz, "The Jewish Secret and the Dalai Lama," *Conservative Judaism*, v. 43 (4) (Summer 1991).

3. *Tosefta*, ed. Lieberman, Yebamot 8.

4. BT Gitin 90b.

5. BT Yebamot 62b.

6. See Patrick Riley, *Chastity and the Common Good* (Washington: Dissertation Pontificia Studiorum Universitas A. S. Thoma Aq. in Urbe, 1991).

7. This study, made in 1985 by Sid Groenman for B'nai B'rith Women, was reported by Sylvia Fishman in the 1989 *American Jewish Yearbook* as having been withheld from the *B'nai B'rith Monthly*.

8. *Newsweek*, op cit.

THREE

Homosexuality and the Order of Creation

You shall not copy the practices of the land of Egypt or the land of Canaan: Do not have carnal relations with your mother, your daughter, your sister, with a beast, with one of your own sex. It is an abomination. Do not sacrifice your child to Molekh. It is an abomination. Let not the land vomit you forth for defiling it, as it vomited forth the nation that came before you.

–Leviticus, chapters 18 and 20

Homosexuality is a violation of the order of creation.

In the passage cited above, the Bible forbids homosexuality and other illicit sexual expressions because it affirms heterosexuality as the way in which humans were made and intended to behave. This affirmation is laid out in the first chapters of Genesis.

Male and female He created them (1:27). In taking up the emergence of the human species, heterosexuality is at once proclaimed to be the order of creation.

It is not good for man to be alone (2:18). Man is in need of a companion. Who will it be? First the animals are considered. Man *names* them, that is, he understands their nature and comprehends why none is a fitting mate for him. Here we have an implicit rejection of bestiality. Woman is formed and becomes his partner. In her, man finds completion. So, the Jewish sages instruct that a woman should not be without a husband; a man should not be without a wife; and both should not be without the Divine Presence.

Be fruitful and multiply and fill the earth (1:28). Replenishment of mankind through propagation and companionship are the purposes of heterosexuality.

Therefore shall a man leave his father and his mother and cleave unto his wife, and they shall become one flesh (Gen. 1:27–28; 2:18–24). The husband-wife relationship is axiological. It takes precedence even over the elemental parent-child bond.

Male and female He created them and called their name adam. Again, it should be stressed that the name *adam*, which means in this context a human person, is given to the man and woman together and not separately. In other words, we are only fully human, fully *adam*, when male and female are met in a social bonding, in marriage. Therefore, it follows that the blessing, "Praised are You, O Lord . . . Creator of *adam*," is not recited at a male birth, as one might expect, but at the Jewish wedding service when male and female are joined and the intention of creation biologically completed.

The early biblical narratives can be read as a continuous attack on the widespread sexual deviance that challenged and often seduced the Israelites, whose fallings away Scripture scrupulously records. Thus, arguments are advanced against homosexuality in the story of Sodom and Gomorrah (from which tale derives the pejoratives "sodomy" and "sodomites"); against voyeurism at least and homosexuality at worst in the case of Noah and his sons; against incest in the incident of Lot and his daughters; and against rape in the Dinah episode.

What has not been sufficiently noted, however, is that the principal story of this type, one which includes all forms of sexual deviance, including homosexuality, is the Flood, a catastrophe that far outreached other stories limited to family or community.[1] What crime was of such magnitude to have evoked a divine regret over the creation of humankind and require the destruction of almost every living creature? According to the most ancient understanding of the biblical story found in rabbinic sources, it was the violation of the natural order of sexual life. Sexual deviance was so pervasive and so struck at the heart of God's plan for the world, that a reconstitution of that order could only come from a new creation. But, how do we know that the cause of the Deluge had to do with the corruption of the sexual order, since Scripture only tells us that its justification was *man's wickedness* but not what this "wickedness" was? Let us examine the text.

> *When men began to increase on earth and daughters were born to them, the divine beings saw how beautiful the daughters of men were and took wives from among those that pleased them. . . . The Lord saw how great was man's wickedness on earth, and how every plan devised by his mind was nothing but evil all the time. And the Lord regretted that He had made man on earth and . . . said, "I will blot out from the earth the men whom I created."* (Gen. 6:1–2, 5–7)

The episode of the Flood is introduced with the story of the seizing of human women by heavenly creatures (Gen. 6:2). This enigmatic tale of *divine beings* has puzzled biblical scholars who usually understand it as a remnant of the pagan mythology of the life of the gods that somehow escaped the eye of the biblical censor and found its way into the canon. That may very well be, but, whatever its source, it would seem to be used here to explain the origins of the catastrophe of the Deluge. It suggests that the immoral life of the gods was aped by humans, the disastrous effect of which was of such measure that it called into question God's plan for creation. By transgressing the bounds of nature, the performance of the *divine beings*, Nahum Sarna observes, signals the calamitous breakdown of the biblical "world order."[2]

The Jewish sages clearly understood the story as a polemic against the dissolute ways of the pagan gods and pagan society. They ascribed to the "divine beings" the most lurid sexual crimes: the rape of virgins before marriage (*jus primus noctis*), the rape of women already married, and copulation with other males and beasts.[3] If lust invaded heavenly creatures, what cravings must humans have suffered? For *the Lord saw how great was the wickedness of man on earth* (Gen. 6:5).

While other crimes are listed among the catalogue of misdemeanors of the generation of the Deluge, the rabbinic understanding of the flood story affirms that their *wickedness* was primarily sexual. The key verse is *all flesh had corrupted their way on the earth* (Gen. 6:12).

Flesh corrupting its *way* is taken in a sexual sense. Examples that are cited are whoredom,[4] incest,[5] and sodomy.[6] Reflecting the custom common among the Greeks, "The men of the generation of the flood used to take two wives, one for procreation and the other for sexual gratification. The former would stay like a widow throughout her life, while the latter was given to drink a potion of roots, so that she should not bear, and then she sat before him like a harlot."[7]

"All" flesh included the beast. The natural barriers of sexual distinction had broken down, as had those separating man from the brute creation, so that all

were now on the same level. *On the "earth"* implies that even the order of the plant kingdom was corrupted.

The rabbis described the perverse condition thus:

> While humans manipulated the coupling of wild beasts with the domesticated cattle, they themselves copulated with both . . . ;[even] the earth yielded unnaturally ["went a-whoring"]. . . . Each of these [mismatches] returned to their proper species [as a result of the ordeal of the Flood].[8]

> The generation of the flood was not blotted out from the world, until they took to composing nuptial songs for marriages between man and man and man and beast as for man and woman.[9]

> God is long-suffering of all manner of crime, save sexual immorality. [Two examples are given: the Flood and the case of Sodom, where Lot's prayers delayed the punishment of the Sodomites, until they made their homosexual desires known–*Bring them out that we may have intercourse with them* (29:5)–after which Lot and his family are told to flee for their lives from the destruction which then swiftly follows.][10]

So appalling were the sins of the generation of the Flood, according to the rabbis, that the Divine Presence that had come to dwell among men fled heavenward, while the sublime light God had made on the first day of Creation was secreted in the world to come in which those who perished in the Flood would have no share, nor be judged, nor be mourned for by the angels who sang even at the drowning of the wicked Egyptians.[11]

What may have begun as a pagan cultic crossbreeding to encourage fertility[12] exploded into a fury of sexual license that shattered the most ancient, guarded and fundamental of barriers. Thus, the Flood was caused, say the sages, by a violation of the laws of natural mating through all branches of creation. Only the most drastic measure might save the human experiment: destruction and a new beginning–but a beginning that would be centered upon the sexual paradigm of husband and wife.

A careful analysis of the story of the Flood bears out this focus upon sexual order and disorder. Scripture takes pains to tell us that of those who entered the ark each male had a female companion: Noah and his sons are never mentioned entering or exiting from the ark except with their wives (6:18, 7:7, 13, 8:16, 18). This fivefold repetition is emphatic. A further examination of these texts reveals that husbands and wives are listed separately upon entering but together upon leaving, which leads the sages to conclude that sexual relations were not permitted in the ark, the better, perhaps, to dwell upon the cause of the Flood which led to their incarceration and salvation.[13]

This focus upon the sexual order points to the family. Continuation of human life was threatened by the quality of that life. Promiscuous sexual relations between man and man, man and woman, human and beast, would inevitably cripple the institution of the human couple and that of the human family. Therefore, when humans are chosen to repopulate the world, it is not simply a group of men and women that are designated, but a *family*. Not Noah and "others," but Noah with his wife, and their sons with their wives, which is to say, an entire family unit. So firmly is this teaching embedded in the Flood story, *that every animal, every creeping thing, and every bird, everything that stirs on earth came out of the ark "by families"* (8:19).

Nor must the monogamous element be overlooked. Noah and his sons each have a single wife. Their children are born from these wives and not from additional wives or maidservants. In this, the pattern of Adam and Eve in the Garden of Eden is replicated. The message seems clear: human society is meant to be composed of families–of monogamous families.

Further, and quite remarkably, this concern to restore sexual normality to humans, through the pairing of Noah and his children into husbands and wives, was extended even to the animals. They, too, are brought to the ark *male and female* and each according to *its species* (6:20, 7:14), to reconstitute them into their proper groupings, just as the humans. Most curious is the fact that the animals, upon entering the ark, are not simply described as *male and female* and according to their *species,* but *each with his wife*–the only such usage in Scripture (7:20)[14]–and, upon exiting, as we have noted, according to their *families!* These last delineations are taken by the sages to mean that the only animals allowed in the ark to constitute the new society and reestablish sexual order were those who had not violated their "species" in the past and the only ones allowed out were those who promised not to do so in the future.[15]

In the Genesis story, the crossbreeding between "heavenly" males and earthly women prepares the way for the destruction of the Flood. According to the sages, generative crossing-over was the paradigm for the subsequent mixing of sexual lines among humans, among animals, and between them both, a transgression that extended upwards to include divine beings and humans and downward to encompass even the plant kingdom. The disarray was so complete, so total, as to embrace the supernal, the biological, and botanical realms. Corruption of the intended order of creation, we are told, had insinuated itself into the very first generations of humans to such chaos as to prove intolerable to the divine will. Catastrophe and a new creation were called for–the Flood! The Deluge swept away both man and beast, leaving only the inhabitants of a small ship to restore order for the new world that would emerge. Divine mismating had been joined with that of the human, animal, and plant worlds to shatter the harmony of the universe.

What lies behind the drama of the Flood, if this supposition is correct, is the avowal that sexual misconduct may open the floodgates of destruction. There comes a time when society can no longer abide the violation of the laws that bind it together: a point is reached when constant batterings finally unravel the cords, and everything falls to pieces. Scripture spells out the dynamics of that deluge in Leviticus chapters eighteen and twenty (cited above), where a cataclysm of smaller proportions transpires. There the Israelites are warned that just as *the land vomited forth* the Canaanites for their sexual debauchery and child sacrifice, and replaced them with the Israelites, so will it treat the Israelites themselves should they so behave. Note that Scripture takes care to tell us that it is the *land* which becomes defiled through such behavior and the *land* which has "vomited forth" its inhabitants (and may do so again). Divine compassion accounts for human frailty, but the moral law is so set into the very fabric of creation, that, when the measure of toleration is exceeded, it spews forth sinners, whether pagan or Hebrew.

The Bible and the Talmud are replete with the requirements, admonitions, and prohibitions set down to encourage the sexual morality expected of the post-Flood humanity. One series of laws which may relate to the Flood, found in the holiness chapter of the Bible and carried further in an entire tractate of the Talmud, is that forbidding a "mixing of kinds": *You shall not let your cattle mate with a different kind; you shall not sow your field with two kinds of seed; you shall not put on cloth from a mixture of two kinds of material* (19:19). Could this admonition be a reflection of the rabbinic opinion that the crossbreeding which they claim brought about the Deluge reached to the very plant kingdom? To this very day, pious Jews are careful in not wearing clothing in which wool and linen are mixed (*sha'atnez*), though few can offer a rationale. Maimonides, however, records a striking Middle Eastern practice consistent with the connection of magic, mingling of diverse species, and immorality.

> [The Sabians] mention that when one species is grafted upon another, the bough that is meant to be grafted ought to be held in the hand of a beautiful girl and of a man who has come into her in a disgraceful manner that they describe, and that the woman must graft the bough upon the tree while the two are performing this act. There is no doubt that this [practice] was generally adopted . . . especially in view of the fact that in this custom the pleasure of sexual intercourse is joined to the desire for the benefits in question. Therefore the *mingling* [of diverse species] . . . is forbidden, so that we shall keep far away from the causes of idolatry and from the abomination of their unnatural kinds of sexual intercourse [emphasis added].[16]

Despite the havoc wrought by the Flood, Scripture sees it as only an interlude in the moral chaos that prevailed in the ten generations that preceded it and the ten that followed, until the advent of Abraham and Sarah. The patriarchs and matriarchs, Abraham and Sarah, Isaac and Rebekah, Jacob and Rachel–reminiscent of Adam and Eve–attempt to replicate within the mortal and fallible portals of history the monogamous model of the Garden of Eden. With the patriarch-matriarch paradigm, the Bible establishes the human couple as the fulfillment of the order of creation and the archetype for all generations. Their model is refuted neither by the concubines, who are only brought to Abraham and Jacob by the barren matriarchs that they may raise the children, nor by Leah, whose position is anomalous and incongruous, a foil for monogamy.[17] It is the institution of marriage and the consequent features of the family–home, permanence, fidelity, and mutuality–which become the national treasure of the Jewish people, the bulwark and irreplaceable center of their society, and which Judaism surrounds with all manner of support and protection. The home that housed the Jewish family became both a school of parental instruction and a sanctuary-in-miniature (as the Talmud calls it), where the family rites were enacted.

Compare the two home occasions, the Jewish Sabbath table with its family presence, its traditions and its religious joy, with the common form of the Greek symposium from which the excluded family was replaced by drink, conversation, and sexual liaison with prostitutes or young boys. Both the Greeks and the Jews possess myths that explain love as the reconstitution of two creatures into their preexistent unity. One is found in Plato's *Symposium*, the other in the classic work of Jewish mysticism, the Zohar. The contrast between them, however, is conclusive. In the *Symposium*, Aristophanes cites the celebrated fable of immensely proportioned preexistent humans with two heads, four arms, etc., whom Zeus severs in half in a moment of anger, pulling their skins together and setting them free in the world. Ever-after they are destined to seek their other half: those who were androgynous searching for one of the opposite sex, while those who were of a single sex, whether male or female, searching for a same-sex mate.

The Zohar presents a countermyth of reunification.[18] According to its account, human creation was of a single person with two faces. "God sawed them in two, separating the female from the male and brought them together, so that they would be face to face. And when she was gathered in to man, then God blessed them, as at the wedding service."

Note the two differences in this version from that of the Greek legend: first, the preexistent state is only androgynous and never all-male or all-female, thus rejecting the homosexual option; and second, the reconstitution of the primeval unity is not simply the working of biological tropism, the blind yearning for another body as the Greek myth would have it, but the solemn union of husband and wife. The Zohar's fable finds its source, of course, in the biblical story of creation: *Male and female He made them* [androgyny]. *He blessed them, and called "their" name adam* [marriage] (5:2). It is here argued that only in the male-female relationship are we fully human beings; only then is adam, the human person, fully created.[19] Furthermore, the male-female relationship is sanctified in the institution of marriage. Until marriage, the individual is said to be incomplete, unfulfilled. As the Zohar puts it, "The Divine Presence rests only upon a married man, because an unmarried man is but half a man, and the Divine Presence does not rest upon that which is imperfect."[20] Similarly, the Talmud proclaims, "Whoever is not married is without joy, blessing or good, [and some add] without Torah or peace."[21] Indeed, so important was it to establish marriage as the norm that the Midrash suggests that God Himself performed the first wedding ceremony for Adam and Eve.

Few mitzvot are so richly developed in Jewish literature and Jewish life as marriage. A good part of the Talmud deals with its wider ramifications. The Bible already exempted those eligible from army service in the first year of marriage that a man might *rejoice with his wife* (Deut. 24.5). At the circumcision, the following prayer is recited: "As he has entered the covenant of Abraham, so may he enter the study of Torah, the marital state and the practice of good deeds." It was considered a parental duty to arrange for an early marriage for children. "One who reaches the age of twenty and has not yet married," warns the Talmud, "spends all his days with sinful thoughts."[22] Indeed, to protect the holiness of Jerusalem from being contaminated by the presence of unmarried men, those between the ages of twenty and sixty were forbidden to reside there according to an ordinance of 1749.[23] Hesitant young men might be compelled by the Jewish court to marry.[24] Social pressure was exerted in a variety of ways. For example, an unmarried man does not wear a talit or a kittel (prayer garments) in the synagogue, nor does an unmarried woman cover her hair, by which habits their marital status is clearly identified. Sephardim or those who follow the Spanish rite call a married man to the public reading of the Torah as *gevir* or "gentleman," otherwise he is merely *bahur* or "young man/bachelor." In the competitive list of those who had priority rights to the honor of being called to the reading of the Torah, the bridegroom stood first. The most precious of Jewish possessions, the Torah scroll, cannot be sold, except to pay for a wedding. Jewish society was so structured as to encourage, arrange, and maintain marriage, and, in the event of death, remarriage. In the writings of church fathers, on the other hand, not only was celibacy preferred to marriage, but once married, if one's spouse died, widowhood was the chosen state.[25]

An unspoken principle in Jewish life emerged quite early: whatever strengthened the family is to be affirmed; whatever hinders it is to be opposed.

What the doctrine of creation was to the Hebrews, "natural law" was to the Greeks. While popular practice, exemplified by Aristophanes' myth of the divided human searching for his other half, be it male or female, reflected the wide acceptance of homosexuality during certain periods, the philosophic-legal opinion was quite different. Aristophanes' myth, after all, was spoken in the give-and-take of dialogue, and need not represent Plato's view, which, following Aristotle, finds that homosexuality is "unnatural."[26] The Greek thinkers understood certain features to be characteristic of man "by nature," while others are not. Recent scholars, some of whom have their own private sexual agendas, have bridled at Plato's terminology and try to soften it. Thus, in the *Republic* (571b), Plato speaks of dreams in which one,

> as if freed from every restraint of shame and reason, attempt[s] to have intercourse with his mother or with any other creature, human or divine or animal . . . and in a word to go to any length in madness and shamelessness.

The translation of Plato's term for such longings, *paranomoi*, clearly means "against *nomos* or law" and not simply "convention," as one recent author would have it.[27] Thus, Herodotus (i.61) speaks of one who, wishing to have no children by his new wife, had intercourse with her in a way that was not in accordance with *nomos*. Furthermore, in Plato's *Laws* we find:

> Were one [legislator] to follow the guidance of nature and adopt the law of the old days before Laius—I mean, to pronounce it wrong to have to do carnally with youthful male as with female, and to fetch his evidence from the life of animals, pointing out that male does not touch male in this way because the action is unnatural [not by *physis*], his contention would surely be a

> telling one, yet it would be quite at variance with the practice of your societies.[28]

The example of animal behavior cited in this passage hardly lends itself to explanation as a violation of "convention," but quite decisively describes homosexuality as unnatural, yet widely practiced–precisely the Greek conundrum.

This conundrum is expressed, on the one hand, in the spread of homosexuality in the Greco-Roman world. Thus, one scholar describes Periclean Athens as "a society dominated by men who sequester their wives and daughters, denigrate the female role in reproduction, erect monuments to the male genitalia, have sex with sons of their peers, sponsor public whorehouses, and create a mythology of rape,"[29] while another authority sees the later Greco-Roman society as exhibiting "all the symptoms of a great national disease, a kind of moral pestilence. . . . In very truth, the whole of society was infected with it, and people inhaled the pestilence with the air they breathed. . . . By the time the last days of the free republic were reached, the vice had attained a fearful degree among the Romans."[30]

On the other hand, the previous reference to the time of the early king, Laius, as the watershed of homosexuality in Greece suggests a more complex attitude to homosexuality there. We are, of course, familiar with the centerpiece of Freud's theory of the parent-child relationship, the Oedipus complex, in which the killing of one's father to marry one's mother is paradigmatic. Oedipus is the famed character in Sophocles's play *Oedipus Rex*, where the story is played out to a horrified audience that witnesses the killing of his father, King Laius, and the marrying of his mother in ignorance of her true identity. Less well-known is the mythic origin of the story. According to a legend, homosexuality was unaccustomed in Greece before the time of King Laius, the father of Oedipus. The tale goes that a boy, whom Laius had abducted for sexual purposes, committed suicide out of shame, whereupon the boy's father placed a curse upon the king: either he should have no son or that son would kill his father. The myth adds that Hera, the goddess of marriage, fearing that homosexuality would undermine her dominion, sent the Sphinx to destroy Thebes, the city of Laius. Thus, the story of Oedipus, the classic tale of family tragedy in Greek drama, has its source in the spread of homosexuality, whose introduction into Greek life was understood to have brought on a familial catastrophe, personal and communal, which, though smaller in scale, has its parallel to the Flood myth among the Hebrews that some explain is the result of sexual confusion.[31]

Heterosexuality is, then, for the Greeks (at least, theoretically and legally) a human characteristic "by nature"—as it is for the Hebrews, who would argue the same for the family, which is established and nurtured by marital sexual union.

The debate over the argument from normality is illustrated by Roger Scruton's amusing parable of the lion without a mane. It seems that a plague struck and left lions without manes. Two opinions soon formed. One argued the obvious: that while lions may not have manes for the time being as the result of a plague, the real lion, the normal lion, the one intended by the order of creation or nature, of course has a mane, while those presently without them are deviants. The other replied with equal aplomb that today's modern maneless lions are quite happy as they are, delighted to be rid of those mangy manes. And, all this talk about plagues, creation, natural law, and normality is sheer nonsense, an insidious effort to pull us back into the past.[32]

Nevertheless, homosexuality is abnormal in the sense that it violates the natural constitution of humans. Even in those cases where it is no fault of their own, one can say that homosexuals are abnormal in the same way the blind and the deaf are abnormal. As the existence of such persons does not deny the fact that humans hear and see "by nature," so humans are heterosexual "by nature," though individual persons may be homosexual, whether by constitutional orientation or environmental influence. Whether one views marriage as a part of the divine order of creation or of natural law, one who is unable to enter into such a sexual relationship is abnormal.

Certainly for the preponderance of homosexuals today, those "by choice," Jaffa's observation applies:

> All normal people have within themselves, at one time or another, desires which they know they ought not to gratify. The difference–by and large–between those who live moral and those who live immoral lives, is that the former refuse to indulge their passions merely because they have them. By habitually doing what is right, and habitually abstaining from what is wrong, the bad passions gradually lose their power, and the good ones become increasingly pleasant. This is what moral education is all about.[33]

> Why is sodomy against the natural law? . . . Because man is a species-being and the species which defines his nature is both rational and social. . . . The inclination of many men . . . to take their sex where they find it (whether their partners consent to it or not) and ignore the consequences, must be subordinated to their higher nature, which includes the interest of society. For in no other species are the young so helplessly dependent for so long. Hence the

importance . . . of both the moral and civil laws governing the institution of marriage and of the family. We know that the relaxation of these laws leads to disorder, disease, and death, no less surely in the most advanced cultures of modernity than in the most primitive. . . . All friendship, all society, indeed all of human existence, arises from the physical difference of male and female human beings. From this physical difference arises the ground and purpose of human life, because it is the ground and purpose of nature. . . . Equally with rape and incest, homosexuality strikes at the authority and dignity of the family. The distinction between a man and a woman is a distinction as fundamental as any in nature, because it is the very distinction by which nature itself is constituted. It is the ability of two members of the same species to generate a third, that confirms them as members of the same species. It thereby confirms male and female members of the human species in that equality of rights to which they are entitled as members of that species.

. . . A wife does not expect to be in sexual competition with other women, and a husband does not expect to be in such competition with other men. Nor does a wife expect to be in sexual competition with other men, or a man with other women. Where such competition exists, there can be no confidence and no love; in short, no family. Nor–odious as it is to say–does a wife expect to be in competition with her daughter, or a husband with his son. Sexual competition, whether from without or from within the family, destroys the friendship between man and wife, and thereby destroys the basis of all other forms of friendship. Confining sexual friend-

> ship to its proper sphere—between man and wife—is the very core of that morality by which civilization is constituted. It did not require Freud to instruct us in the fact that the sexual passion in its primal force is anarchic, and that the "discontents" of civilization may be traced to its imperfect sublimation. Nevertheless, without the control of the libido by the super ego, all the interests of civilized existence are at risk.[34]

When the Bible associates homosexuality in Leviticus, chapters eighteen and twenty, with other sexual deviations, it assumes that the heterosexual marital state is the normal condition for sexual relations. Once the argument from the order of creation and natural law is abandoned and heterosexuality within the marital bond as a norm is dismissed, then how can adultery, pedophilia, incest, or bestiality be rejected? I have not been able to find a single argument in opposition to, for example, incest, in the literature that advocates homosexuality. The reason for this is the simple fact that "someone who cannot say that sodomy is unnatural cannot say that incest is unnatural."[35] After all, if pleasure is the measure of all things, sexual pleasure the measure of all pleasures, and deferred sexual pleasure the ultimate sin—and unhealthy to boot—then how can one object to any means to achieve it, including the above itinerary?

To say that bestiality, pedophilia, sadomasochism, fetishism, necrophilia, and homosexuality are perversions is to posit a norm from which these deviate. But, this is precisely what is denied by present-day sexual nihilists. For them there are no norms. Yet, none of our contemporary sexual expressions are new to history. Over the centuries peoples have suffered the full measure of sexual experimentation and have testified against them, sometimes going so far as to mete out the death penalty when social cohesion was in jeopardy. The most fundamental code of even primitive societies included at the very least rules about the improper uses of force and sex. When through civil edict, religious instruction, and family sanction, sexual codes developed and were progressively internalized—though regularly violated—it was a sign of advancing culture. That culture, the "funded wisdom of the ages," is grounded in traditional family values, which modern society, in its attempt to turn civilization back to zero, neglects at its peril.

> The dissolution of the family is at the root of nearly all the social problems afflicting contemporary American society. The high rate of divorce is making emotional cripples out of children at all levels of society. And the children of divorce become divorced themselves at much higher rates than others. Crime, drug abuse, alcoholism, mental illness, venereal disease, low educational achievement, lack of job-related skills, all of these things—and many more—can have their causes traced to the disintegration of the traditional family. And at the root of the disability of the contemporary American family is the ethic that says that sexual preference is, and should be, only a matter of personal preference and personal choice. The traditional family, the embodiment and expression of "the laws of nature and nature's God," as the foundation of a free society, has become merely one of many "alternative lifestyles." . . . A free people who succumbs to such a teaching cannot long endure.[36]

Endnotes

1. See Jack. P. Lewis, *A Study of the Interpretation of Noah and the Flood in Jewish and Christian Literature* (Leiden: Brill, 1968) for a survey of Jewish and Christian understandings of the Flood.

2. N. Sarna, *Genesis* (JPS, Philadelphia, 1989), 145. One Midrash suggests that these angels belittled carnal temptation and said that were they to descend to earth, they would remain immune. They descended and succumbed. M. Kasher, *Torah Shlemah*, vol. II, p. 371, no. 16.

3. Genesis Rabbah, 26:5. See Theodor-Albeck ed. note to this verse.

4. Leviticus R. 23:9

5. *Pirkei de-Rabbi Eliezer.*

6. B. Sanhedrin 108a; Genesis R. 27:3.

7. Genesis R. 23:2.

8. TB. Sanhedrin 108a.

9. Leviticus R. 23:9. Genesis R. 26:5 adds marriages to beasts.

10. Genesis R. 26:5. Cf. *Tanhuma*, Genesis 12; Leviticus R. 23:9.

11. Genesis R. 19:7; Song R. 5.1. TB. Hagigah 12a; Ruth R. intr. 7.5; Exodus R. 35.1. Genesis 28.8; TB. Sanhedrin 108a; Lamentations R. introd. 24.

12. See EJ "Mixed Species," esp. references to Maimonides and Nahmanides.

13. Genesis R. 31.12;34.7. Cf. Philo, *Quaestiones et Solutiones in Genesis*, ii 49.

14. The Targum resolves the difficulty by translating the phrase, male and female, as in 7:3. Cf. Maimonides, *The Guide to the Perplexed*, III 6.

15. Rashi ad. loc.

16. Maimonides, *The Guide of the Perplexed,* III 37. In the same section Maimonides notes that "most of these magical practices [found in the Middle East] pose the condition that those who perform them should necessarily be women. . . . They mention [for example] that if four women lie down upon their backs, raise their legs, holding them apart, and say and do certain things while in this disgraceful posture, hail will cease falling in that place."

17. Leah was more a foil for monogamy than a case of polygamy. See the chapter on Leah in my *Rachel* (Minneapolis: Augsburg Fortress, 1994).

18. Zohar III 4b. This is based on numerous earlier rabbinic passages. See Ginzberg, *Legends*, V, 88–9 for sources and comparisons.

19. "A man without a wife is not a man, for it is said, *male and female He created them. He blessed them and called their name adam.*" TB Yevamot 63a.

20. *Zohar Hadash* 4,50b.

21. TB Yevamot 62b; Gen. Rabba 17.2.

22. TB Kidushin 29b, 30b.

23. D. Feldman *Birth Control in Jewish Law* (New York: New York Univ. Press, 1968), 31, n.53.

24. Ibid., 27.

25. D. Bailey, *Sexual Relation in Christian Thought* (New York: Harper and Bros., 1959), 20, 31–2, quoted by Feldman, ibid., 23.

26. Plato, *Laws*, Bk. 8, 835d–842a, especially 836d, 838b,c. Cf. Jasper Griffin, *NY Review of Books*, 29 March 1990, 10.

27. John J. Winkler, *The Constraints of Desire: The Anthropology of Sex and Gender in Ancient Greece* (New York: Routledge, 1989). Cf. Griffin, op. cit., 9–11.

28. Plato's *Laws*, translated by A.E. Taylor (The Everyman Series, Dutton, 1934), 223, quoted by Griffin, op. cit., 9. See ahead for further explanation of Laius.

29. Eva Keuls, *The Reign of the Phallus* (New York: Harper and Row, 1986), 267, 8.

30. Jack Lindsay, *The Ancient World: Manners and Morals* (New York: Putnum, 1968), 54.

31. Griffin, op. cit., 10.

32. Roger Scruton, *Sexual Desire: A Moral Philosophy of the Erotic* (New York: Free Press, 1988); Richard Neuhaus, "The Maneless Lions," *National Review* (8 May 1987): 5.

33. Harry V. Jaffa, *Homosexuality and the Natural Law* (Montclair, Calif.: The Claremont Institute, 1990), 25.

34. Jaffa, *Homosexuality*, 33–37.

35. Jaffa, *Homosexuality*, 34.

36. Jaffa, *Homosexuality*, 38.

FOUR

Goddess Feminism

What happens when the feminist accusation that male domination is the reason for society's failures runs up against the Bible? In that case, a growing body of thinking today argues, traditional religion and its Scriptures must go. This, at least, was the verdict issued at a conference at Indiana University, sponsored by their Women's Studies Program and entitled Feminist Search for Religious Alternatives. The focus was upon neo-paganism.

The major papers of the conference were published in a fifty-page "special section on neo-paganism" in the *Journal of Feminist Studies on Religion*, spring 1989. Among the themes taken up in these papers are the rejection of the Bible for neopaganism, the goddess and the witch, polytheism, and the fertility cult. These papers provide a shocking bird's-eye view of what is transpiring in one of the fastest growing and most radical religious movements today. They are written by young academics or leaders of the feminist movement whose influence is, and will continue to be, considerable among students and others. It is a movement that, surprisingly, has received little critical comment from scholars.

For some time, a debate has been raging between those feminists who believe one can function within the confines of a reinterpreted Judaism or Christianity and those who do not. Thus, the frantic altering of gender words in new editions of liturgies and Scriptures on the one hand, and the proliferation of altogether new liturgies and cult practices on the other. Rosemary Ruether has criticized "that branch of the feminist spirituality movement that has rejected biblical religion and turned to the alternative religion of the Goddess."[1] "On what basis," she asks, "do Goddess feminists totally reject the Bible? . . . And how helpful is the specific alternative they offer?" Opposing "separation and rejection," Ruether calls instead for "synthesis and transformation," and finds "the key to authentic feminist critique of culture . . . in the discovery of the liberating potential of traditional religion," using, for example, the prophetic cry for justice against what she considers to be oppressive biblical texts.[2]

Even Ruether, however, is not opposed to the exploration of paganism as a "religious alternative," if only its adherents be as critical of their new faith as of the old.[3] This was not good enough for Carol Christ, who argued that "contemporary oppression of women is a logical outcome of the core symbolism of God/He," that "patriarchal attitudes of the majority of those whose religious faith is based on the Bible will not be changed until the image of God is changed," and that "real feminists are revolutionaries who reject the biblical tradition in favor of a journey to the Goddess."[4] Catholic feminist Mary Daly, who gained notoriety by leading women students, exodus-like, out of the Harvard University Chapel in 1972, summed up the belief that God the "Father" guarantees a patriarchal society with the slogan, "If God is male, then male is God!" "By 1979," writes Jo Weaver, "old icons like Mary, the mother of Jesus, had no place in the women's movement."[5] Attempts to locate in Mary qualities of independence and majesty, as found in the goddesses—as well as other efforts to adjust traditional religion to the requirements of the new feminism—were denounced as "casuistry," for she had been used too long "to relegate women to subservient positions."[6]

The call to seek feminist symbols outside the accepted religious traditions was growing louder. "The Bible was a political weapon used by men against women," argued Elizabeth Stanton.[7] The reason they have had no history is because they have always been "wives, mothers and whores."[8] Thus, in the European Christian tradition, "a witch . . . is a woman who sleeps with the devil, and a nun is a woman who married her god. Wives, mothers, witches, mid-wives, nuns or whores are described almost exclusively in terms of their sexual function."[9] Mary Daly claimed that "men were naturally necrophilic, their religions inexorably patriarchal, and their world on the verge of collapse." She urged women "to reclaim their creative, biophilic natures" in a goddess religion.[10]

Less strident and more influential in her early years, certainly among Catholic women, Ruether published her *Womanguides* in 1985. Arguing that women cannot find fulfillment in the church "from the existing base of the Christian Bible," which should now serve as only one among other texts in search for "a new textual base, a new canon," her book is a compilation of such texts. It includes a prayer to the great goddess of Babylonia, and a picture of the goddess Isis leading Queen Nefertiti, beneath which is the caption, "Hand in hand, women guide each other as they claim their buried past and journey to the place of the death of patriarchy and the beginning of new possibilities of womanbeing." It became clear from the middle 1980s that when one spoke of "feminist spirituality," some kind of religious experiences clustered around goddess worship and witchcraft was intended. Not only were more books on goddess religion being printed by leading publishers, but popular expressions were being reported throughout the country. Ohio housewives were described offering up harvest fruits to Isis, and in *Women's Sports and Fitness* women of South Pacific islands were depicted claiming that their skill exceeds that of men because of powers they alone had from "an ancient Goddess from the underworld."[11]

From a reading of these reports of the Indiana conference, one concludes that while some feminist scholars still feel that one can retain the Bible and the biblical religions by means of radical reinterpretation, the majority seem to be of the opinion that it is a useless task. What it comes down to, according to Mary Jo Weaver, is the fact that "feminist theologians have to show either that the core symbolism of Christianity [or Judaism] is not hopelessly sexist, or they have to abandon it in search of a new religion."[12]

In their pursuit through history for examples of "female empowerment," feminists have found them in the goddess and the witch[13] (itself a form of goddess religion, according to Starhawk). The burden of Naomi Goldenberg's *Changing of the Gods*, for example, is to set "the revival of goddess worship in the context of a female quest for power, noting that all legitimate power for women is based on the great pagan goddesses of the ancient world."[14] Indeed, it is "the energy of Goddess religion and the rise of modern witchcraft [that] gave much of the excitement to the field of feminist theology," Weaver tells us.[15] Goddess worship, which first emerges as a female quest for power, has in the past decades grown into a full-blown religious alternative to Judaism and Christianity. God, it is claimed, is a symbol that has outlived its usefulness, whereas the goddess possesses principles of liberation not only for women but for all humanity. "I had given up on the Judeo-Christian tradition [with] its hierarchy of God, man, woman, children, animals, and earth on the bottom," one Jewish goddess-feminist explains.[16] Another, Rev. Lesley Phillips, who rejected Judaism for the Unitarian Universalist Church whose Covenant for Pagans she helped to found, tells us that "the concept of the Goddess made the Divine work for me–I don't need a male god."[17]

Far from applauding the Israelite conquest of Canaan and its ongoing struggle with paganism, we are instructed to lament the Hebrews' introduction of a male god who sought to eradicate the alleged former goddess worship. "That is, the Israelite displacement of the Canaanites is commonly perceived as a conquest of male over female, of 'patriarchal warriors' obliterating a peaceful 'matriarchal' people. Monotheism is viewed as promoting 'one right way, and that way is ours,' while polytheism is embraced as religious pluralism."[18] For, goddess worship brings with it, the argument continues, a halt to the rule of violence and force that male dominance must by its very nature foster and advocates peaceful and even utopian social and political goals. According to Diane Eisler (whose work Ashley Montagu calls "the most important book since Darwin's *Origin of the Species*"), "the only ideology that frontally challenges [a male-dominator female-dominated model] of human relations, as well as the principle of human ranking based on violence, is, of course, feminism."[19] (That the ancient goddess was anything *but* nonviolent is not touched upon in these studies.)

A line of understanding can be drawn from the Enlightenment's criticism of Christianity and Judaism to today's neopaganism. "In a phrase," Peter Gay writes, the eighteenth century "philosophes . . . were modern pagans."[20] Feminist neopagans must be pleased to hear this, but they do not quite agree for an interesting reason: while the Enlightenment left its secular advocates with "no use for sacred symbols and rites," religious feminists claim that, in rejecting traditional religion, they do not reject the need for religious values, community, or cult without which life would be intolerable. Accepting the Enlightenment's criticism of traditional religion, the new paganism questions its conclusions, claiming they do not go far enough: traditional religions seem to have been quite able to adapt to the Enlightenment's notion of a monotheistic religion of reason, but neopagan polytheism of our day dooms traditional religion once and for all, contending "that polytheism is more tolerant than any form of monotheism, . . . celebrates diversity and multiple truths, and is the logical conclusion of the Enlightenment's critique."[21] "What is truly radical of goddess feminists," writes Weaver, "is not their rejection of God but their determination to embrace religious experience in rite and community." In this sense, neopagans resemble the thinkers of the Enlightenment more in the latter's espousal of nature-worship which, it was believed, releases the elemental forces bottled up in the human psyche–Hayden White's "wild man" or Rousseau's "natural man"–and celebrates, for example, the free expression of sexual energy. In addition to the divinity of earth and nature, the new paganism respects female deities, homosexuality, and native peoples and promotes a dogmaless spirituality (each element of which can be found in the program for the "Jewish" Woodstock cited later).

"An attempt to salvage the Enlightenment critique of Judaism, which saw no fundamental differences between Judaism and savage religion," is the way anthropologist/rabbi Eilberg-Schwartz sums up the purpose of his book, *The Savage in Judaism*.[22] He attempts to "collapse the distinction between Judaism and savage religions,"[23] by professing to locate elements of the "savage" in the practices and teachings of ancient Israel. Furthermore, as is the case with goddess-feminists, he takes umbrage at the negative connotations of the term *savage*, arguing that the distinctions which have heretofore been made between Judaism and pagan religions derive more from bigotry against paganism and favoritism towards the Bible, than from fact. Against the biblical single-mindedness in rooting out idolatrous practices and the fuss repeatedly raised by the prophets against backsliding Israelites, Schwartz poses the allegation that the Israelite faith itself was shot full with savage elements. Furthermore, according to the new science, the connotation of the term *savage* as barbarous or uncivilized is passé and demands correction. In our author's opinion there are no "savages." The populations of the Congo or New Guinea "are not 'savages' whose cultural and religious practices are inferior to those of the West."[24]

One is reminded of the efforts of Delitzsch in his *Bibel and Babel* and Frazer in his *Golden Bough* and *Folklore of the Old Testament* to flatten the distinctions between biblical and pagan religions, as well as the efforts of later scholars such as Wright and Albright to restore them. For example, in his short but incisive and not sufficiently known study, *The Old Testament Against Its Environment*, Wright rejects the developmental thesis of Frazer and others which argues that the "earlier the literary source material, the more primitive should be its religious teaching and the nearer it should stand to the pagan environment in which it arose." For, in the opinion of Wright, "the faith of Israel even in its earliest and basic forms is so utterly different from that of the contemporary polytheisms that one simply cannot explain it fully by evolutionary or environmental categories. It has been assumed that . . . [Israel] borrowed from many sources, and her uniqueness consisted in the alterations and improvements which she imposed upon what was borrowed." (William James distinguished between "origin" and "validity.") "But," Wright asks, "what led to these 'alterations' and 'improvements'? . . . What . . . in early Israel . . . predisposed . . . the course of Biblical history? . . . What . . . made the particular and peculiar evolution of Biblical faith a possibility? This is precisely what the environmental and developmental hypotheses have been unable to define." Wellhausen himself confessed that "why Chemosh of Moab never became the God of righteousness and Creator of heaven and earth, is a question to which one can give no satisfactory answer." Wright's response to the failure of these theories to examine these questions is to the point: "*the inability to take seriously . . . God's revelation and covenant at Mt. Sinai*" (emphasis added).[25]

Judith Plaskow agrees with those who see the biblical description of paganism as a "caricature," a "distorted portrait of the Canaanite religion," and she does not find the biblical battle against the pagan cults altogether a cause for celebration. To the contrary, she laments over "what was lost in the Jewish victory over paganism . . . a wide range of male and female images . . . women [serving] as dancers . . . diviners . . . priestesses."[26] But, one must ask, would not the cost of giving up "dancers," "diviners," and "priestesses" by the ancient Israelites in their struggle against paganism have been relatively painless if it meant they might also be free of cultic practices, such as, for example, child sacrifice?

For despite the biblical outrage against the horrific idolatrous institution of child sacrifice, it made inroads among the Israelites, along with other pagan institutions:

> You shall not sacrifice any of your children to Molekh. . . . After the doings of the land of Canaan shall you not do . . . For in [this] the land was defiled. . . . I visited their iniquity upon them and the land vomited out her inhabitants. (Lev. 18:20, 24, 25)

> The people of Judah have done evil in my sight, saith the Lord . . . to burn their sons and their daughters in the Valley of Ben-Hinnom [in Jerusalem]. (Jer. 7:30)

> They rejected the commandments of the Lord . . . and served Baal. They consigned their sons and daughters to the fire. (2 Kings 17:16–17)

> [King Josiah of Judah] destroyed Tophet in the valley of Ben-Hinnom, so that no one might consign his son or daughter to the fire of Molekh. (2 Kings 23:10)

Was the biblical abhorrence of child sacrifice simply a "caricature" or a "distorted picture" conjured up to present a better argument for "us" against "them"? Archeological evidence, scant in relation to most of the biblical claims, is considerable in this case. Stager and Wolf present the data in their comprehensive study *Child Sacrifice at Carthage: Religious Ritual or Population Control.*[27]

On view in a major exhibit at the New York Museum of Natural History several years ago were the shocking remains of child sacrifice in Carthage, the chief outpost of Phoenicia, with whose powerful culture the early Israelites had to contend. The importation to North Africa of the practice by the Phoenicians, the preeminent travelers and traders of the time, seems clear. The sacrifices were offered to the goddess of Carthage, Tanit, and her consort, Baal Hamon. "Tanit was identified as Astarte, the Canaanite goddess of love and war,"[28] in the ivory plaque of the seventh century B.C.E. discovered by Pritchard on the Mediterranean coast not far from Sidon; it reads, Tanit Ashtart.[29] "With the discovery of this inscription, scholars now know that Tanit was originally a Near Eastern deity who ultimately received her greatest veneration in Carthage, where she was the leading goddess."[30] The grave site in Carthage is referred to as Tophet, reminiscent of the infamous spot in the valley of Ben-Hinnom in Jerusalem where the Israelites themselves once performed the abomination of burning their sons and daughters. The Carthaginian grave site contains children's bones as early as the seventh century B.C.E., continuing into Roman times, even after the Romans had forbidden child sacrifice and crucified its priestly perpetrators. This is not simply a huge cemetery of infants; it is quite simply "the largest cemetery of sacrifices of humans ever discovered."[31]

Rejecting former suppositions that the sacrifices were offered by the lower classes, or sporadically, or only in an early period and gradually phased out, it now seems to have been an ongoing upper-class practice that grew, rather than diminished, with time and was concurrent with a highly developed civilization. Alarmed at this apparent disparity, one excavator of the site wrote,

> This is a dreadful period of human degeneracy that we are now unearthing in the famous Temple of Tanit, but such is archaeology! In one spot we may be uncovering works of priceless art and traces of the advancement of civili-

> zation, and in another spot the contrasting decadence shown in the revelation of such a cult as found at . . . Carthage in Africa.[32]

Stager goes on to point out that child sacrifice seems to have been only one form of infanticide that continued to be practiced for many centuries and had purposes other than ritual. It had advantages over abortion (sex selection and the health of the mother) and was common in France, for example, until the eighteenth century. The first foundling homes were established by the Church to meet the distressing dilemma of the large number of abandoned children. "Because so many women were throwing their children into the Tiber,"[33] Pope Innocent III established the hospital of Santo Spirito at the end of the twelfth century. In the eighteenth and nineteenth centuries, the major cities of Europe had large children's hospitals for this purpose but could hardly cope with the demand. "Instead of being a protection to the living," wrote John Brownlow, referring to the London children's hospital in the mideighteenth century, "the institution became . . . a charnel house for the dead."[34] The innovation of the "turntable" ascribed to Napoleon was a new feature that, by assuring the mother's anonymity, was meant to encourage her not to destroy the child but keep it alive. Thus, "the mother or her agent could place the child on one side, ring a bell, and have a nurse take the child by turning the table, the mother remaining unseen and unquestioned."[35]

I have discussed this item at some length not because all the problems associated with child sacrifice by the Israelites and the Phoenicians are now clarified,[36] but because in this case we have abundant evidence of a comparable practice prohibited in Scripture, in which the nature of the "abomination" is fully evident in a unique archeological find of almost unparalleled range in time and depth. With this evidence, we can not only better assess the struggle against a particular idolatrous practice which the Israelites early succumbed to, yet were tenacious enough to overcome, but we are more adequately able to understand the stubborn battle the Israelites waged to root out the pagan cult in general. As a consequence of the biblical encounter, infanticide–ritual or otherwise–never posed a problem in later times to the people-Israel, for the offense struck at the infinite worth of the child in their central institution, the family.

One of the three objectives of the Indiana conference was "to introduce the university to a practicing witch."[37] Starhawk (Miriam Simof), America's best known practitioneer, was invited to address a standing-room only crowd. A short passage from one of her books gives the reader some idea of what she is about:

> The old woman carries a basket of herbs and roots she has dug: it feels heavy as time on her arm. Her feet on the path are her mother's feet, her grandmother's, her grandmother's grandmother's. Always the people of the village have come to her: her hands are healing hands . . . ; her murmuring voice can charm away pain. . . . She believes she has fiery blood in her veins, blood of the Old Race who raised standing stones to the open sky and built no churches.[38]

With the development of witchcraft, "feminists have done a noble thing," says Starhawk, for "to reclaim the word 'Witch' is to reclaim our right, as women, to be powerful; as men, to know the feminine within as divine. To be a witch," she continues, using Holocaust propaganda language much as homosexuals and prolifers have done, "is to identify with 9 million victims of bigotry and hatred."[39] As neopagans "internalize the [witch] antitype," so they internalize other human antitypes such as the "Wild Man" of nature, as well as the androgynous individual. "Men are used to thinking of themselves only as men, and women think of themselves as women, but the psychological facts [sic!] indicate that every human being is androgynous."[40]

"Priestess of the Old Religion of the Goddess, witch, religious leader, writer, counselor, women's spirituality superstar,"[41] Starhawk travels the college circuit and presided recently at a women's ritual at the University of Pennsylvania's Christian Association. A *Washington Post* reporter described the event, which began with setting an altar in the center of the room, supporting candles encased in glass.

> Before casting the formal circle that so many women's rituals start out with, Starhawk encourages the youngest and strongest in the group to form an inner circle around the altar. . . . As participants form a larger ring around the inner one, she "casts" the ritual circle, theoretically making the space within it a special place. Candles representing the four directions and the Earth's center are lit. Earth, air, fire and water are invoked. Women stand and sway as she drums, urging them to find their centers, their connectedness, often against the background of a simple chant: "rising, rising, the earth is rising. Turning, turning, the tide is turning. Changing, changing, she changes everything she touches. Changing, changing, and everything she touches changes . . ." The session ends with a grand finale "spiral dance"—clockwise to invoke, then counter-clockwise to release. "Anything you want to do involves both," she says. . . .
>
> In person, the 40ish priestess looks not unlike the onetime tall Jewish girl from Los Angeles she used to be. But her soft-voiced, authorita-

> tive presence and staccato chanting and drumming, command her sessions with surprising power. . . .[42]
>
> Two hundred people . . . were ready to join Starhawk at the three-hour $40 event. Another couple of hundred men and women arrived later that evening for Starhawk's lecture. . . .
>
> G. R., a rabbinical student, was one of the event's organizers.[43]

It comes as no surprise, then, that reports of pagan rituals are beginning to reach the public. Still, readers of the *Boston Globe* (27 April 1992) were startled to find a feature article pointing to pagan clubs at MIT, University of Massachusetts, and elsewhere, but concentrating on a description of a woman's "moon circle" (a celebration of the full moon) in a Cambridge Unitarian Universalist church. Seated on cushions, surrounded by candles, the women chant, "The earth, the fire, the air, the water, turning, turning, turning, turning . . . The goddess is alive and magic is afoot." After the smudge stick or burning incense is passed around, they rise for the spiral dance and howl joyously at the moon.[44]

Neopagans celebrate the surprising revival of witchcraft in America: no longer illiterate outcasts of Western civilization, their books are brought out by leading publishers; noted colleges invite them to their campuses. Naomi Goldenberg even offers a phenomenology of modern witchcraft.[45] On a more mundane level, the recent judgment in Rhode Island granting witchcraft tax deductible status as a "religion" is a sign of political and legal recognition. Witches "are now recognizable and respectable members of our society. . . . Anyone who cultivates the power of his or her will," Margot Adler tells us, "can become a witch."[46]

Author of the best-selling *Drawing Down the Moon: Witches, Druids, Goddess-Worshippers and Other Pagans in America Today*, of which more than one hundred thousand copies are in print, Adler was described in the *Washington Post* article as a "journalist, an elder with Covenant of the Goddess, a priestess, the granddaughter of analyst Alfred Adler. 'I think it would be fair to say,' " Adler observed in describing her journey, " 'that none of this would have happened to me if I hadn't been hit over the head in the seventh grade by studying the gods Artemis and Athena. This was the late '50s, and there weren't a lot of powerful images of women. What was interesting was we studied Greece for a whole year, and this was my religion. But I think way down deep I didn't want to worship these goddesses–I wanted to *be* them.' "[47]

Adler's *Drawing Down the Moon* and Starhawk's *The Spiral Dance*, both published in 1979, have been among the most influential in the movement. Harper & Row in San Francisco finds that goddess literature is among the hottest items in its list and boasts of some thirty-four titles which seem to sell "with little or no promotion."[48]

To gain credence, creators of religious movements usually maintain that they are not begetting something novel but, in fact, are only returning to more ancient and authentic forms. So it is with goddess advocates who assert that theirs is not a new faith at all, but simply a restoration of the old. Patriarchal religion, they claim, appeared on the historical scene, bringing with it violence and destruction by tragically defeating what had previously been a harmonious woman-centered world. The task now, it would follow, is to sweep away the errors of history and reclaim the pre-patriarchal society where matriarchs ruled and the Great Goddess held sway, a time of peace and justice. That there are no historical facts to support these bizarre claims seems not to deter their circulation. No evidence is adduced to testify to the curious contention that a supposed pre-patriarchal female-dominated epoch in which the goddess reigned supreme ever existed,[49] while the supposed harmonious, matriarchal, goddess society is contradicted by the portrayal of the goddess in the ancient texts as a bloodthirsty warrior. Feminists present a variety of responses to such arguments. Rosemary Ruether "criticized Goddess feminists for the absence or misuse of historical evidence; for articulating a simple-minded anthropology in which males are necrophilic whereas females are biophilic; for writing what amounted to escapist fiction."[50] While such censure has had a moderating effect on some, it has failed to deter the zeal of others for whom veracity must bow to ideology. Thus, despite anthropologist Margaret Mead's frequent denial–"All claims so glibly made about societies ruled by women are nonsense. We have no reason to believe that they ever existed. . . . Nowhere do I suggest that I have found any material which disproves the existence of sex differences"–sociologists seem so committed to the rejection of the physiological in favor of the environmental nature of male and female behavior that an examination of recently published textbook introductions to sociology finds that thirty-six of thirty-eight of them begin their chapters on sex-roles by citing her study at Tchambuli as evidence.[51] Naomi Goldenberg goes further in choosing "to ignore historical problems in favor of the psychic reality Goddess religion has for its adherents."[52] Undaunted by arguments, there is the insistence among some writers that "*the historical data on goddesses should be ignored if they do not present an image that is helpful for modern feminists seeking an alternative spirituality*" (emphasis added).[53]

Feminine politics draws from and parallels the

politics of sex and blackness. Thus, certain anthropologists reacted to Derek Freeman's refutation in 1983 of Margaret Mead's sensational revelation of teen-age promiscuity in Samoa by explaining that in creating "myths for society to live by," Mead was in pursuit of "a higher truth."[54] And, after the so-called rape of Tawana Brawley (heralded by Al Sharpton and Alton Maddox as characteristic of white oppression) was exposed as a hoax, Stanley Diamond wrote in *The Nation* that "it doesn't matter whether the crime occurred or not"; even if the incident was staged by "black actors," it was staged with "skill and controlled hysteria" and described what "actually happens to too many black women." Further, attorney William Kunstler opined that "it makes no difference anymore whether the attack on Tawana really happened" and applauded the actions of black militants who "now have an issue with which they can grab the headlines and launch a vigorous attack on the criminal justice system."

Another theme enunciated at the Indiana conference was a call for a reconsideration of the fertility cult in the life of the goddess and in ancient history. When historians of antiquity speak of Canaanite religion, they often do so in terms of what they call the "fertility cult." Thus, John Bright in his standard textbook of the period wrote,

> Canaanite religion . . . presents us with no pretty picture. It was, in fact, an extraordinarily debasing form of paganism, specifically of the fertility cult. . . . [The goddesses] represented the female principal in the fertility cult. They are portrayed as sacred courtesans or pregnant mothers, or with a surprising polarity, as bloodthirsty goddesses of war. . . . As the myth was reenacted in the mimetic ritual, the forces of nature were thought to be reactivated, and the desired fertil-

> ity in soil, beast, and man thereby secured. As in all such religions, numerous debasing practices, including sacred prostitution, homosexuality, and various orgiastic rites, were prevalent. It was the sort of religion with which Israel, however much it might borrow of the culture of Canaan, could never with good conscience make peace.[55]

Martin Noth writes similarly, as does Bernhard Anderson, observing that the goddess was known "for violent sexual passion and sadistic brutality,"[56] while Albright notes that "the three goddesses [Astarte, Anath, and Asherah] were principally concerned with "sex and war. Sex was their primary function."[57] These four, among the best known scholars of the biblical period, from their studies in comparative religion and archeology, find evidence pointing to a cult that was devoted to fertility. Of late, critics have questioned whether the fertility cult as described ever existed, or whether cultic prostitution was not prostitution pure and simple(!),[58] though the sexual-centeredness of the pagan world, and the biblical and rabbinic consuming abhorrence of the consequences, can hardly be denied.

The agitation over the fertility/sexual characteristic of the goddess, however, is more than a scholarly debate to be decided on the basis of historical evidence. Having acquired the goddess as an "empowering," liberating force, some feminist writers are now warning fellow feminists to beware that they not unwittingly buy into this fertile understanding of her, for to do so would be to reduce the goddess to just another "sexist model rather than a liberating one."[59] Most feminists decry the goddess as sexual symbol in the belief that that is precisely the fate to which women have been sentenced in the past and from which they now need to be redeemed. Judith Ochshorn, on the other hand, admires the fertility goddess for the example of "free sexuality" for women that the goddess celebrates.[60] As Starhawk put it,

> Sexuality is sacred, and potentially an act of worship. The women in pagan temples did not consider themselves to be prostitutes, but were reenacting a great mystery. All acts of love and pleasure are rituals of the Goddess. Judaism [however] gives a double message: sex is good, but menstruation is unclean. Sex is a mitzvah, but only with your husband.[61]

But, how do feminists who dispute the association of the ancient goddess with fertility/sexuality deal with the evidence? They deny its credibility, suggesting that these theories have been concocted out of secondary sources by those unable to read the Canaanite texts, or, if they can read them, that they write out of masculine bias. After all, who first came up with the notion of a "fertility cult" but men? The whole construction of fertility religion vs. biblical religion is nothing more than a web of "fears and fantasies" of Western male scholars, "many of whom are"–and this is the ultimate put-down–"Protestant clergymen."[62] To those who are sympathetic to paganism, biblical religion is simply another one of the cults of antiquity, better than pagan cults in some ways, worse in others. Biblical fulminations comparing religious apostasy with adultery and prostitution are simply dismissed by Hackett as a "metaphor: the good guys and the bad guys . . . a metaphor nineteenth and twentieth century [male] scholars identify with. . . . They fail to recognize the propagandistic function of much of biblical literature."[63] Hackett continues,

> Scholars have exaggerated the connection between fertility and female deities in the religions of the ancient Near East, and I think they

> have done this because, as Martin Noth said of the Israelites, they are profoundly uncomfortable with *female* deities, and find it easier to deal with such power if it is restricted to the sphere of fertility. . . . Modern scholars are . . . perpetuating the biblical polemic when they describe the rivals to Israel's official cult as debased and degrading.[64]

In their attempt to claim black Egypt as the source of Western civilization, Afrocentrists (e.g., Molefi Asante's *Afrocentricity*) are not averse to explaining away the presence there of art which testifies to the reverse by ascribing it to fiendish Western forgeries perpetrated to "mislead people into thinking that the ancient Egyptians were white."[65] Similarly, in confronting the absence of evidence attesting to an Ur-matriarchal society, Mary Daly accuses male scholars of having doctored the translations of the primary goddess texts to suit their fancies; it was a case of male malevolence. "The patriarchs destroyed the records, burned the women, and set humanity on a collision course with self-destruction."[66] (The possibility that some modern scholars, male and female, uneasy with moral mandates, may be embarrassed by and seek to downplay the prophetic and rabbinic outrage with sexual perversion is not dealt with.)

What are Jews to make of all this? Is there any ground for special Jewish concern? Yes, there is and on several levels. It has not been adequately appreciated that, amidst the larger scene of feminine awareness and achievement, a movement is afoot to embrace a pagan and polytheistic goddess cult, and that in this effort it is the Hebrew Bible that bears the brunt of the attack. Further, Jews figure prominently among goddess-feminists, both among the rank and file and among authors who play a central role in the growth of this movement.[67] Most serious is the relative silence on the part of Jewish thinkers and biblical scholars in defense of Judaism. There is hardly a single significant book by a Jewish biblical scholar that attempts to refute the neopagan, goddess claims which by now include a considerable number of articles, books, and conferences.

How shall we explain this failure? Is it because Jewish scholars are not aware of this burgeoning movement, or, aware of it, agree with its claims? I would prefer to consider three more compelling reasons.

One reason is academic. Those who have attained a high level of learning may wave the goddess literature aside as unstudious and a distraction from more important work. A double standard seems to be at play here in taking seriously what one considers a properly scholarly undertaking while ignoring most of the issues raised at the Indiana conference. Although this may be understandable within the constraints of tight research schedules, it cannot be excused for the simple reason that there is a growing population who, reading this literature, may take it at face value, including people whom we want to educate, including future Jewish scholars.

A second reason is objectivity. Some scholars want their work to be considered "value-free." They see themselves as not taking sides, believing it to be unscientific to make distinctions between, for example, the mythological goddess of the neopagans and the God of Israel. But, there is precious little scholarship or teaching that is value-free. Every scholar brings to his or her work a system of values. Of course, students or readers must draw their own conclusions, but does that mean that scholars are not to draw conclusions of *their* own in favor of one point of view or another? Not doing so could be a way of side-stepping responsibilities. Can one discuss Genghis Kahn vs. Socrates or murder vs. just wars in a totally antiseptic manner? People were killed by the Germans at Auschwitz and by the allies in WWII, but not even the most objective scholar will fail to modify the word "killed" in each of these events. Teaching inevitably involves making judgments. Our very language compels taking sides: right from wrong, creative from destructive.

Some see being free from theological bias as an advantage over so-called theologically committed or partisan writing. But, the opposite may be the case. And, lacking the tools of theology and of ethical conceptualization, they may miss the most important "facts" they analyze. Scholars such as Frank Cross and William Albright, Protestant clergymen to be sure, had no trouble in using terms of opprobrium in describing pagan religions. What is the Bible if not a struggle to wrest the people-Israel from the clutches of the pagan gods and the cultures they spawned? Mordecai is emphatically called a Jew "because he abjured paganism [*avodah zarah*], for everyone who abjures paganism is called a Jew" (Megillah 13a).

Are Jewish scholars unused to wielding the tools required to deal with these issues? Has the neglect of theology for the pursuit of the "history" of ideas or "comparative" religion—the shying away from the concepts of the Bible in favor of its literature, its history, its philology, and its archeology—hampered a mastery of the theological and intellectual claims of the Bible and of its rabbinic successors? Have Jewish scholars by their training in the science of Judaism been denied an education in the values of Judaism and so frustrated their mastery of the weapons of response?

Perhaps the bias against theology and competing value systems has been encouraged by the honest confusion caused by specialization, whereby the wider context of questions such as what is right and wrong, or the claim of Judaism to present a world outlook that is superior to that of the pagan world in which it arose, came to be deemphasized. In the days of the prophets, there were no doubt people who were value-free experts in both the pagan cult of Ashtoret and the worship of the God of Israel, but who left no imprint upon human civilization. The prophets of Israel, however, who may have lacked "scientific objectivity" have left a lasting impression upon the world up to and including our own time. Perhaps contemporary Jewish scholars should bear this in mind as they pursue their serious and worthwhile intellectual endeavors.

A third reason for the relative silence of Jewish scholars to neopaganism one might describe as something between caution and cowardliness. I hope I am mistaken in using this worrisome word, but it describes at times the behavior of some academics today who strive to achieve what has come to be known as PC (Political Correctness) on campus. The disease of PC seems to have spread into many of our institutions in a way that stifles traditional academic freedom. There is the fear of getting into trouble, of offending the sacred cows. British historian Paul Johnson goes further. He tells us in *The Spectator* that Political Correctness is

> entirely a university invention . . . the new form of totalitarianism. It is a myth that universities are nurseries of reason. They are hothouses for every kind of extremism, irrationality, intolerance and prejudice. . . . The virulent outbreak of black antisemitism, which has [Crown Heights] Brooklyn in violent uproar, was bred on campus in the fraudulent "Afro-American Studies" departments.

The arrival of PC should come as little surprise

when we consider what academics were writing about as shown in the recent Arts and Humanities Citation Index for the years 1976-83. The most commonly cited authors were Lenin, Freud, Noam Chomsky, Roland Barthes, and Heidegger, in that order.

Freedom of expression is on the campus books, of course. It is the eleventh commandment. But, in reality everyone knows that you dare not speak your mind on certain issues, including, affirmative action, reverse-discrimination, homosexuality, and feminism. Much as white guilt turns a blind eye on whatever blacks do, regardless of their excesses, so anything that parades under the name of feminism goes unchallenged, irrespective of the consequences. For our purposes, Jewish scholars may think they can avoid distress by distancing themselves from the troublesome issue of goddess feminism. The hesitance to speak out is understandable, but it is not pardonable. Safety is no substitute for honesty. History will ultimately judge those who failed their responsibilities as scholars and human beings.

It reminds one uncomfortably of German and Russian scientists, who knew better but were silent at Hitler's racial theories or at Lysenko's biology in order to avoid being put into a predicament. In America, one can offer no such excuse. It is true that one of the problems of the devotees of Judische Wissenschaft was that, in an effort to demonstrate to the world that Jews possess something to be proud of, they were, at times, given to exaggerated apologetics: on the other hand, hiding one's virtues in the attempt to appear objective is even more damning. Scholars are more than chroniclers of ancient texts.

The "basic idea of Israelite religion," wrote the Israeli scholar Yehezkel Kaufman in the 1930s in his great polemic against paganism, is monotheism, the belief that

> God is Most High, over all. . . . In short, the religious idea of the Bible, visible in the earliest strata, which even permeates the "magical" legends, is that of a supreme God who stands over every cosmic law, every destiny and every compulsion: unborn, uncreated, knowing no passion, independent of things and their powers, a God who does not fight against other deities or powers of impurity, who does not sacrifice, predict, prophesy and practice witchcraft; who does not sin and needs no atonement; a God who does not celebrate the festivals of his life. A free divine will which transcends all that is—that is the characteristic of biblical religion, and that makes it different from all the other religions on this earth.[68]

Where is the Yehezkel Kaufman of the 1990s?

Endnotes

1. Rosemary Ruether, "A Religion for Women," *Christianity and Crisis* 39 (10 December 1979): 307–311; cited by Weaver in "Who Is the Goddess," *Journal of Feminist Studies in Religion* (Spring 1990), vol. V, issue 1 (hereafter *Journal*) 54, 55.

2. Weaver, "Goddess," 55, 56.

3. Weaver, "Goddess," 55, note 23.

4. Ibid., 54–55.

5. Ibid., 51.

6. Ibid., 52.

7. Ibid., 59.

8. Jo Ann Hackett, "Can A Sexist Model Liberate Us? Ancient Near Eastern 'Fertility' Goddesses," *Journal of Feminist Studies in Religion* (Spring 1990): 66.

9. Cited by Hackett in "Sexist Model," 66.

10. Weaver, "Goddess," 51.

11. Mary Nelson, "News from the Field," *Women's Sports and Fitness* 9 (March 1987), cited by Weaver in "Goddess," 54.

12. Weaver, "Goddess," 59.

13. Ibid., 53.

14. Ibid.

15. Ibid., 54.

16. Judith Antonelli, "Paganism's Allure Draws Women Alienated From Judaism," *The Jewish Advocate*, 29 May 1992, interview with Thelma (Levy) Henner.

17. Anthony Flint, "Paganism Seeing a Resurgence," *Boston Globe*, 24 April 1992.

18. Antonelli, "Paganism's Allure."

19. Riane Eisler, *The Chalice and the Blade*, 164, cited by Weaver in "Goddess," 63.

20. Peter Gay, *Enlightenment*, 8, XI, cited by Howard Eilberg-Schwartz in "Witches of the West: Neopaganism and Goddess Worship as Enlightenment Religions," *Journal of Feminist Studies in Religion* (Spring 1990): 80.

21. Eilberg-Schwartz, "Witches of the West," 88.

22. Howard Eilberg-Schwartz, *The Savage in Judaism: Anthropology of Israelite Religion and Ancient Judaism* (Bloomington: Indiana University Press), 240.

23. Ibid., 1.

24. Ibid., 2. In his review, David Biale tells us that Eilberg-Schwartz "is entirely correct in his claim that doing away with the old apologetic dichotomy between Judaism and 'savage' religions is a profoundly political act. It forces us to consider Judaism as one of the many world religions, with no special privilege born of lofty monotheism or refined ethics."

25. G. Ernest Wright, *The Old Testament Against Its Environment* (London: SCM Press, 1950), 10, 7, 15.

26. Judith Plaskow, "Jewish Anti-Paganism," *Tikkun*, vol. 6, no. 2, 66-68.

27. Lawrence Stager and Samuel Wolf, "Child Sacrifice at Carthage: Religious Ritual or Population Control," *BAR* (Jan/Feb. 1984): 31–51. A comprehensive study of the subject is now available in J. Day, *Molech: a god of human sacrifice in the Old Testament* (Cambridge: Cambridge University Press, 1989).

28. Stager and Wolf, *Child Sacrifice*, 45.

29. Ibid., 50. See J. Pritchard, "The Tanit Inscription from Sarepta" in *Pheonizeir im Westen*, ed. H. G. Niemeyer, *Madrider Beitrage* 8 (1982), 83–92; cited by Stager.

30. Stager and Wolf, *Child Sacrifice* 50.

31. Ibid., 32.

32. Ibid., 32.

33. Ibid., 51.

34. Ibid., 51.

35. Ibid.

36. See B. Levine, *Leviticus* (Philadelphia: JPS, 1989), excursus 7, pp. 258–60, for a summary of the issue.

37. Weaver, "Goddess," 48.

38. Starhawk, *Dreaming the Dark*, 183–4, cited by Eilberg-Schwartz in *Journal*, 85.

39. Starhawk, *Dreaming the Dark*, 18; cited by Eilberg-Schwartz in "Witches," 86–87.

40. J. Sanford, "Projecting Our Other Half," in *Challenge of the Heart*, ed. John Welwood (Boston: Shambhala, 1985), 82; cited by Eilberg-Schwartz in "Witches," 86.

41. Judith Weinraub, *Washington Post*, "The New Technology-SHEology: Mystical Women's Spiritual Movements, Gaining Momentum . . . and Adherents," 28 April 1991.

42. Ibid.

43. Ibid.

44. Anthony Flint, "Paganism."

45. See her *Changing of the Gods.*

46. Eilberg-Schwartz, "Witches," 84.

47. Weinraub, "New Technology-SHEology."

48. Ibid.

49. See Weaver, "Goddess," 56.

50. Ibid.

51. Steven Goldberg, "Feminism Against Science," *National Review* (18 November 1991): 30. "Jesse Bernard . . . pointed out that, if the reader ignored the adjectives, the Tchambuli did not seem very different from other societies. 'Effete' headhunters and 'comradely' women feeding their children are still male headhunters and women feeding their children, and it is only the adjectives provided by Margaret Mead that even begin to suggest otherwise" (ibid.).

52. Weaver "Goddess," 58,

53. Hackett, "Sexist Model," p. 67, note 6, citing Christ and Plaskow.

54. Nicholas Davidson, "Was Socrates a Plagiarist?" *National Review* (25 February 1990): 47.

55. *A History of Israel*, 3d ed. (Philadelphia: Westminster Press, 1981), 118–19; cited by Hackett in "Sexist Model," 71.

56. *Understanding the Old Testament*, 3d ed. (Englewood Cliffs, N.J.: Prentice-Hall, 1975), 142; cited by Hackett in "Sexist Model," 72.

57. William F. Albright, *Archaeology and the Religion of Israel* (Baltimore: Johns Hopkins University Press, 1942), 142. Cited by Hackett in "Sexist Model," 72.

58. Cf. Gruber, "Hebrew *Qedesah* and Her Canaanite and Akkadian Cognates," *Ugaritsche Forschung* 18, 133–148.

59. Weaver "Goddess," 48.

60. Judith Ochshorn, *The Female Experience* (Bloomington: Indiana University Press, 1981), 127–129; cited by Hackett in "Sexist Model," 67, note 5.

61. Antonelli, "Paganism's Allure," interview with Starhawk.

62. Hackett "Sexist Model," 68.

63. Hackett, p. 73. "No one really knows what Canaanite religion was," advises Starhawk. "I would question what the Talmud says about it, just as I would question what Julius Caesar wrote about the Druids, what the white man wrote about Native Americans, or what a Catholic priest in the 15th century wrote about Jewish theology" (Antonelli, op. cit.).

64. Hackett "Sexist Models," 75.

65. Davidson, "Was Socrates a Plagiarist?" 45.

66. Weaver, "Goddess," 57, citing Mary Daly.

67. One "ex-pagan" who returned to Judaism tells us that in the seventies she was a "goddess-worshipper" but now she is married, has children and belongs to a synagogue. In 1971, during her college years, a Witchcraft Museum opened in town that she visited "out of curiosity," but when her dying father asked his children to go to temple and pray for him, they went to the Witchcraft Museum instead "for some incantations." Drawn to paganism for feminist reasons, she joined a "coven" of 13 women for "women's power and healing," which included "color healing, aura cleansing, astral travel to past lives, organizing and educating women to bring them to goddess worship."

Turned off to paganism by "psychic manipulation," "the institution of a High Priestess," and her growing awareness of anti-Semitism, and encouraged by a visit to Israel, "it wasn't until I started building a Jewish home that I slowly incorporated Jewish spirituality back into my life." Paganism, she said, had denied her "Jewish roots . . . with women who thought their roots went back to ancient Egypt, when

I knew mine didn't. I was hanging out with Hagars instead of Sarahs." She felt that she "could have achieved the same spirituality reading about the Jewish matriarchs." Before, she had "wished there was a book to give me the answers. [Now she knows] there is . . . the Torah. It's the key to civilization and peaceful life. . . . When I was a pagan, I didn't believe in monogamy. Sex was an expression of freedom. [But] promiscuity is not healthy [or] holy."

She says she is raising her children so that there will no possibility for them to become pagans. "If I had been given a deeper and richer understanding of my own religion, I wouldn't have had to go in that direction. I am teaching my children to thoroughly enjoy and understand Judaism. They're getting the full education that I didn't get." (Antonelli, "Paganism's Allure.")

68. Y. Kaufmann, *The Religion of Israel* (abridged version translated from the Hebrew by M. Greenberg), Chicago 1960, 60, 121.

Around the same time in America the doyen of Christian biblical authorities, William Albright, summed up the idea of God in early Israel.

"The belief in the existence of only one God, who is the Creator of the world and the giver of all life; the belief that God is holy and just, without sexuality or mythology; the belief that God is invisible to man except under special conditions and that no graphic nor plastic representations of Him is permissible; the belief that God is not restricted to any part of His creation, but is equally at home in Heaven, in the desert, or in Palestine; the belief that God is so far superior to all created beings, whether heavenly bodies, angelic messengers, demons, or false gods, that He remains absolutely unique; the belief that God has chosen Israel by formal compact to be His favored people, guided exclusively by laws imposed by Him." *Archaeology and the Religion of Israel* (Baltimore, 1942), 116.

FIVE

The Return of Paganism

Encouraged by feminist spirituality groups that focus their attention on goddesses, some Jews, as I have pointed out in the last chapter, have turned to a world of pagan rituals in order to supplement an allegedly sexually impoverished Jewish tradition. All of this is often legitimized with the simple explanation that the more "woman oriented" folk religions of the ancient world were able to avoid the patriarchal pitfalls of monotheism.

Why is all this threatening? The mention of goddesses and images within a Jewish context will probably sound strange to most Jews–but is not likely to seem much of a hazard in the century of concentration camps, Arab terrorists, and scud missiles. But, we are dealing here with values that ultimately are deeply antagonistic to what I would describe as the healthiest aspects of the Jewish tradition. Having gathered material for some years now for a study of the sexual aspects of ancient paganism and its modern revival, I was at once stunned and unsurprised by these developments. I was stunned because it had surfaced so close to home, but I was not surprised because it was inevitable that it would surface somewhere soon, considering the confluence of the sexual revolution, expanding and extremist feminist claims, the considerable representation of Jews in both the feminist scene and the sexual revolution and–of particular importance–the failure of competent scholars to bring those concerns into the categories of Jewish teaching. Even if some critics are correct and the ancient fertility cult was not quite as it has been described–having at least as much to do with male deities as female, etc.–that would not affect the use of a similar term today. What better way is there to describe our sex-saturated society in which carnal performance has been elevated to the status of a religion? The revived pagan outlook responds, it is claimed, to a perceived need, and a review of this outlook may suggest what kind of a threat it poses to the Jewish (and Christian) way of life. To explore the ancient fertility religions in more detail we must treat books and subjects considered pornographic only a few years ago–but not by some ancients, nor a growing number of moderns.

The Fertility Cult

What upset the ancient Hebrews about pagan deities was not the art form the pagans used, but the life form they represented. Female divinities played a prominent role. These power-hungry goddesses of the pagan agricultural cult were anathema to the Hebrews. One ritual of this cult was sexual intercourse between the gods and goddesses and/or with the priestesses of local shrines (Herodotus); these acts were meant, through the convolutions of sympathetic magic, to encourage a divine mating of the male and female gods, which was to insure the fertility of the land. The pagan worship of sexual prowess, releasing as it did one of the most uncontrollable of human impulses, quite naturally gave rise to explicitly erotic art and poetry and to excesses far beyond the limits of the cult practice itself (homosexuality, for example, which certainly could make no contribution to fertility).

From the successful efforts of archeological research and linguistic advances over the past century, we are able to piece together into a startling mosaic the individual bits of evidence that have been unearthed. We understand more now about the cryptic, idolatrous terms that the Bible frequently uses but rarely defines—terms such as "high places," "beneath leafy trees," "Asherah," and "pillars." We now better recognize the sexual-centeredness of the pagan religions of biblical times against which the Bible is arraigned in bitter and constant conflict.

Part of this conflict involved a biblical response to myths associated with the pagan religions, which can be divided into three basic types: myths of fecundity, myths of passion, and myths of divine marriage. The myths of fecundity taught that procreation, the elemental need of a pastoral-agricultural society, was to be achieved through the coupling of the gods. The god-father, most often associated with the phenomenon of the storm (rain signifying the fertilizing sperm), impregnated the god-mother, personified by the earth, thus germinating not only the plant world but also the animal and human, and serving the interests of both shepherd and farmer. In the myths of passion, the goddess-lover seduces in archetypal fashion her male partner, or rather, partners, for she has many. Ishtar, the Babylonian counterpart of Aphrodite, has a central lover; Tammuz, the dying and reviving deity of vegetation, has a number of them, including the horse, the bird, the shepherd-bird, the keeper of the herd, and her father's gardener—liaisons which span the divine, the human, and the bestial. The last of the three types of myths, depicted in Ugaritic and other texts, consists of myths of divine marriage. These myths tend to focus attention on the nuptial union itself.

While the myths offer divine archetypes, their accompanying rites are more significant. These rites, often of a sexual nature, are characterized by a belief in sympathetic magic by which the acts performed are somehow efficacious. Thus, the divine marriage enacted with pomp and ceremony on the new year between the king, who represents the community–Marduk of Babylon, for example–and a chosen priestess, is meant to stimulate the male fecundity of human, beast, and land. The rite of the monarch sets a royal pattern for the members of the cult, who were said to visit the priestess-prostitutes (at times castrated males) in their sanctuaries, and whose acts may suggest and even reenact the divine union. Around the primal sexual rite, fantasized ceremonies no doubt proliferated, accompanied by frankly sexual art forms. A religion characterized by such myths and rites must have unleashed the erotic fantasy into a torrent of behavior beyond the prescribed forms of the cult.

Despite recent efforts of some scholars to downplay the fertility cult, contrary evidence continues to mount. At Medinet Habu, for example, the site of the temple of Ramses III of Egypt (1182 to 1151 B.C.E.), a major excavation was undertaken from 1927 to 1933 under the direction of the leading Egyptologist of the period, James Breasted of Chicago, and supported by other international scholars. Only in the summer of 1993, however, did Chicago's Oriental Institute receive the lost field notes that had been housed in East Berlin. Many small beds about one foot in length decorated with religious symbols had been discovered, accompanied by figurines of women with extremely large breasts and men with highly exaggerated phalluses–clear examples of a fertility cult. However, what was previously thought to be limited to the nobility or the temples now seemed to represent the religion of the common people. Egyptologists conclude that

> by determining which objects came from commoners' homes, we gain whole new insights into the Egyptian way of life. Now we are sure that the votive beds are a reflection of an ancient fertility cult enacted in private homes. The material is an intriguing reflection of the cares of women and their families in ancient Egypt. . . . This material allows us to see the art and ritual objects of the common man and woman and to see how most of the society lived.[1]

With a better understanding of the nature of these pagan cults, we may gain a fuller appreciation of the unremitting struggle of the biblical prophets to root out what the scholars have labelled almost euphemistically "polytheistic idolatry." Only in this context will we come to understand why the Bible uses the verb *zonah*–"to whore after"–when referring to foreign gods; the verb is not used only metaphorically. We know that the Scriptures do not countenance idolatry, but we have not adequately known why. And, we have not known why, because we did not fully appreciate the character of the threat posed by the pagan cults. This seems not to have been the case with the Talmudic sages. Rabbi Judah said in the name of Rav: "*The Israelites knew there was no substance to pagan idolatry. They took it up only to engage more freely in forbidden sexual practices.*"[2]

Biblical Response

As the people were enticed away to pagan rites, the prophets railed against them, no more impressed by the charm of the pagan priestesses or the drama of the goddess than they were with the splendor of the "ivory palaces" of Samaria, which were cursed by Amos because they were built from the sweat and blood of the poor. The danger of pagan religion challenged the essence of the prophets' humanity.

The ancient Israelites viewed the sacralization of human impulses as their enemy, the seductive work of an ingenious, dazzling, smothering, primeval demon. The powers of nature were not divine forces to be feared, worshipped, or manipulated. Unlike the pagan pantheon of gods and goddesses that invaded every aspect of human life, the Lord of Israel was not nature's creature, subject to its laws and whims. He was its sovereign Creator, the Master of all. The stars in the heavens did not represent divinities to be adored, but served to "declare the glory of God." In a single stroke, the authority of the pagan deities was destroyed. And, in place of the pagan rituals with their focus upon worship of the forces of nature, a regimen of mitzvot was established to civilize man by governing human impulse. This was a central difference between paganism and the religion of the Bible. Scripture's unequivocal label for this sort of cult was "abomination," and the Hebrews attempted to stamp it out, sometimes ruthlessly, in an ongoing battle of culture and practice, the record of which is a central theme in the Bible and Talmud.

The eighteenth chapter of Leviticus, the scriptural reading for the afternoon of Yom Kippur, the day of fasting, atonement, and contrition, the holiest day of the Jewish liturgical year, leaves nothing to the imagination when spelling out the challenge:

> *You shall not copy the practices of the land of Egypt where you dwelt, or the land of Canaan to which I am taking you: nor shall you follow their laws. My rules alone shall you observe. . . . I am the lord. . . . You shall not have intercourse with your mother . . . your sister . . . your granddaughter . . . your sister-*

> *in-law . . . with a man as with a woman . . . with a beast. Nor shall a woman submit herself to have intercourse with a beast: that is a violation of nature. . . . You shall not sacrifice your children to Molekh. Do not defile yourselves in any of these ways, for it is by such that the heathen that I am casting out before you defiled themselves. . . . So let not the land spew you out for defiling it, as it spewed out the nation that came before you. All who do any of those abhorrent things–such persons shall be cut off from their people. . . . I am the Lord your God.*

The poison of pagan culture, as they understood it, was to be feared, expunged, or, at the very least, avoided. Canaanite spouses were not to be taken by the patriarchs, Isaac and Jacob, since these critical transmitters of the covenant of Abraham might thereby be seduced into the paths of idolatry. Therefore, the long and dangerous treks across the desert to relatives in far-off Haran in search of Rebecca and Rachel, who, like Sarah, were to become worthy partners in sustaining the covenant. That these measures were not unreasonable is attested to, for example, by the fact that the king of Moab almost succeeded in his plan to destroy Israel by using Moabite women to entice the Israelites into worshipping the Baal of Peor, one of the most sinister and powerful of the pagan cults. *While Israel was staying at Shittim, the people profaned themselves by whoring with the Moabite women, who invited them to the sacrifices for their god* (Num. 25:1–2). The later rabbis expound this passage in lurid fashion:

> At the bazaars huts were built for harlots. Old women sat at the doors to drum up business for the girls inside, enticing passers-by to enter by offering discounted merchandise. Once within, after some sweet talk, the Israelite would be encouraged to drink sufficient wine, until Satan burned within him and led him astray. As it is

written, *harlots and wine capture the heart.* [3] (Hos. 4:1)

To halt the orgy, Pinhas, the priest, entered the tent of the Israelite prince and put a spear through him and the Moabite woman who lay beneath, *pinning them together* (Num. 25:8). It required the death of thousands more Israelites to stamp out the revolt, the seriousness of which must have been considerable in view of the lethal means used to halt it. The grave nature of the incident is evidenced by the fact that it is dealt with over several chapters in the Book of Numbers and referred to in other parts of the Scriptures. Of Edom who attacked with the sword, Israel is told *Do not abhor them,* but of Moab who attacked with sin, Israel is told, *Do not come into marriage forever.*[4]

Victory over pagan idolatry was never complete. Every generation had to struggle against the threat. The momentous reform of King Josiah, recorded in the Book of Kings and chosen for the prophetical reading on the second day of Passover, demonstrates how closely Israel came to being swallowed up by the powerful cults. The Book of the Covenant (Deuteronomy?) was "found" in the temple, as if it, along with its laws, had been lost, and at a solemn convocation the people renewed their covenant with God, promising to fulfill the commandments *with all their heart and all their soul.* As the text continues,

> *The king ordered the high priest . . . to remove from the Temple of the Lord all the objects made for Baal and Asherah [i.e., the "sacred post"]. . . . He brought the image of Asherah from the House of the Lord . . . and burned it in the Kidron valley outside Jerusalem; he beat it to dust and scattered its dust over the burial ground of the common people. He tore the cubicles of the male prostitutes in the House of the Lord, at the place where the women wove vestments for Asherah. . . . He brought all the priests from the*

> *towns of Judah and defiled the shrine where the priests had been making offerings. . . . He also defiled Tophet, which is in the Valley of Gehinom, so that no one might consign his son or daughter to the fire of Molekh. . . . The king also destroyed the shrines facing Jerusalem . . . which King Solomon had built for Ashtoreth, the abomination of the Sidonians, for Chemosh, the abomination of Moab, and for Milcom, the detestable thing of the Amonites.* (2 Kings 23)

The biblical excoriations very closely identified sexual license, idolatry, injustice, and child sacrifice. A similar association can be found in the prophets.

> *Long ago you broke your yoke. . . . On every high hill and under every verdant tree, you recline as a whore. . . . How can you say, "I am not defiled, I have not gone after the Baalim"? Look at your deeds in the Valley [of Hinnom, where child-sacrifice was offered]. Consider what you have done! Like a restless she-camel in heat . . . None that seek her will grow weary– In her season they will find her.* (Jer. 2:20–22)

> *I will be a swift witness against the adulterers, and against false swearers; and against those that oppress the hireling in his wages, the widow, and the fatherless, and that turn aside the stranger from his right, and fear not Me, said the Lord of hosts.* (Mal. 3:5)

> *These are the words of the Lord God: "Alas for the city that sheds blood within her walls and brings her fate upon herself, the city that makes herself fetishes and is defiled thereby! the guilt is yours for the blood you have shed and for the fetishes you have made. . . .You have treated your fathers and mothers with contempt, have oppressed the alien . . . ill-treated the orphan and the widow . . . and desecrated my Sabbaths. You have feasted at the mountain shrines and committed lewdness. You have exposed your father's nakedness, violated women during their periods, defiled your sisters . . . accepted bribes to shed*

> *blood . . . oppressed your fellow for gain. And you have forgotten Me. . . .*
>
> *"I, the Lord, have spoken and I will act. I will disperse you among the nations and scatter you abroad; thus will I consume your filthiness out of you altogether . . . And you will know that I am the Lord."* (Ezek. 22:1–15; see also chapter 23)[5]

Greco-Rabbinic Period

The Jewish struggle for sexual morality and for the family, which is such a clear presence in the Bible, remained a constant motif well into the later talmudic period, as evidenced by an extensive rabbinic literature devoted to these themes. During the talmudic period, however, the threat was posed by aspects of the dominant Greco-Roman culture, as well as by the local cults which had represented the major threat of the biblical period. The threat presented by the Greco-Roman world is taken up in a recent study of Greek sexuality by classicist Eva Keuls.[6] Her book offers a startling picture of Greek sexuality, not in the later, decadent Hellenism, but in the high culture of Athens. Keuls describes Periclean Athens, long revered for its contributions to philosophy and drama, as "a society dominated by men who sequester their wives and daughters, denigrate the female role in reproduction, erect monuments to the male genitalia, have sex with sons of their peers, sponsor public whorehouses, [and] create a mythology of rape." When Keuls speaks of a society marked by an "open display of the phallus," she is

> not referring, as Freudians do, to symbols that may remind us of the male organ, such as bananas, sticks, or Freud's cigar. In Athens no such coding was necessary. As foreigners were astonished to see, Athenian men habitually displayed their genitals, and their city was studded

> with statues of gods with phalluses . . . erect. The painted pottery of the Athenians, perhaps the most widespread of their arts, portrayed almost every imaginable form of sexual activity.[7]

While most of this pottery had been hidden away in museums and rarely discussed, like much of the statuary found at Pompeii, 350 pieces are reproduced in Keuls' book. They depict scenes that are, if possible, even more revelatory than the pagan hymns from Sumer. The artifacts of Inanna's time, some three thousand years ago, are hardly discernible today. Furthermore, Inanna describes the mythic rites of the gods, while the Greek representations, also in some measure portraying divine fantasies, depict actual scenes of daily life in classical Athens, which for the historian of culture, is their greatest value. Keuls' analysis of Greek literature illustrates her theory. She writes,

> The comic drama of the classical age is so steeped in far-fetched genital allusions and imagery that no scholar can hope to decipher it unless armed with complete sexual single-mindedness and a formidable vocabulary of obscenity in ancient Greek. If Philip Roth could read Aristophanes with full understanding, he would blush. Classicists teaching Aristophanes tell their students that if they fail to find an obscenity in any one phrase, they probably are not getting the point.[8]

But, most enlightening for our present discussion is Keuls' sketch of the sexual education of the "model Athenian gentleman." This gentleman, Keuls writes,

> probably started his sexual experimentation in youth as the "beloved" of a mature man, who would copulate with him and offer social and intellectual favors. The youth was introduced to heterosexual intercourse at a symposium, where he could develop a supremacist stance by mak-

> ing slave prostitutes submit to dorsal sex. The practice of humiliating and battering older prostitutes at drinking parties helped him overcome the lingering mother image in his soul. Soon he began going to brothels and private pimps to rent a succession of prostitutes, with whom he engaged in revels and symposia. Society afforded him a long rope of tolerance. Promiscuity, group-sex, [and] drinking . . . were standard ingredients of this phase. When no longer very young, our hero brought home a child bride whom he had not previously met. His new wife entered his home, cowed and terrorized, both by the separation from her own family and the overdramatized prospect of defloration. If she survived the hazards of teenage motherhood, she probably developed as a mature woman feelings of frustration and hostility against her husband. By then our hero was a full-fledged member of the male community and was probably taking his turn as a lover of boys–getting even, in a sense, for the humiliations of his own youth. With the onset of middle or old age he began to yearn for more tender attentions, regular companionship, and personal care; at that time, he would take a concubine. With her he entered into an informal, essentially monogamous, quasi-marriage of undetermined duration, in which he held all the power.[9]

This new portrait of the model Athenian sheds light on the gravity the rabbis assigned to their continuing battle for sexual morality and for the family, and it explains the forcefulness and the stridency of their tone. It is, in part, in the context of a Greco-Roman world such as that described by Keuls that the rabbinic teachings continue the campaign initiated by the Bible. From a random selection of rabbinic teachings one can find the pagans described as "drowning in lewdness–*sh'tufey zimah.*" And, one can also find the following caution. "Lest she be attacked, it is forbidden for a Jewess to be alone with a pagan even in the presence of his wife, since heathen women are accustomed to such behavior."

"At least pagan homosexual couples do not undergo a marriage ceremony," observes the Talmud, alluding, perhaps, to the notorious wedding of Emperor Nero to his male consort. Roman circuses and theaters were proscribed by the rabbis as places of perversity and cruelty. And, Shimon ben Yohai, in response to another's praise for Roman architecture, remarked, "Selfishness is the purpose of all their building: baths they build to delight their flesh, roads to collect tolls, and market-squares to station harlots. Whereupon he was sentenced to death."[10] The sharp divide which separated Jewish values from those of the Greco-Roman world is tragically demonstrated in the record relating that "after the conquest of Palestine a shipload of boys and girls, being taken to Rome for lewd purposes, drowned themselves."[11]

According to the rabbis, the reason the eighteenth and nineteenth chapters of Leviticus are juxtaposed is because the eighteenth chapter contains the central biblical catalogue of sexual proscriptions, while the nineteenth begins with the verse, *You shall be holy, because I the Lord am holy* (19:1), thus teaching that the first lesson of holiness is to remain sexually pure. The Talmud, written in the Greco-Roman period, explains that the strategy of the biblical Moabites, in attempting to seduce the Israelites to immorality at Baal Peor, was based on the presumption about the Hebrews that "their God despises lewdness" and would surely punish them. Abraham, the principal patriarch and the first to enter the covenant of the flesh, was said to have been stationed before the gate of Gehinom to deliver the circumcised from entering, except for those who had illicit relations, especially with Gentiles, for "the God of Israel forgives all, save sexual sin."[12] Josephus, finally, provides us with insight into the talmudic dictum that "Jews were above suspicion of sodomy" when he tells us that even Herod, highly assimilated into Roman ways as he was, balked at dispatching his brother-in-law, Aristobulus, to the Roman court, because "he did not think it safe to send so handsome a man to Anthony, the principal man among the Romans, who would abuse him in his amours" (*Antiquities*, XV 2, 6).

As we have seen, Judaism contended with the sexual ethos of its neighbors, the rabbinical teachings continuing the biblical struggle. We can summarize the biblical stand against sexual paganism by identifying four aspects of that struggle that became essential to the Jewish way of life:

1. *De-mythologizing the divine.* The Scriptures rejected the ancient mythological biographies of fighting, seducing, incestuous, cannibalizing deities that are born and die, couple to fertilize the earth, and that are symbolized by "pillars" on "high places" or sexually graphic statues. The pagan gods, from Egypt to Babylonia to Greece to Rome, appear to have been fashioned, to an extent, in the human image, that is, in the subhuman image, reflecting subconscious drives for violence and passion. The gods in fact do what humans fantasize doing, and, through veneration and imitation of them–for they are the gods–humans find license to violate restraints and do similarly. In contrast, the Bible presents one supreme, eternal spirit, Who forbids images, Who creates the world and demands fidelity and righteousness from His creatures.

2. *De-sexualizing the cult.* The Scriptures provide no place for the sympathetic magic of pagan sexual worship. In one sweeping move, the ancient, ubiquitous and compelling link between sexuality and ritual was sundered, and it was sundered in part by placing religious worship in the hands of a single gender. Even God, Who is beyond all gender, is referred to in male terms.

3. *Sanctifying sexuality.* Two institutions were established. For the male, circumcision, understood not simply as a national rite, but also a covenant of sexual morality; for the female, the laws of "family purity," featuring the mikveh. Both institutions, emerging in the Bible, found full expression in rabbinic law and remained central features of Judaism over the centuries. The new institutions helped to consolidate the home and family.

4. *Confirming the family as the basic unit of society.* The Bible, as we have indicated, lays down as one of its central objectives, from which it was never for very long to be diverted, the spiritual and legal development of the family, including such values as fidelity, monogamy (ultimately), the home, the Sabbath, parenting of children, and honor for the parent. In the rabbinic literature, these values are fleshed out in the ethical teaching (agadah) and law (halakhah). But, this can be traced back to the Bible, which typically conveys its message not by theological discourse but by emblematic family episodes that offer themselves as paradigms for living.

Biblical morality was not spelled out formally in syllogistic splendor, but found its medium in the trivial and the momentous, the failures and successes, of individual families: Abraham's finding the proper wife for Isaac, Jacob's love for Rachel, and Joseph's rejection of temptation and revenge. A careful reading of a number of the Genesis stories and the rabbinic commentaries on them–the sin of Adam, the Flood, the sons of Noah, Sodom and the daughters of Lot–reveals that each was meant to repudiate the practices of homosexuality, adultery, and incest linked to the surrounding cultures. In the Talmudic period, the victory of the Jewish family against its environment was virtually complete. Roman writers noted the strange quality of visiting Jews, who did not behave as other travellers but remained faithful to their wives. Roman matrons were even known to light the Sabbath candles in emulation of the Jewish Sabbath.

To understand Jewish history is to appreciate the priority given throughout to the Jewish family, for one of Israel's most important guiding principles is: *Whatever is supportive of the family is to be favored. Whatever is harmful to the family is to be opposed.* Once we recognize the axiomatic nature of this principle, we can better perceive Judaism's attitude to practices that were seen as disruptive to the family, such as premarital and extramarital sexual relations, homosexuality, and casual divorce. It was not that other forms of sexual life were impossible, but that over the long course of human history these other forms proved self-defeating, while the family seemed to be the most successful institution in containing the sexual impulse and providing the basic unit of society. One of the most remarkable achievements of biblical-rabbinic Judaism was the single-minded goal of creating the moral, eventually monogamous, family within which the sexual impulse was validated and sanctified. This goal is in the very order of creation, as Scripture tells us: *He created them male and female, and He blessed* (married?) *them, and called THEIR name ADAM.* In the Jewish view, then, the human person is not whole until male and female become family through the mitzvah of marriage.

Family imposes responsibility for one's actions. As Allan Bloom has pointed out in *The Closing of the American Mind*, man's naturally promiscuous sexual desire is restrained; he accepts these restraints when beauty and character evoke a lasting love for a single person. And, such love, expressing itself in poetry and song, leads to sublime–or sublimated–sex. The free choice of such a partner and the willing acceptance of the responsibilities and obligations of family is the mark of culture–in Bloom's phrase, "desire informed by civility." Only within the context of family bonds, which provide love and permanence, the miracle of procreation, and the gentleness and sacrifice of parenting, can sexual desire be sublimated and civilized.

That lesson is painfully clear today in our society which has seen the disintegration of the family, and which now suffers from AIDS, a sexual disease whose destructive power has reached appalling proportions. It is well to keep in mind that sexual promiscuity and crime are least among children of two-parent homes. Furthermore, it is in the family that our egocentric struggle of each against the other is transformed into a pattern of mutual concern. The family views our unfinished natures not as a shortcoming but as a blessing to be consummated in marriage.

The fact that Judaism, by identifying the family as one of its first concerns, was able to overcome the formidable challenge of a hostile and corrupt environment and produce one of history's noblest communities, is an encouraging sign for our own twentieth-century society, which finds itself in a dilemma not without ancient parallels.

Feminism

Two movements that have especially affected women over the past decades are feminism and the sexual revolution. Each of them emerged as a response to what some women considered to be repressive conditions, and each has achieved a number of its original goals–not without cost, however. Considerable advance has been made, for example, in opening the marketplace and the academy to women, but as they have experienced the new demands that job responsibilities make on their time, energy, and family life, and as the growing percentage of unmarried and, what is more serious, apparently unmarriageable, women populate the scene, the real price for these victories becomes clearer. The once triumphant cry about "superwoman having it all" has been modified with more sober talk about "tradeoffs."

A polarizing of views is perceivable. On the one hand, husband, home, and family have risen in esteem for a number of women. Some, with successful careers, regret the sacrifices they made. Others are planning more carefully how best to cope with both family and career at the same time; and, still others have decided to opt out of a career altogether. On the other hand, there is a hardening of position among extremists, an eagerness to consolidate victories and push forward, regardless of the cost. If family commitments present a problem, then do without, or, better, substitute a pseudofamily with nonhusbands, or without men altogether. Convinced that gender persecution has been, and will be, the inevitable lot of women unless they gain "power," some feminists are moving to an exclusively female society, even to the point of incorporating a belief in witches and goddesses.

In her brilliant book, *Who Stole Feminism*, Christina Sommers distinguishes between the older "equity" feminism, which argued with considerable logic against discrimination, and the newer "gender" feminism, which declares war against "patriarchy," that supposedly has enslaved woman. An example of "gender" feminism's irresponsible method is the fantastic claim made in the books by Gloria Steinem, Naomi Wolf, Joan Rumberg, and repeated even by columnist Ann Landers, that 150,000 women a year die from anorexia, a disease ascribed by these authors to male dominance and expectation. That is more than three times those who suffer auto fatalities! Sommers, surprised by the figures, did what the others did not do–she sought to validate the source. She discovered that the National Center for Health Statistics said the number was fifty-four, not 150,000!

Or, take the case of Andrea Dworkin. She finds the crux of women's problems in *Intercourse,* the title of her book. "The political meaning of intercourse for women," writes Dworkin in summing up her argument, "is the fundamental question of feminism and freedom: can an occupied people–physically occupied inside, internally invaded–be free?" One pauses to allow her words to sink in. "People" must mean women, and "physically occupied inside, internally invaded," must mean sexual intercourse, presumably even that between husband and wife. According to this philosophy, then, woman, without doing or being anything special, but simply by virtue of her biological nature, has been, and must continue to be, a victim rather than a partner in any sexual relation with man. To put it differently: she suffers perennial and constant rape, because all sex is rape–invasion, violation, occupation. For a woman to be "free," then, must mean, according to Dworkin, quite simply that she not have intercourse!

Is this an argument for celibacy? Yes, but with a twist. Women are to be celibate, but only from men. It argues for lesbianism, not because one is born that way and can do no other–the common justification for homosexuality–but because, on principle, one should avoid men. Believing women to have been dominated by the male since the beginning of history, Dworkin and others propose that the yoke be broken once and for all; women should rid themselves of the male, find love with other women and, if they wish, have children by grace of the new chemistry.

Among this militant element in the women's movement, the language becomes more strident, more demanding, and more anti-male. One finds parallels with the black movement. Just as it began as a struggle for rights in a colorblind society and has moved on to demand black power for black enclaves (an official training manual on racial sensitivity for teachers in the New York school system advised that "all whites are racist!"), so the push for women's rights has given way, among some, to the demand for women's power and women's separate place. I have cited the Dworkin example only to give the reader a notion of the distance some women have traveled from the benign purpose of equal rights and opportunities. It is in this general context that one may see the goddess model, powerful and authoritative, expressing commandingly two central human passions–sex and aggression.

A summary statement of Jewish teaching on sexuality may be helpful at this point. The way of exploitation, characterized by pagans both ancient and modern, argues for the worship of the forces of natural impulse and unleashes human passion; in it the other is solely an object for the gratification of the self. The way of escape, characterized by ascetic religions, glorifies celibacy, sees sex as sinful, and frustrates the natural human desires. Judaism, rejecting both the ways of exploitation and escape, has understood sexual desire neither as holy nor unholy, but waiting to be made holy, and sublimates it, through a system of mitzvot that focus on marriage and the home, to the service of God.

Some Jewish feminists strike out against Judaism when they mean something else and propose bizarre solutions instead of working out the issues within the norms of Jewish teaching. That is not to say that aspects of the image of woman in Judaism, or, better, their halakhic manifestations, are not without problems. But, the conceptual framework is conducive to a resolution of these problems, and, in fact, considerable progress has been made to resolve them, especially among the nonorthodox. (Paradoxically, orthodox women seem less, not more, disturbed by "problems.") Jewish obsession with sexual repression as an all-inclusive problem, which lumps Jewish and Gentile approaches together, is like Jews preaching to Jews about zero population growth at a time when they had just lost one third of their numbers in the Holocaust! The sexual issue, so prominent in our day and so prominently participated in by Jews, is hardly a Jewish issue at all.

The Jewish theologian Abraham Heschel identified "two extreme views" on human sexuality, one "deifying" desire, the other "vilifying" it. He wrote,

> There were those who, overwhelmed by the dark power of passion, believed that they sensed in its raving a manifestation of the gods and celebrated its gratification as a sacred ritual. Dionysian orgies, fertility rites, sacred prostitution are extreme examples of a view that subconsciously has never died out. The exponents of the other extreme, frightened by the destructive power of unbridled passion, have taught man to see ugliness in desire, Satan in the rapture of the flesh. Their advice was to repress the

> appetites, and their ideal, self-renunciation and asceticism. Some Greeks said: "Passion is a god, Eros"; Buddhists say: "Desire is evil." To the Jewish mind, being neither enticed nor horrified by the powers of passion, desires are neither benign nor pernicious, but, like fire, they do not agree with straw. They should be neither quenched nor supplied with fuel. Rather than worship fire and be consumed by it, we should let a light come out of the flames.[13]

Over the centuries, Judaism has dealt profoundly with the sexual issue, encouraging individuals not simply to find objects for their personal gratification but partners for mutual love and responsibility. And, Judaism teaches that through love, marriage, and family, a biological act can be sanctified. How, then, do we explain the antifamily strictures espoused by some Jewish feminists? I think that Susan Handleman has accurately identified their source when she suggests that Jewish

> attacks on the Jewish family are not from a depth of true Jewish commitment and understanding but from an all too American ethic of self-gratification, narcissism and antinomianism. Being Jewish is not to be defined by whatever makes one feel good and self-justified. *The lifestyles of Jews should not determine the Jewish style of life* (emphasis added).[14]

Handleman quite correctly distinguishes between Jews and Judaism. Judaism represents a legacy of wisdom, but many Jews, for whatever reasons, have chosen to ignore that legacy, so that the "Jewish style of life" and the "lifestyles of Jews" come into conflict. But, it should be clear that the former is not determined by the latter, even if the latter should become a majority in the Jewish community. What is so disturbing about the problem today is that it also transpires within part of the religious community of Jews. It is one thing for the *Village Voice* to wave as their banner certain radical causes, but quite another for institutions of Jewish learning to do so—when those causes violate the most central teachings of Judaism. To cloak perversion with piety has a frightening ring, conjuring up memories of the Asherah in the temple and the antics of Jacob Frank, precisely because it blurs the distinctions between the Jewish style of life and the lifestyle of Jews, between what Judaism prescribes and what some Jews regrettably choose to do. It tends to validate the position that *whatever* Jews say or do can be identified as Judaism. It cripples the ability of Judaism to address the doings and sayings of Jews. How can a religion that is based four-square on marriage and the home countenance the revival of the sexual lifestyle of ancient (and modern) idolatry?

Jews have, as well, played a less than admirable role in the sexual revolution. That, however, does not mean that they speak for Judaism, any more than antifamily Jewish feminists do.

The Jewish style of life is not androgynous. While it argues for the rights of women, it argues too that women remain women. Equality does not mean sameness. Achieving equality with men in areas in which this was not previously the case need not mean acquiring men's faults—for example, the rising incidence of lung cancer among women suggests that they have taken on the smoking habits of men with a vengeance. "We have become the men we once wanted to marry," remarked a reformed feminist. Nor should it mean that women abandon qualities uniquely theirs. The movement of women into the uncharted waters of the clergy presents both opportunities and perils. Unisex, the homogenous blurring of gender, is not the answer. There is work to be done. And, men and women must do it. Some of the work is to be done in the same way by both, some differently; some is to be shared, some is not. To insist on fitting women exactly into the mold forged by and for men over the millennia may not be the wisest course. Regardless of how we twist and turn, biology speaks to destiny. Feminine qualities should not be abandoned but utilized, enhanced, and celebrated.

Better than most specialists in Jewish studies, writers such as Allan Bloom, Leon Kass, and Daniel Bell have plumbed the shallowness of the modern scene and seem to understand that the collapse of the modern age's substitution of culture for religion has opened us to traditional and, in many ways, Jewish values.

> In the old dispensation [writes Bloom] modesty was *the* female virtue, because it governed the powerful desire that related men to women, providing a gratification in harmony with the procreation and rearing of children, the risk and responsibility of which fell naturally–that is, biologically–on women. Although modesty impeded sexual intercourse, its result was to make such gratification central to a serious life and to enhance the delicate interplay between the sexes, in which acquiescence of the will is as important as possession of the body. Diminution or suppression of modesty certainly makes it easier to attain the end of desire–which was the intention of the sexual revolution–but it also dismantles the structure of involvement and attachment, reducing sex to the thing-in-it-self. This is where feminism enters.
>
> Female modesty extends sexual differentiation from the sexual act to the whole of life. It makes men and women always men and women. The consciousness of directedness toward one an-

> other, with all the attendant attractions and inhibitions, informs every common deed. As long as modesty operates, men and women together are never just lawyers or pilots together. They have something else in common— . . . "life goals." Is winning this case or landing this plane what is most important, or is it love and family? As lawyers or pilots, men and women are the same, subservient to the one goal. As lovers or parents they are very different, but inwardly related by sharing the naturally given end of continuing the species. Modesty is a constant reminder of their peculiar relatedness and its outer forms and inner sentiments, which impede the self's free creation or capitalism's technical division of labor. It is a voice constantly repeating that a man and a woman have work to do together that is far different from that found in the marketplace, and of far greater importance.[15]

Kass concludes his splendid essay on Rebekah thus:

> We have come a long way from the days of Rebekah, and yet, we face her situation afresh in each generation—and today, more so than for many years: how to transmit the way of life directed and sanctified by the God of Abraham, Rebekah, and Jacob, amidst the natural dangers and cultural temptations that stand in the way? Today, the fatal attractions for Jewish fathers (and not for Jewish fathers only) are more prevalent and tempting than [Isaac's] venison: money, power, and status; board rooms, country clubs, and ESPN; the Ivy League, the Chicago [Bulls], the bottom line; and, alas, for a growing number, alcohol, promiscuity, and even cocaine. These fatal attractions, thanks to our newly found equality, are also open without discrimination to women. What will become of the children of

> Israel (and, again, of children generally) if women, too, live only for the here and now, if they opt only or mainly for personal self-fulfillment? Whatever might be the case for America or for the world, the way of the Jewish people, now and forever, depends absolutely on the right ordering of the household, devoted wholeheartedly to the noble and sacred task of rearing and perpetuation. For this task–and there is, for Jews, none higher–women, we learn from the Bible, have special access and special gifts, especially if they hearken to . . . the transcendent voice.[16]

But, the views of Bloom and Kass are little heard in the welter of voices raised on these and related issues. Indeed, a return to pagan models is being seriously considered among precisely that body which has historically been at the forefront of the struggle against it: the clergy.

Seminary

In a privately distributed, mimeographed article, "Wine, Women, and Shabbas," written by Arthur Waskow (until recently a teacher at a rabbinical seminary), the author illustrates the program of the new "messianic halakha," which he advocates.

> We begin the Shabbas service [at Kibbutz Micah, a farm in Pennsylvania] with a purifying Mikveh in the creek. A dozen of us, men, women, children, naked, exhilarated, join hands in a circle, chant the mikveh prayers, go deep under, let ourselves float into the water, the World. Rise up, laugh, sing, pray, immerse again. Three times, as prescribed by law; and then another four, from ecstasy. . . . The sexual energy high but/and spiritually directed: among us, between us and the universe. We walk singing up the hill

> to greet . . . the Sabbath . . . Deep, high, sexually alive, open to the knowing of God. Coming back to the farmhouse for a Shabbas meal of cheese, nuts-and raisins-in-cinnamon, wine. Staying sexually/spiritually alive through maariv. Then, as we separate from the community into couples, feeling the traditional mitzvah of Friday night sex as indeed for the first time a holy act.[17]

In Waskow's updating of the Passover haggadah, *The Freedom Seder* (published in 1969 through the Micah press and copyrighted by the religious community of Micah), he included in his celebration of "freedom" Allen Ginsburg's foul poem.

> Holy! Holy! Holy! . . . The world is holy! The soul is holy! The skin is holy! The nose is holy! The tongue and —— and hand and a— holy! Everything is holy! everybody's holy! everywhere is holy! . . . Everyman's an angel! The bum's as holy as the seraphim! The madman is holy as you my soul are holy . . . Holy Peter holy Allen . . . holy Kerouac . . . holy Burroughs. Holy my mother in the insane asylum! Holy the —— of the grandfather of Kansas . . . Holy the jazz bands marijuana hipster peace and junk and drums . . .

Carrying forth Waskow's theme of the "messianic halakha" is Zalman Schachter, who has been associated with the same rabbinical college as Waskow and has told us that he has "apprehensions when [he] is asked to marry a couple who has *not* lived together" (emphasis added).[18] In an article, "The Future Shabbat," from the journal of the commune he founded called *P'nai Or* (originally *B'nai Or*, now apparently too sexist a name), Schachter provides us with the most explicit description of his sexual model. In answer to the question, What can we hope for sexually in the future Shabbat? he replies:

> An adolescent or otherwise single person who wanted to give hirself [sic!] pleasure and waits to do it likhvod Shabbat [in honor of the Sabbath], and/or a loving pair who make sure to take their time enacting the union of the Holy One and Shekhinah and do so lavishly and tenderly.

Waskow's and Schachter's bizarre juxtapositions of the holy and the profane, of piety and perversity—turning the welcoming of the Sabbath into a sexual orgy thought to celebrate a divine cohabitation eerily reminiscent of the Mesopotamian pagan cults, and transforming the Passover seder into a feast of liberation from "middle-class" morality, featuring vulgarity, crude pantheism, and the invoking of homosexual gurus—were early signs of the present pagan explosion. They conjure up painful memories of the infamous seventeenth century false messiah Sabbatai Tzvi or his successor, Jacob Frank. Their coming was to mark a new age when the rule of Torah was to be superseded—"What was forbidden is now permitted"—and transgressions would become mitzvot. Is that the "messianic halakha" Waskow had in mind? Is that the new age envisioned by Waskow, who has, through books on social action and celebration, and as leader of an antiwar center, worked hard and creatively to find a Jewish home for what he has retained from the political-radicalism, commune-sex-drug life-style of the sixties, flavored with a touch of mysticism?

The name of the celebrated novelist, Bashevis Singer (who I shall treat in detail later), surfaces at this point. In his fraudulent focus upon the so-called sexual and demonic underground of East European Jewry, Singer declares his early "fascination with Sabbatianism," which, he tells us, early in his life became the anchor to his spiritual mooring. One wonders whether one of the factors that prepared the ground for the new Jewish paganism is the present awakening to sexual and female themes in Jewish mysticism. A central attraction of Sabbatianism, to which Gershom Scholem has given such extended and sympathetic treatment, is its antinomian character, its break with law and tradition. Scholem's obsession with Kabbalah in general and Sabbatianism in particular was due in considerable measure, according to Schweid and others, to his own break with Jewish tradition.[19] His denial of a "normative" Judaism in favor of a series of "Judaisms"–Karaism, Sabbatianism, etc.–each as authoritative as the next, may not be unrelated to the present-day denial by some Jews of the normative–i.e., "heterosexual, nuclear"–family, in favor of a number of alternate, equally valid family styles. "Anarchism" is the term Scholem himself used. For those who seek the forbidden in Jewish guise, Sabbatianism points the way. For centuries–and especially following the Frankist heresy–Kabbalistic works were generally restricted to an elite who were known for their piety, talmudic learning, and observance, and who, irrespective of the erotic symbolism which characterized that literature, were themselves highly moral in their private lives and followed the law in all its details. We now face the wide dissemination of these texts, readily available in translation, to a post-Freudian generation of students and others, mostly untutored and often disgruntled.

All of this seems to have come together in the summer of 1992 with the opening of the first Jewish Woodstock, "The Woodstock Center for Healing and Renewal," the moving spirits behind which are Waskow and Schachter with a heavy sprinkling of rabbis from the Reconstructionist College serving in various capacities (though the college found it necessary to deny their official sponsorship). The confluence of feminism and goddess worship with sexual experimentation, mysticism, and a back to nature drive is manifest in their impressive booklet. It signifies the full-blown arrival of the New Age movement among Jews. This major "happening" featured, according to its brochure, some forty courses, among which were "daily yoga"; "a week for Lesbian, Gay, or Bisexual Jews"; "Depth Hasidic Journey . . . a week of devekut"; "Encountering the God/dess–An Exploration of Jewish Feminist Identity" with "Starhawk, a High Priestess who wanted to be a rabbi when she was sixteen, but has chosen a goddess-affirming path outside of Judaism"; "Torah and Dharma . . . Ram Dass and Zalman [Schachter], two Dharma-Bums, grandfathers of the *New Age* [who] meet again to . . . share their passion in the service of the planet." The staff of fifty included a Cherokee Indian, the creator of "Dyke Shabbas," "a specialist in the spiritual dimension of weddings, [who] is also a licensed massage therapist, now studying for the rabbinate," the rabbi of "Bet Shekhinah" of San Francisco, an instructor of "Sexuality and the Sacred and Theologies of Liberation," including the reigning American witch, Starhawk.[20]

Among the non-Orthodox rabbinical schools, the Reconstructionists (with the Reform closely behind and the Conservative also on the move) have been particularly indulgent of alternate lifestyles, accepting homosexual candidates for the rabbinate. When the dean of academic administration was asked about his reaction to the interest in paganism among the students, he explained that Reconstructionism is based on the thought of Mordecai Kaplan, who argued that Judaism is not more than the civilization of the Jewish people; so, too, is its notion of God. One might recognize "a variety of attitudes of what God is," the dean asserted. Consequently, "it is difficult to define what a rabbi should do and believe. . . . We are open to people experimenting with new ideas and practices, as long as people are honest."[21]

Clearly, Judaism is tied to land, language, and culture, elements, to be sure, of a civilization. But, does it follow from this that Judaism is *anything* Jews say it is, as long as they are "honest," that there are *no* fundamental beliefs or patterns of behavior without which Judaism ceases to be Judaism? If the majority of Jews suddenly affirmed a belief in Inanna as their personal savior, would that make her the goddess of Judaism? Is that really what Mordecai Kaplan meant when he equated Judaism with the civilization of the Jewish people? If it is "difficult to define what a rabbi can do and believe," does that mean that a rabbi can do or believe *anything*? Are there no limits to pluralism?

There are those who represent an interest in the forgotten pagan past as expressing the "cutting edge" of Judaism. But, the pursuit of the cutting edge dare not become an end in itself. The administrator cited above sees no problem with "experimenting with new ideas and practices," as long as "people are honest." One wonders if "honesty" mandates making known the sexual "preference" of ministerial candidates to congregations, who may have some apprehension over a spiritual leader who will not discourage–and may even encourage–lesbianism and/or homosexuality, and who may raise the worrisome problem of whether two married homosexuals (male or female) can sue the congregation if dismissed because of their liaison. Do congregational families not have a right to feel betrayed? This would seem to be the view of one noted psychoanalyst, Mortimer Ostow, who has studied such behavior for decades:

> I believe that some people will be homosexual no matter what experiences they encounter, and others will be heterosexual no matter what experiences they encounter. However, there are many individuals who observe within themselves inclinations toward homosexuality and who can be influenced one way or the other by not only childhood, but pubertal and adolescent experiences. It is common for pre-pubertal and early postpubertal boys particularly, but sometimes girls, to engage in homosexual contacts. Unless there is a seduction by an important adult, their decisive option is for heterosexuality. *In other words I believe that at critical periods, the influence of an adult relative or family friend or casual contact can bring about a permanent option for homosexuality* [emphasis added]. *(Conservative Judaism)*

How far does "experimentation" go? Does it include nakedness in Sabbath retreats? Does it entail a new type of rabbi who will expect a couple to live together before marrying them? Does it include worshipping a goddess or becoming a witch? Does it mean that the sign of successful sexual training for the "future Shabbat" will be "an adolescent . . . who wanted to give 'hirself' (sic!) pleasure and waited to do it in honor of the Sabbath, [or] a loving pair who make sure to take their time enacting the union of the Holy One and Shekhinah and do so lavishly and tenderly?" Does it include homosexual or lesbian rabbis? Will there be new liturgies for intermarriage or for the marriage of single-sex couples, for the circumcision of a child born to lesbian rabbinic partners, or for keeping "sexual energy high"? Where will it end?

The Reconstructionist Rabbinical Seminary affirmed that "the process of defining limits must regularly proceed simultaneously with our efforts to expand our horizons." Though this seems irreproachable on the surface, does this tendency to "expand horizons" without sufficiently defining limits point to a weakness in the Reconstructionist philosophy, which had its origins in the popular naturalist-positivism of seventy years ago and was directed to nonbelieving Jewish ethnics, who were told that "Jewish civilization" could replace their lost faith? Today, however, the ground rules have changed. Secular Jewishness is dead and its ethnic ghetto long gone. Young Jews now ask for reasons to retain their Judaism, *religious* reasons. But, a Reconstructionist naturalism that denies a personal God and Jewish chosenness finds that task increasingly difficult.

Nor are these issues limited to a single institution. In part, what gives rise to the situation in which the Reconstructionists and others find themselves is the powerful influence of moral relativism, described by its modern apostle, Max Weber, as a "fact-value dichotomy." What that means and what is wrong with it, is suggested by Leo Strauss:

> Science, including social science would hereafter focus all its attention on facts, because only facts constituted true knowledge; values would be consigned to the private sphere because they were inherently subjective. [But] if all values are entirely subjective, this means that no solution is morally superior to the other, and therefore the decision has to be transferred from the tribunal of ethics to that of convenience or expediency. According to modern social science, our natural sense of right and wrong must be artificially suppressed for the purpose of reigning scientific objectivity. . . . In avoiding value judgments, where reason cries out that such judgments be asserted, is not truth sacrificed to pro-

> cedure? How can one give an account of the morally turbulent creature called man, without making certain value judgments?[22]

Our generation is the bewildered inheritor of that valueless philosophy, which by now has filtered down to every level of society. To the level of politics: a presidential candidate who commits adultery is only guilty of "bad judgment" (while the paper that broke the story is "repugnant to decent social conduct"). To the level of the family: homes housing a husband-wife-child, a live-in couple, or a gay couple with an adopted male child are promoted as equally valid family lifestyles. To the level of education: teachers are told to present the facts of a "life-situation," such as teen-age sex, and then "even-handedly" to moderate the students discussion about how they might deal with it, which procedure is called–"Values-Clarification"! To therapy: not "Do you think that is right or wrong?" but "Does it make you feel comfortable?" To disease: AIDS is viewed more as a problem of discrimination against homosexuals than of homosexual behavior. To religion: "It is difficult to define what a rabbi should do and believe. . . . We approve of people experimenting with new ideas and practices as long as people are honest."

At a conference of Jewish academicians several years ago, I was sitting next to a young Catholic theologian, the author of a fine book on a Jewish thinker, who had come to the conference to see and hear the Jewish scholars "discuss Torah." The speaker of that session was explaining why there is no "essence of Judaism," not even God or Torah; no essence, only survival. The Catholic, visibly disappointed, turned to me and uttered the most Jewish statement of the evening: "I don't understand. If there is no essence, not even God or Torah, then why should the Jews survive?"

Those who object to Judaism's heterosexual and monogamous approach to sexuality as being too narrow to embrace the alternate and "creative" way of the pagan goddess religion are hardly prepared to advance the cause of the Jewish family. How would a clergy intrigued by the power-hungry goddess, or who view sex as rape, deal with pastoral family problems, such as the raising of children, adultery, illegitimacy, or, for that matter, any family tension? How could they transmit the ideal of the woman as wife, mother, Akeret Habayit and Eyshet Hayil, and the father as Baal Habayit? And, if not, are we willing to abandon those ideal types?

At a sparsely attended session of the convention of conservative rabbis in 1980, Allan Miller, prominent rabbi and analyst, raised these questions:

> The worship of the Mother Goddess was opposed by the spiritual leaders of the [Jewish] people. What were the reasons for this opposition? Are those reasons still currently valid? If not, why not? What is the significance of the reemergence of the female principle, God as Woman, in Jewish mystical literature? Should it be encouraged? . . . How will the ordination of women as rabbis affect the important issues contained in these ancient disputes, if at all? Was woman kept away from ministering to the people in high places and holy places because she was deemed to be inferior or because she was deemed to be too powerful and hence dangerous?[23]

Miller's questions are filled with foreboding today, as extreme feminist positions of ten years ago–militant lesbianism, rejection of the family, the goddess as cult and model, and witchcraft–gain acceptance. Ignored then, Miller's questions should be dealt with now, certainly by those who are already engaged in or who aspire to such a career. Enough time has passed for a preliminary assessment on the Reform and Conservative movements' decision for women rabbis.[24] While a rich infusion of talent has entered the rabbinate, is the decline in the number of men applying for rabbinical school a cause for alarm?

If the age-old division of roles is to be modified because of the new technology that released woman from bondage to her body and home, and because she has alerted herself to new opportunities, then careful consideration must be given to a primary reason for that original division: to counter the corrupting influence of paganism, old and new, of woman's power as well as her impotence. While Judaism stands behind the demand that women be treated with full respect, contemporary versions of feminism should receive neither automatic approval nor automatic rejection, but a careful weighing of all concerns from the perspective of Jewish teaching. But, such a weighing out must be guided by the understanding that within Judaism there are certain fundamentals which, if abandoned, threaten its very core. The family and sexual morality are just such fundamentals. We weaken those fundamentals at our peril. At the same time that certain new roles for women should be affirmed, the notions that the goddess might serve as a model or that the nuclear family is only one of a series of alternate sexual lifestyles must be rejected. Indeed, the gains achieved by women in their new roles in Jewish religious life may be in jeopardy, unless they themselves are prepared to speak out on what they are against in contemporary feminism as well as what they support.

Endnotes

1. "Lost Notes Provide Key to Finds," *New York Times*, 21 September 1993.

2. TB Sanhedrin 63b.

3. Numbers R. 10:33.

4. Numbers Raba, 21:4.

5. For a rabbinic association of idolatry with sexual immorality, see the Talmud, B Sanhedrin 82b.

6. Eva Keuls, *The Reign of the Phallus* (New York: Harper and Row, 1985), 72.

7. Ibid., 2.

8. Ibid., 79.

9. Ibid., 267–8.

10. B. Shabbat 33b.

11. B Gittin 57.

12. Genesis R. 26:2; see note there in Albeck ed. for further references.

13. Abraham J. Heschel, *Man Is Not Alone* (New York: Giroux, Straus and Cudahy, 1951), 262–3.

14. Sh'ma, 20 March 1987, 17/330.

15. Allan Bloom, *The Closing of the American Mind* (New York: Simon and Schuster, 1987), 102.

16. Leon Kass, "A Woman for All Seasons," *Commentary* (September 1991).

17. While Waskow objects that this incident occurred many years ago, as if it were a one time occurrence, which, nevertheless, inspired an attendant to pursue a rabbinical career, the president of the RRC in the article on sexuality describes the event as ongoing.

This article is cited by Mayer Gruber in a highly technical study on sexual license in biblical times. He refers to the prophet's fierce condemnation of fornication: *They profane my holy Name* (Amos:2:7); *He consults his stick* [phallus]; *his rod* [penis] *directs him. A lecherous impulse has made them* [Israelite men] *go wrong. They have strayed from submission to their God* (Hos. 4:12); *They debauch over new grain and new wine* (Hos. 5:3–4, 7:14). Gruber then proceeds to write an unusually contemporary footnote.

"For a modern parallel to that which Hosea condemns cf. *mutatis mutandi* Arthur Green, 'A Contemporary Approach to Jewish Sexuality,' in *The Second Jewish Catalogue*, ed. Sharon and Michael Strassfield (Philadelphia: Jewish Publication Society, 1976) 96–99, especially the following (p. 97). 'While these circles [havurot] have . . . rediscovered liturgy as a means toward personal religious expression . . . our lifestyle [i.e., the lifestyle of the havurah or fellowship] is hardly to be considered halakhic. . . . It is in the areas of sexuality and the place of women that this discrepancy between fully halakhic traditionalism and the neotraditionalism of these "new Jews" is most clearly seen.' Hence, Green explains further, 'When a havurah [i.e., fellowship] schedules a retreat and announces that 'spouses and lovers' including homosexual lovers of haverim [members of the fellowship] are welcome to attend the weekend event, it is clear that approval has been given to an open flouting of the halakhic norm.' For the prophetic condemnation of fornication see also Jer. 5:7–9." Mayer Gruber, "Hebrew *Qedesah* and Her Canaanite and Akkadian Cognates," UF 18, p. 134–5.

18. Zalman Schachter, *The First Step* (New York: Bantam Books, 1983), 45.

19. Eliezer Schweid, *Judaism and Mysticism According to Gershom Scholem* (Atlanta: Scholars Press, 1985).

20. *Eilat Hayyim*, The Woodstock Center for Healing and Renewal, Woodstock, 1992.

21. *Advocate*, op. cit.

22. D. D'Souza, "The Legacy of Leo Strauss," *Policy Review*, Spring 1987, no. 40, p. 39.

23. *Proceedings of the Rabbinical Assembly* (New York: Rabbinical Assembly, 1980), 50.

24. In 1993 and 1994, these denominations did in fact hold conferences for this purpose, but rather than a sober analysis of achievements and failures, they turned out to be little more than feminist "rallies."

SIX

Bashevis Singer

> Tell me . . . did you ever actually see such Polish Jews [as Isaac Bashevis Singer describes]? Were Jewish daughters in Poland really so available? What's going on here? And we keep silent! Is there no one to say a word against this mockery of the crown of our people—the Polish Jew? Shall we allow a fool to convert all of Polish jewry into one brothel!?

Thus, a secularist writer, Leo Finkelstein, wrote in the Canadian Yiddish journal, *Tint un Feder*, in 1950.

I am not concerned so much with Singer himself. No doubt he was a brilliant storyteller who could delight his audience. Nor do I wish to deny that some of his work will find its place in future anthologies of Yiddish literature. Still, writers use their gifts in a variety of ways. Some have their eyes glued on what is most marketable. It should not surprise us that a talented artist devoted a substantial part of his life's efforts, even after the Holocaust, to exploring the erotic behavior of East European Jewish beggars, wives, businessmen, and scholars; to finding "realism" in reducing human beings to their physiological functions, delighting in opening Yiddish literature to the scatological. Singer has reaped the rewards of fame and wealth for all this. What he is selling is eminently marketable: it has, after all, brought the Nobel Prize.

One can only ponder whether part of the reason non-Jews are so taken with his stories, written by a Polish Jew in the language of Polish Jews and widely applauded by Jews, is that they mitigate a measure of the Gentile uneasiness over the Holocaust. Six million of Singer's Jews may be somewhat less of a burden to bear. Some of them even seem to resemble the "vermin" described by Julius Streicher. Perhaps the Gentiles delight so in Singer, at least subconsciously, because he gives them the Jews they prefer to have–Jews who fit the old stereotype. This may be one explanation why, over the past few years, a leading Protestant journal, *The Christian Century*, has published appreciative studies of two contemporary Jewish "thinkers"–Woody Allen and Bashevis Singer!

I am, however, concerned more with the Jewish reaction to Singer than with Singer himself; less about what his writings say about him than what the Jewish response to his writings says about them. How does it happen that of the plethora of articles by Jews that have appeared on Singer in the past years, especially since the awarding of the Nobel Prize, there is only adulation, ecstasy, and reverence? Singer has been raised to the level of a veritable oracle. One hardly hears a critical word. Even the most hushed reservations evoke an avalanche of abuse and are often retracted. What is going on here? Why do Jews keep silent? Why is there no one to say a word against this mockery of "the crown of our people, the Polish Jew"?

Jews were not silent when the Yiddish writer, Scholem Asch, turned his considerable talents to novels about Jesus and Mary, some say in an effort to win the very prize that Singer received. Jews were not silent at Hannah Arendt's depreciation of the six million. Jews were not silent when Philip Roth reduced Jewish motherhood to Portnoy's neurosis, and Jews to lechery and worse. Gentile writers who, until then, had let Jews alone, perhaps out of respect for Auschwitz, now believed that if Roth could paint Jews with itching fingers and limbs, the moratorium was over.[1] But, about Singer there has only been silence–hardly a voice of protest or a cry of outrage. And, that is the very point: the absence of outrage has been the worst outrage of all.

In Abraham Heschel's paean to East European Jewry, *The Earth Is the Lord's*, he wrote:

> The little Jewish communities in Eastern Europe were like sacred texts opened before the eyes of God, so close were their houses of worship to Mount Sinai. In the humble wooden synagogues, looking as if they were deliberately closing themselves off from the world, the Jews purified the souls that God had given them and perfected their likeness to God. There arose in them an infinite world of inwardness, a "Torah within the Heart," beside the written and oral Torah. Even plain men were like artists who knew how to fill weekday hours with mystic beauty. They did not write songs, they themselves were songs. . . . The Jews had always known piety and Sabbath holiness. The new thing in Eastern Europe was that something of the Sabbath was infused into every day. One could relish the taste of life eternal in the fleeting moment. In such an environment, it was not difficult to maintain the neshama yeterah, the Additional Soul, which every Jew is given for the day of Sabbath. There were no concerts or operas in their little towns; yet what they felt when attending the Third Sabbath Meal, no

> songs were eloquent enough to express. Jews did not build magnificent synagogues; they built bridges leading from the heart of man to God.... Has there ever been more light in the souls of the Jews in the last thousand years? Could it have been more beautiful in Safed or in Worms, in Cordoba or Pumbeditha?
>
> How do we appraise the historic significance of a period? By what standards do we measure culture? It is customary in the modern world to evaluate a period by its progress in general civilization, by the quality of the books, by the number of universities, by the artistic accomplishments, and by the scientific discoveries made therein. As Jews, with an old tradition for appraising and judging events and generations, we evaluate history by different criteria, namely, by how much refinement there is in the life of a people, by how much spiritual substance there is in its everyday existence. In our eyes, culture is the style of the life of a people. We gauge culture by the extent to which a whole people, not only individuals, live in accordance with the dictates of an eternal doctrine or strive for spiritual integrity–the extent to which inwardness, compassion, justice, and holiness are to be found in the daily life of the masses.
>
> In this period, our people attained the highest degree of inwardness. I feel justified in saying that it was the golden period in Jewish history–in the history of the Jewish soul.

When Heschel's book was published (1950), few favorable reviews appeared. Most critics labelled it unrealistic, exaggerated, untrue. Perhaps it was an exaggeration, if one took it to mean that every East European Jew was a scholar and a saint. Heschel, let us remember, was silent on the horrors of the Holocaust. He believed that the story of the lasting values of that civilization deserved our attention more than the tales of the destruction. Yet, the book, venerated today as an impressive monument, was misunderstood then and derided as untrue.

Are Singer's writings "true"? The corruption, the adultery, the demonic, the philandering, the decay, the perversion that pervade Singer's picture of Polish Jewry–is it all "true"? And, if it is not "true," then why has someone not said so? Why, at the very least, has the issue not been raised to encourage an exchange of views? And, where are the contemporary counterparts to the protesting critics who met Heschel's book some forty years ago?

Is it "true," as Singer argues, that "the sexual organs express more of the human soul than all other parts of the body, even the eyes"?[2] Is it "true," as Singer tells us, that if only "Tolstoy could have described Anna Karenina's sexual relationships with her husband and later with her lover," we would really know her? "All the details about Anna's visits, friendships and journeys did little to reveal her situation. How much better it would have been to learn her erotic relation with the two men."[3] Does Tolstoy fail to provide the reader with a genuine understanding of one of modern literature's great heroines because he omits a voyeuristic analysis of her during sexual intercourse? Is it "true" that if we "take away . . . sex, there is no literature"? Or that "Sholem Aleichem was a good middleclass man who knew little about the darker aspects of life"?[4]

At the beginning of one of Jules Romain's twenty-four volumes that comprise *The Men of Good Will,* he proposes a principle not unlike Singer's: that we cannot know a person unless we know his sexual behavior in physical detail. He then proceeds to describe this briefly for one of his many characters. But, the reader is struck by the fact that he does it for no other character and that, apart from a few generalities, he does not really do it even for this one. Indeed, no writer has ever done it in all of world literature. Still, authors have managed to give us real characters. Singer's sexual scenes are merely shocking, not at all revelatory. Indeed, the so-called principle seems to be nonsense: just so much hypocritical posturing and sensationalism, at the expense, of course, of human dignity.

In his article, Finkelstein describes a gathering of the Polish Jewish writers' association, the Jewish Pen Club, to deal with a situation for which Singer was in large measure responsible. It seems that he had become involved with the Yiddish afternoon paper *Radia*. His method was to adapt French *boulevard romans* by peppering them with erotica and vulgar language. The success of this genre led to a spate of imitators.

> Other publishers, seeing that Bashevis's product had a growing market, were jealous of *Radia* and decided to introduce a similar section of trashy literature into their own publications. In time a whole crop of trashhacks appeared, a descent into the lowest sort of junk. Writers rolled up their sleeves and spared no effort in turning out salacious novels. Bashevis, however, had them all beat. Things reached such a point that the poetess Kadya Maladowski asked the executive committee of the Jewish Pen Club to call a general membership meeting for the purpose of considering ways of driving the plague of trash from the Jewish street. I remember the meeting quite well. Kadya Maladowski made a fiery speech. She bewailed the fact that we were being consumed by obscene literature. She de-

> manded that the Pen Club should take responsible action. I can still picture the meeting, the audience listening with head cast down. Another writer suddenly spoke up, bursting into tears: "What can we do if the reader demands it and we must make a living?" Bashevis was sitting to the side, his bluegreen eyes afire, the thin red hair on his bumpy head getting even redder. Later, a derisive smile spread over his narrow, pointy, little satyr face. He said nothing, but soon picked himself up and went into the neighboring hall. Later when I entered the room, I heard Bashevis saying to someone in a loud voice: "Get this, just get this! They're going to tell me what I should write? They can go to hell!" . . . Dismissing them all, he continued with great success his work with *Radia*.[5]

Singer was little affected by such criticism. Indeed, once freed from the restraints of the Polish-Jewish moralism and finding his American audience more accepting, his lust for acclaim led him to pursue his tawdry task even more single-mindedly, despite the fact that his writings appeared during and after the Holocaust. The dean of Yiddish literary criticism, Shin Niger, in reviewing *Satan in Goray* (published in Poland in 1935 and in 1943 in the United States), tells us that "in Poland Singer had visions of sanctity as well as profanity: however, when he reached these shores his nightmare was converted into pure profanity, the highest form of Satanism." Singer's fascination with the scatological as the key to all else fit in quite nicely with the American literary mood of the time. Morris Freedman describes it thus:

> Like medieval peasants, we have become awed by supposedly holy fragments of bones and rags, relics, intimate revelations. Or is it that we de-

> rive from them the satisfaction of the leveler. We now have a library of books and articles, some admittedly speculative, some actually plausible, some irresponsible and disreputable, some just distasteful or ill-advised, all in some measure demeaning of respectable, rigorous literary discussion—on Shakespeare's, Kipling's, and Hemingway's putative homosexuality; Milton's sexual naivete; . . . Emily Dickinson's abortion; [etc., etc.]. It is not a matter of putting into a portrait the warts and other blemishes which properly provide particularity, shading, and depth; it is a matter of painting a new portrait that distracts, blurs, titillates, and that can help us little or not at all in understanding a writer's words.[6]

How does one react to an author whose first story "ends in a shocking scene. The ailing father is asked by his daughter, a prostitute, to roll over in bed so that she might use the other half for her trade,"[7] or to the critic who sees the author as only "a rather puckish character"?[8]

Over the past fifty years Singer has given us ample evidence of his eagerness for sensation. The beginning of his career found him delivering softcore pornography to a Warsaw newspaper. The close of his career finds him recommending none other than Henry Miller for consideration as the next Nobel laureate for literature. If it is questionable whether a writer with such a pervasive and enduring mania for sexual exhibitionism is capable of telling the "truth" about East European Jewry, why do we keep silent?

Those who were not philanderers, adulterers, murderers, seducers, or religious fools, whose faith was neither in demons nor in sex—surely not a minority—are lying in unmarked graves throughout Poland. What of them? If Singer's picture of Polish Jewry is accepted—and his immense popularity makes that at least a possibility—what image of that civilization will be left for those who survive and for their children? Indeed, if Singer's picture is authentic, Jews must ponder if they should survive at all—to perpetuate *that*!

Of course there was ugliness among Polish Jewry. Of course there were prostitutes and beggars. But, Singer's stories are like describing a field filled with lovely flowers and verdant bushes by looking only at the worms under the rocks. We have come too far from Freud for prudery, for closeting sex in the Victorian mode. Indeed, the classical Jewish literature of the Bible and Talmud had no hesitation in dealing openly with sexuality. But, there is a difference between a serious concern with sexuality among the Jews of Poland, or anywhere else for that matter, and what Singer is about. Singer's sexual obsession is dishonest because it is less an attempt to reflect Polish Jewry than to titillate by fabrication, to the frantic applause of the public. To what extent has he shed any light on Jewish behavior in Eastern Europe with his imps and pimps, his demons and prostitutes? One might even argue that, despite language and locale, Singer is not a Jewish writer at all. Singer has a right to say what he wishes, but to claim that what he says provides an understanding of Polish Jewry of the past centuries is nonsense. It would be more correct to say it reflects current middle America, which, by the way, is the source for the sales of his books.

The noted Yiddish poet and novelist, Chaym Grade, told me that he had had an editor at Knopf who was the descendent of a Pilgrim minister noted for being one of those who argued for Hebrew as the official language of the new land. Once, their discussions turned to Singer, whose novels the editor had not read. When the editor asked why Grade's aversion to Singer was so violent, Grade replied in this fashion: Long ago there was a people in a far-away land who, upon hearing of the noble Pilgrims who founded the United States, wanted to meet one. After a trying search throughout their remote land, they at last found an American, himself a descendent of those Pilgrims. They asked the American to describe his ancestors. Having noticed the local citizens' penchant for demons, sexual exploits, and pornography, the American decided that his fame would be most enhanced by describing the Pilgrim fathers in this way.

That is what Singer has done in his novels, explained Grade. The Jews of Eastern Europe that Singer writes about in his demeaning manner are no more. There is hardly anyone to testify against his description of them. People will have to take my word or his word, my books or his books.

It is almost as if Singer had taken the stories of Boccaccio's *Decameron*, removed the trappings of the early Renaissance and replaced them with traditional Jewish garb–beards, sheitels, tzitzit, and kapotes–entertaining, to be sure, but totally false. In 1949, Grade concluded, Asch wrote him about Singer: "We must drive out the yellow plague. He will bring us shame and disgrace."

What was so holy about Bashevis Singer? Why did he become such a Jewish oracle? Readers would follow him around, hanging on his every word as if he were a holy Rebbe. The endless interviews with him, sometimes printed in great detail, are often ridiculous, probing for opinions about Kabbalah as if he were an expert in mysticism; querying him about prayer and God as though he were a theologian; demanding to know if he "really" believes in hobgoblins as if he were a wizard; asking, because he wrote *Yentl*, whether he approves of women being admitted to rabbinical schools. This man, who on the "Dick Cavett Show" said, "There is no evidence whatsoever that [a human being] is more valuable than a mouse,"[9] was invited to lecture on his notion of the deity, which was then printed in the op-ed page of the *New York Times*.

Singer tells us of his first mistress, Gina, a woman

> perhaps twice as old as I but a woman I could love and from whom I could learn. In a moment of exaltation I promised that we would have a child together, but the forces that ruled did not want Gina to be the mother of my child. . . . Yes, this woman might easily have been my mother, but not the mother of my child. . . . Would it be possible to describe in Yiddish the kind of relationship I had with Gina? . . . [For] Yiddish literature had remained provincial and backward.[10]

In other words, describing his intimate relationship with a woman old enough to be his mother was the way Singer believed he could modernize Yiddish literature and bring it up to date from "backward" writers like Sholem Aleichem. "I lusted after women and yet at the same time I saw their faults, chief of which was that they were amazingly like me–just as lecherous, deceitful and egotistical."[11]

The Baal Shem Tov taught that when a man beholds evil, it has been shown to him because he possesses part of it.

Consider Singer's fascination with Sabbatianism, which, he tells us, early in his life became the anchor to his spiritual mooring.

> Rummaging through the bookstores and libraries, I encountered a number of books that steered me in the direction I was to follow later. I found Professor Kraushaar's works about the

> False Messiah, Jacob Frank, and his disciples. I read whatever I could about the era of Sabbatai Zevi, in whose footsteps Jacob Frank had followed. . . . In these works I found everything I had been pondering, hysteria, sex, fanaticism, superstition.[12]

What is significant here is not that Sabbatianism provided a frame for some of his stories, but that it had become the ground for his thinking and believing. Nor is he the last modern Jew to have turned to Sabbatianism, the one movement in Jewish history that not only broke the moral yoke of Sinai but provided a theological justification for it: "in the transgression is the mitzvah." The growing interest in Sabbatianism is more than a literary or scholarly phenomenon; it may be raising the curtain upon a new and frightening drama in Jewish life. Is it not strange, then, that the meaning of the rebirth of Sabbatianism in modern dress as an alternate faith for the modern Jew–a rebirth that Singer in some ways symbolizes–has not been a topic for serious discussion?

Singer's writings revolve around a fascination with sexuality and the demonic. These were precisely the two dominant environmental realities of ancient Israel: the fertility cult and the demonic myth. Their defeat, by sanctifying the sexual urge within the family and the home and looking behind the mystery of the demonic to the Creator God who demands justice from man, marked the emergence of biblical Judaism. Now a writer resurrects these two elemental forces of paganism in a series of novels and stories and is congratulated, not simply by those who inhabit the fringes of society, but by representatives of the Establishment itself, by those who allegedly profess Judaism. Why? What does it mean? Does no one see the incompatibility of Singer's values with Jewish teaching? Is there no one to hold up a mirror of Jewish doctrine against Singer's views?

Israeli writers have been far more restrained in their estimate of Singer. Further, it is difficult to find copies of Singer's books in Yiddish, for he is not the darling of the Yiddish-reading world. Most Yiddish readers were too familiar with Jewish life in Eastern Europe to accept Singer as more than a clever charlatan. Thus, one such reader writes, "It is a sad state of affairs in world literature when a man like Isaac Singer . . . who throughout his writing life distorted Jewish life in Poland with his sick mind, perverted fantasies and filth . . . receives the Nobel Prize! Any one who lived in Poland will testify to that."[13] Another, disputing the enthusiastic report in a Canadian Jewish paper that "Jews everywhere are thrilled that the Nobel Prize was awarded to a Yiddish writer," wrote,

> One must ask why previous masters [such as] I.L. Peretz, Sholem Aleichem, H. Levick, [or] the great Yiddish novelist and poet, Chaim Grade, did not receive the award. . . . It is ironic that a man who approaches Jewish life in Poland with cynicism should be so honored. Those familiar with Jewish life in Poland . . . know that Singer's description was not true. . . . Perhaps the "sitra akhra," the evil demons who perform all sorts of dirty tricks with pious and naive people in his stories, assembled in Stockholm to honor the Satanic novelist.[14]

With the passage of time, however, Yiddish readers who knew where to draw the line have gone to their eternal reward, except for a tiny enclave whose voice hardly carries beyond their own narrowing circle. Where is the thunderous denunciation of Singer from the English-reading Jew?

Outrage at the appearance of a book by Singer was, indeed, expressed in an extended *New York Times* review of *The Penitent* (1983) by the celebrated critic, Harold Bloom. *The Penitent*, he tells us, is Singer's "worst book"; it is "without any redeeming aesthetic merit or humane quality" and "ought not to have been translated at all."[15] What so upsets Bloom about *The Penitent* to have evoked so harsh a verdict? It is not, as one might have expected, Singer's persistent enslaving of Polish Jewry to a pervasive underworld of the spirit, but, as we shall see, just the reverse.

An admirer of Singer's earlier volumes, Bloom is outraged because the book's hero, having tasted a variety of transgressions and fashionable ideologies, abandons his sinful life in Poland and America for one of piety and study as a hasid in the innermost recesses of Jerusalem. Affirming a biblical, or better a Talmudic morality, he condemns the world of corrupt modernity he knew with its homosexuality, adultery, and general sexual promiscuity, with its "Jewish reds," "liberalism," and "dirty plays and films," rejecting so totally the values of contemporary society as to refuse to read the daily newspapers. Bloom is disturbed that the Singer he respected–whose treatment of "sexual obsessions and the demonic" provided a fictional counterpart to Gershom Scholem's (one of Bloom's icons) studies of "messianic apostasy and Gnostic demonology"–has become nothing more than a "strident moralizer." Citing the hero's regard for the more normative Baal Shem Tov over the moral renegades of Jewish history so popular in earlier volumes, Bloom observes, "It is as though Singer is a Sabbatai Zevi who becomes . . . an orthodox bigot." If Singer really believes, argues Bloom, that "Darwin and Marx did not reveal the secret of the world," he must be guilty of creationism, and "worthy to be taken up by the Reverend Jerry Falwell." It is a sign of "Moral Majoritarian hovering in each of us."

Take, for example, the following passage from Singer's novel, which Bloom cites.

> A pure, decent woman can provide a man more physical satisfaction than all the refined whores in the world. When a man sleeps with a modern woman, he actually gets into bed with all her lovers. That's why there are so many homosexuals today, because modern man is sleeping spiritually with countless other men. He constantly wants to excel in sex because he knows that his partner is comparing him to the others. This is also the cause of impotence from which so many suffer.

What the reader might find to be an insightful observation into the malaise of modern sexuality, Bloom rejects outright as another example of Singer's descent into cheap moralizing. He compares it to the "simply satirical" rantings Saul Bellow might put into the mouth of a "minor character."

Or again:

> There is no such thing as morality without religion. If you don't serve one idol, you serve another. Of all the lies in the world, humanism is the biggest. Humanism doesn't serve one idol but all the idols. They were all humanists: Mussolini, Hitler, Stalin.

Here, Singer seems to have touched a raw nerve in Bloom: "The last of those sentences crosses over from extravagance into nonsense but is consonant with everything else asserted by Singer [in *The Penitent*]." What, after all, has religion to do with morality? And, how can he degrade the holy word *humanism*, the etymological emblem of humanity? Is not the "humanist" the embodiment of the best in our culture, the symbol of the Renaissance man? But, it is clear that Singer is using it here to describe one who holds that there is nothing more than the human. To the humanist's claim that man is the measure of all things, Heschel responded, but "what is the measure of man?" *The Penitent* is telling us that morality is grounded in the divine, and, with the loss of the transcendent, modern man is in danger of being reduced to the animal, the prime examples of which have been the "humanist" cults of fascism and communism, which have brought our century to its very knees.

Bloom brightens for a moment to record one redeeming item in the book, a description of the difficulty of having sex while in flight.

> It is hard to sin physically on an airplane. Passengers kept going to and from the rest rooms, the stewardesses weren't sleeping. . . . I felt some passion for this female, but I also felt revulsion . . . although modern woman is always ready to commit all kinds of abominations, nevertheless she girds herself in such a thorough fashion that it's a struggle to get at her. The desire to appear slim is even stronger than the urge to sin. We fumbled around this way for many minutes.

So far the "old Singer," but, to Bloom's regret, the "new Singer" now takes over.

> Suddenly a man walked by me. He wore a rabbinical hat, had a wide blond beard, long earlocks, and the front of his coat was open to display a ritual garment with fringes. . . . I realized at that moment that without earlocks and a ritual garment one cannot be a real Jew. A soldier who serves an emperor has to have a uniform, and this also applies to a soldier who

> serves the Almighty. Had I worn such an outfit that night, I wouldn't have been exposed to those temptations.

At this point, Bloom cites the passage with which the plane incident begins.

> I sat down, and presently a young woman took the window seat. Aha! The Devil had prepared a temptation for me. It's characteristic of Satan that he never gets tired, never capitulates. One holy book says that even when a person is on his deathbed, Satan comes and tries to lure him into atheism and blasphemy. There is far greater knowledge of mankind in this statement than in all the ponderous volumes of all the Freudians, Jungians, Adlerians.

Agitated, Bloom takes off after Singer for having dared to throw dirt at another of Bloom's icons–Freud–and, after quoting chapter and verse from the master, asserts that "the Talmudic uniform becomes merely Singer's super-ego"; he proceeds to link Singer with Cynthia Ozick in a fraternity of "Jewish literary neo-orthodoxy"! But, could it be that Freud is not the ultimate judge, and that the old-fashioned way of understanding temptation has at least an equal amount of validity? For Bloom, however, the true spokesmen of Jewish culture today are not Moses, Amos, Akiba, Maimonides, or the Baal Shem–not even Rozenzweig and certainly not Heschel–but Freud, Kafka, and Scholem. From that perspective, Singer has fallen from grace. Taking comfort in Scholem's dubious claim that there is no one normative Judaism, only many Judaisms, Bloom proposes that Singer is only talking about "Jewishness" and not Judaism at all. If, however, it is Judaism that *The Penitent* represents, then, Bloom warns, it signals "a reacknowledged rupture or felt discontinuity between the [Jewish] tradition and the contemporary Jewish intellectual."

Non-Jews, too, have their own reasons–which I have suggested above–to be dissappointed at the perceived "new" Singer represented in *The Penitent.* One reviewer, who finds the book lacking "the entertainment values and the curious insights into odd corners of the human personality that have won [Singer] his large audience," considers it "likely to provoke mostly consternation among Singer's . . . English readership" and even "imagines a movement being launched to rescind his Nobel Prize!"[16]

Perhaps what horrified Bloom and others most was the possibility that *The Penitent* signaled a late-in-life repentance by the author himself: the penitent is not just a fictional character repudiating his past, but Singer himself abdicating his former life and work. But, here there is no need for alarm. Singer remained Singer. *The Penitent,* by no means the autobiographical confession of the author, had, in fact, been published in Yiddish years earlier in 1973 and was written long before that. His philosophy, as well as his personal life, changed not a whit. The book should be seen as evidence of the author's ability to present another point of view and address a different audience. Furthermore, as if assuring Bloom and other critics of his steadfastness, Singer brought out a final volume not long before his death, *Scum,* which returns the reader to his old ways of vilifying Eastern European Jewry, this time mixing into the stew of their sins the added spice of white slavery.

Two theories may explain American Jewry's silence to the scandal of Singer. The first is that it reflects a lack of authenticity. American Jews, by and large, have made a caricature out of Judaism, not only by the vulgarism and crass commercialism that pervades their communal life, but, more to the point, by too often abdicating the intellectual life of the faith of Israel to the fads of the time. The true creed of many American Jews, especially the intellectuals, has become whatever happens at the moment to be "in"—Marxism, deconstruction, consciousness-raising, permissiveness, liberation, cults, sexual experimentation, etc.

Authentic Jewish teaching is so little heard because, while providing technical and textual understanding, few institutions offer an adequate view of the profound philosophy of Judaism. If they do, few graduates have absorbed it sufficiently to be able to use that perspective to competently review contemporary fashions; and, if they can, there are few avenues in which to make their opinions known. Indeed, some of those who best reflect Jewish teachings in the public square—Leon Kass, Irving Kristol, and Daniel Bell—are not Jewish specialists at all and publish their works, for the most part, in general and not Jewish journals.

American Jews may well be on their way to becoming new pagans, whose hands are the hands of Jacob but whose voices and minds are those of Esau. Approval of Singer may reflect their spiritual ambivalence, their secret desire to repudiate the moral direction of three thousand years of Jewish history in favor of the worship of sensuality and fear of the demonic, hearing fiendish voices instead of the "still small one" and finding meaning in their animal nature instead of in the power of man to transcend himself.

Can it be that Singer's writings are embraced, at least in part, because they express what Jews secretly desire? After all, legend has it that it was only because the mountain was held over their heads when they stood at Sinai that they accepted the covenant in the first place. And, has Singer, in good Sabbatian fashion, so subtly mixed the "holy" with the "profane," Yiddish with scurrility, the Sabbath with lust, Torah-study with seduction, prayer with magic, God with superstition—all the aromas, melodies, nuances, art, legends, and customs of the Jewish village, the shtetl, the archsymbol of Yiddishkeit, with the debauchery, greed, and perversity of man—that they succumb to the insidious temptation to confuse those who, at the very beginning, were to be forever after set apart: the pagan and the Jew?

Part of Singer's appeal may be that American Jews perceive him to say what many of them would like to hear: that they can be pagan and Jew at once. Like a rope tugged in two directions, man is beset with conflicting impulses, the *yetser hara* and the *yetser hatov*, the tug of passion and the tug of conscience. The people-Israel have been taught that through the disciplined life of the mitzvot, man has the power to ennoble his animal needs: in Buber's words, "to hallow the everyday." That the evil yetser must be conquered by the good has been the unremitting, unequivocal message of Judaism. But, at what a price—how many forbidden delights to be denied, what mountains of instant gratification to be spurned, and how lonely a path to walk! While all around them lusted for power, and pleasure abounded in obedience to the fiendish voices, the people-Israel, bound to a law that insulated them against their environment, strove to remain *a people that dwells apart.*

The twentieth-century Jew, however, stripped of that insulation, finds himself an integral part of the larger world. And, with the enfeeblement of Christianity, that world has become pagan, root and branch. Art, literature, and the mass media all blare a single message: relieve your neurosis by glorying in your animality.

Consequently, Jewish rebellion has broken out on several levels. One is the prominent role of Jews as advocates of sexual experimentation. A spate of books by Jewish "psychologists" encourages premarital and extramarital relations as a guarantee for "mental health." Young people, educated by the films and TV of the eighties, might conclude that husbands and wives never go to bed with one another, only those who are not husbands and wives do–according to a 1991 survey, 93 percent. Some Jewish novelists and screenwriters see no reason not to use an occasional Yiddish word in an effort to spice up their stories, as if the Yiddish language were restricted to describing one's private parts. But, behind this foray of Jews into the forbidden kingdom, there has always hovered over them the condemnatory image of Jewish tradition–thou shalt *not*!

How nice if that old inhibiting naysayer were removed! Singer does just that. If one who writes in Yiddish, reeking with the aura of Eastern Europe–the womb of all supposed restraint and prohibition–says it is okay, then it must be okay. What do you think of the Ten Commandments, Singer was asked in another interview, as if the Ten Commandments depended on Singer. In his puckish way he opined that they "were great," with one exception–adultery–which he would do away with! Well, perhaps that is what many modern Jews want to hear. The enticing appeal of the old Sabbatian revolt resounds: ignore the inhibiting Voice of "thou shalt not" and listen to the demon god who, as of old, subtly changes the words of the prayer from *matir asurim* to *matir isurim*–"the devil permits what has been forbidden!" You can be both pagan and Jew at once!

Heschel writes:

> In the agony and battle of passions, we often choose to envy the beast. We behave as if the animal kingdom were our lost paradise, to which we are trying to return for moments of delight. According to a contemporary scientist, "Man's greatest tragedy occurred when he ceased to walk on all fours and cut himself off from the animal world by assuming an upright position." . . . Man is always faced with the choice of listening either to God or to the snake. It is always easier to envy the beast . . . than to hearken to the Voice.[17]

Instead of declaring war against Singer's attack upon Jewish integrity, some rabbis have themselves, in Cynthia Ozick's words, shown signs of turning "pagan." A few years ago, the American public was treated to a Broadway comedy by Singer called *Yentl.* A yeshiva, which symbolizes learning and piety, is invaded by a female–Yentl–disguised as a male student, thus providing a perfect vehicle and endless dramatic possibilities for Singer to insinuate the profane into the holy and, by distorting, destroy it. The author of an article on the play interviewed an Orthodox rabbi hired by the producer to serve as religious adviser. There was no stringlike talis for Yentl, no Amish-looking Hasidim or other tomfooleries which all too often belittle Jewish ritual as portrayed on TV or films. Nothing but authenticity would suffice. "Rabbi Leonard Kaplan," the writer reports,

> enjoyed advising the cast on ritual and its meaning. He showed them how to sway and bend while they pray, explained what it means to study the Talmud and in general helped the cast understand the outlook of a religious Jew. The bearded rabbi is not upset by his association with a play which contains nudity as well as a

woman dressed as a man. He is philosophical. "*It is an abomination,*" he admits, "*But so what?*" [emphasis added].[18]

Jewish silence may be a sign of a sickness so severe we do not perceive its symptoms. One explanation why the ancient Israelites left Egypt 160 years before the ordained four hundred years of servitude is because so long as they knew they were in exile, God, too, could endure their suffering. When they no longer felt the bitterness, however, God knew He dared wait no longer and redeemed them. Forgetting one was in exile was worse than being in exile itself. Silence to Singer may be a barometer of how ill American Jewry is.

My second theory to explain the Jewish affirmation of Singer is more pragmatic. Consider: if East European Jewry really was what Abraham Heschel said it was in *The Earth Is the Lord's*, if it was even one tenth of that, then American Jews would have to come to terms with the corruption of their Jewish lives, individually and communally. They would be forced to confess that they might be the last generation of Jews, who, still possessing the key to a treasury of the spirit, were abandoning it for the fleshpots of the twentieth century. But, contrariwise, if East European Jewry was what Bashevis Singer said it was, if it was even one tenth of that, then they need feel no guilt; they can go about their way, not much different from other Americans, philandering, corrupting, and making of their faith a sham in the comforting belief that it was, after all, always like that! That's what the Jews of Eastern Europe were–philanderers, adulterers, and corrupters: why should American Jews be better?

Perhaps American Jewry's silence also suggests that it has been denuded of its nobility. Preachers, publicists, professors, philanthropists, artists, and writers there are aplenty, but where are those who will step forward and put to them the searing questions which the prophets and sages of past times asked:

"Are your lives compatible with your destiny? Have you become a messenger who has forgotten his message?"

Who will speak the truth?

Leo Finkelstein was one of the few who tried. Toward the end of his essay, he wrote the following:

> Apparently Bashevis has a special pleasure in always lying under the bed, to spy on his "heroes" and to find out what they do at night. Let it be an important baal-habos, a philosopher, a pious little tailor, a preacher, a meshulah, a Jewess from Palestine—he must "catch" them all at intercourse. From his spying eyes no one can escape. It is his noble, literary-satanic mission to point out: Look here, see what the people really are after all. Peretz in his well-known story "If Not Higher," also has his Litvak hide himself under the bed to see what happens at night to the Rebbe of Nemirov. [The Hasidim explained the "disappearance" of their master during the early morning hours when the penitential prayers were recited shortly before Rosh Hashana, the Jewish New Year, by saying that he went up to heaven. The skeptical Litvak doubted this and stationed himself beneath the Rebbe's bed to find out the truth. Hours before dawn he saw the Rebbe arise, go quickly to the outskirts of town to cut the wood, and light the stove of a bedridden woman, all the while intoning the first prayer, then the second, and so on. Later when the Hasidim recounted how the Rebbe was absent from the selihot service because he went up to heaven, the Litvak added: "If not higher."]

> While Peretz came to the astonishing conclusion that man can climb "even higher" than the Litvak had imagined . . . Bashevis lies regularly under the bed to show with great pleasure that people sink steadily lower.
>
> Everyone finds what he seeks.[19]

Endnotes

1. Gersom Scholem, for example, felt compelled to emerge from his scholarly research to respond to Roth and Arendt.

2. Isaac Bashevis Singer, *A Young Man In Search of Love* (Garden City, N.Y.: Doubleday, 1978), 37.

3. Ibid.

4. Ribalow, "On I.B. Singer, An Interview," *Midstream* (January 1979): 35. Sholem Aleichem's son-in-law, B. Z. Goldberg, wrote *The Sacred Fire: the Story of Sex in Religion* in 1932, a major study at that time.

5. L. Finkelstein, *Tint un Feder* (Montreal, 1950), 43–44.

6. Morris Freedman, "Indecent Exposure," *Commentary* (January 1992): 57.

7. R. Wisse, "B. Singer," *Commentary* (February 1979): 33.

8. Ibid.

9. *The Jewish Week*, 22 October 1978, p. 3.

10. Singer, *A Young Man in Search of Love*, 7.

11. Ibid., 166.

12. Ibid., 37.

13. H. Shapiro, *Baltimore Evening Sun*, 29 November 1978, letter to the editor.

14. Fishl and Leah Kolbo, *The Canadian Jewish News*, 18 January 1979.

15. Harold Bloom, "Isaac Bashevis Singer's Jeremiad," *New York Times*, 23 September 1983.

16. Joseph McLellan, *Washington Post*, 13 October 1983.

17. Abraham Heschel, *Who Is Man*? (Stanford, Ca.: Stanford University, 1965), 102.

18. *Present Tense*, ed. Murray Polner, 1977.

19. Finkelstein, *Tint un Feder*.

SEVEN

Woody Allen

Woody and Mia, "New York's quintessential cultural couple–the king and queen of Manhattan literati–is kaput." A pall of confusion has descended upon the select who clustered about them in local clubs, the many adoring readers of his writings, and the mob who flocked to his films. "The fairy tale is over. The odd couple has become an odious couple" (*New York Magazine*).

In 1985, I published one of the few critical articles on Woody Allen (born Allen Konigsberg in the Bronx), touching on some of the very same issues that have exploded today.[1] It was met with scorn. How could one cast stones at the icon of the jet set? He was so clever, so funny, so intellectual. Allen has long been among the most glamorous members of the cultural elite that promotes the prevailing paganism.

My concern then and now, however, is not so much with Allen himself. He is a talented, ambitious, Jewishly deprived artist, who does, alas, what so many artists do to gain fame and fortune, irrespective of whom or what he hurts. In addition, he uses his work as a kind of free self-analysis (though Allen told *Time* magazine,

"The plots of my movies don't have any relationship to my life!"). My concern is rather with his adoring audience, especially his Jewish audience, for that audience, by its adoration, and even by its neutrality, has ipso facto betrayed its faith and its people.

A Betrayal of Faith

The Heart Wants What It Wants

After taking up with Woody (but not marrying him), Mia Farrow appeared in thirteen Allen films and had a child with him named Satchel (for Satchel Paige, the black baseball pitcher), who was added to the seven or eight Mia had already adopted or borne in former marriages. At the age of fifty-six, Allen fell in love, he says, with Soon-Yi, Mia's nineteen-year-old Korean adopted daughter, whom she had rescued from the streets of Seoul as an abandoned, emaciated, lice-ridden child and whom Allen helped to raise.

The affair seems to have gone on for some time. Mia learned of it when she found a number of spread-leg, nude photos of her daughter in Woody's apartment, each of which included her face and vagina. They were taken by Woody, who later claimed the photos were to further her career as a model, though Soon-Yi said she was studying to be a child psychologist.[2] When she saw them, Mia told others, "I felt I was looking straight into the face of pure evil."[3] Mia accused Allen of violating the deepest family taboos, refused to let Allen see the other children, and permitted evidence to be produced of Allen's alleged sexual abuse of their seven-year-old adopted daughter, Dylan. "I have spent more than a dozen years with a man who would destroy me and corrupt my daughter," wrote Mia, "leading her into a betrayal of her mother and her principles, leaving her morally bankrupt with the bond between them demolished."[4]

Soon-Yi made a statement of her own to *Newsweek*: "I'm not a retarded little underage flower who was raped, molested and spoiled by some evil stepfather–not by a long shot. I'm a psychology major at college who fell for a man who happens to be the ex-boyfriend of Mia"; she added that Mia's anger would have been the same if Woody had slept "with another actress or his secretary."[5] Soon-Yi's long-time tutor in language disability doubts that she could have written such a statement.

> She has trouble processing information, trouble understanding language on an inferential level. . . . She's a very typical L.D. kid, very socially inappropriate, very, very naive. . . . She's very, very, literal in . . . how she interprets things socially. . . . The words [of the statement] were often exactly the same as Woody Allen's.[6]

Mia brought a number of the children together for a meeting with Soon-Yi. She told her, "We want you in this family. We love you. But you are going to have to choose whether you want to be in this family or to be with Woody. And that you can promise me that you will never do anything like this again." The other children spoke as well. Soon-Yi said that it was her fault as much as Woody's and left the apartment.[7]

"Soon-Yi never even dated," says John Farrow, Mia's brother. "Woody got a child. She's not her own woman. It's sad. It's disgusting. How would you like Woody drooling over your eldest daughter?"[8] Soon-Yi's incensed baby-sitter employer complained that "she had never had a boyfriend. She was just in high school. I don't think of her as a woman. She always liked Woody and was intrigued with his movies. She couldn't withstand his wooing."[9] Child therapist Carole West seems to agree, asking, "Does anyone really see Soon-Yi as a consenting equal? Would she feel free to say no to the great Woody Allen? Is she intellectually mature enough?"

Asked, "Do you consider it a healthy, equal relationship," Allen replied with the typical cry of the "me" generation—"The heart wants what it wants!"

As recently as a few months before the scandal broke, the *New York Times Magazine* (September 1991), in awe of Manhattan's most dazzling couple and in evident ignorance of what was really going on, applauded their "idyllic" relationship. They had taken a step beyond twelve years of cohabiting and having a child without the benefit of marriage, a relative commonplace today. What excited the *Times* was the fact that they were not even living together! Each occupied a suite on an opposite side of Central Park across which they could look from one swank terrace to the other. How chic! A new terminology would have to be invented for the Woody-Mia affair—nonmarriage, nonfamily, nonincest!

The affair with Soon-Yi, said Allen, posed no "great moral dilemma. . . . She's over 18." Mia's friend, Leonard Gershe, commented, "Nobody ever questioned that he did anything illegal. He did something immoral, and that's what he can't understand."[10]

If the matter of Soon-Yi was immoral but not illegal, Woody's alleged abuse of seven-year-old Dylan, the details of which came to the surface later, was thought to have involved violation of the law. *Vanity Fair*, in November 1992, published a shocking article based on numerous interviews of friends and employees, describing his alleged intimacies with the child.

For several years, it was asserted, the topic of Woody's "strange" behavior with blond, attractive Dylan had been the topic of therapy sessions. His treatment of Dylan appeared to have been obsessive: ignoring the other children in her presence, coming over each morning to sit on her bed until she awoke, following her about and whispering to her.

> He could not seem to keep his hands off her. . . . Woody, wearing just underwear, would take Dylan to bed with him and entwine his body around her. . . . He would have her suck his thumb. . . . Often when Dylan went over to his apartment he would head straight for the bedroom with her so that they could get into bed and play. . . . Mia has told people that he said that her concerns were her own sickness, and that he was just being warm.

Mia's sister and mother, it was reported, were shocked to see Woody apply sun-oil to the child's nude body one summer day in the Connecticut home, "rubbing his finger in the crack between the buttocks. Mia grabbed the lotion out of his hand, and O'Sullivan asked, 'How do you want to be remembered by your children?' " It was reported that Dylan tried to avoid Woody and would lock herself in the bathroom when he visited the Connecticut house.

Though it had been a rule for some time that Woody was not to be allowed to be alone with Dylan, once, in Connecticut, when Mia was out, they disappeared. Upon her return, Mia found that Dylan had no underpants on. Dylan told a story of abuse, of Woody's taking her into a crawl space and telling her that if she remained still he would put her in his movie and take her to Paris. After which he "touched" her. When Dylan insisted on the veracity of the story, Mia made a video of Dylan's description, which her doctor reported to the police.[11]

Allen said that he would sue for libel, and that the accusation is a conspiracy of Mia's. He claimed on "60 Minutes" Mia told him, "You took my child [Soon-Yi]. Now I will take yours [Dylan]." The case was headed for the courts, where Allen was found innocent.

Woody now maintains that at the time he insisted upon formally adopting Dylan, his long affair with Mia was over. But, if that is so, asks Leonard Gershe, Mia's confidant, why "would you be so anxious to adopt a child with a woman you're not going to see anymore? And would she have allowed it? Maybe it was over in his mind. It certainly wasn't in hers. But if it was over, then it makes his eagerness to adopt Dylan even more sinister."[12]

Mia is one of actress Maureen O'Sullivan's seven children, among whom she acted as a little mother in her youth. Having a large family had long been a dream of Mia's. Her sister said that Mia's successful acting career allowed her to practice her "vocation" of finding, adopting, and raising children. "That is her mission in life." Mia has frequently and publicly been commended for devoting much of her life to saving outcast children, raising and educating them (often in religious schools). Teachers and tutors report that Mia is a conscientious mother, always informed and concerned about the children and not shunting responsibilities on to nannies. Rose Styron, wife of novelist William Styron, said, "I've never known anyone who cared so selflessly about children, and who put so much of herself into them." The children have taken Mia's side in the dispute. They refuse to talk with Woody and are angry with his denial of acting as a father figure to them or that their upset over Soon-Yi was only the result of Mia's stirring them up. A friend observed, "The insensitivity of someone who could say that brothers and sisters would not care that their mother's boyfriend was having an affair with their sister . . . devastated the entire family." Mia was moved not by jealousy but by "moral outrage."[13]

However, lest one consider her another Florence Nightingale bent only on mending the broken, remember that Mia starred in *Peyton Place* as a teen-ager; she pursued and married forty-eight-year-old Frank Sinatra at nineteen; and later, when Roman Polanski, the director of *Rosemary's Baby* (in which Mia was featured), was accused of pedophilia for having drugged a thirteen-year-old girl to have sex, she wrote a character reference for him. About this time, she became attached to a guru and followed him to India. At twenty-two, Mia met conductor Andre Previn, became pregnant with twins, and married him. Previn's wife at the time of the affair suffered a nervous breakdown.

All of which does not add up to the qualifications for a model parent of children–natural, foster, or otherwise. Yet, the courts in their wisdom gave her child after child for adoption. To adopt Dylan, the New York law forbidding a child to an unmarried couple had to be modified; Soon-Yi's adoption required an act of Congress–in the belief that Mia had put her early behavior behind her and was a dutiful mother. On the other hand, Allen's sister and defender asks, "What is this need to keep adopting children? It's a frenzy. At the height of the crisis between Mia and Woody, she adopted two special needs children, a crack baby [Isaiah] and a blind girl [Tami]."

In one of the stories in Allen's book *Side-Effects*, smartly named "Retribution," he startles us with the remark that the hero hesitates before making a pass at his girlfriend's mother. "Banner headlines in the yellow press formed in my mind. . . . I am in love with two women. Not a terribly uncommon problem. That they happen to be mother and child? All the more challenging!"

The following is a scene from the piece (which I cited in my 1985 article).

> The wedding [between Harold Cohen and Emily, the mother of Connie, with whom Harold had

an unsuccessful affair] was held in Connie's apartment and champagne flowed. My folks could not make it, a previous commitment to sacrifice a lamb taking precedence. We all danced and joked and the evening went well. At one point, I found myself in the bedroom with Connie alone. We kidded and reminisced about our relationship, its ups and downs, and how sexually attracted I had been to her.

"It was flattering," she said warmly.

"Well, I couldn't swing it with the daughter, so I carried off the mother."

The next thing I knew Connie's tongue was in my mouth.

"What the hell are you doing?" I said, pulling back. "Are you drunk?"

"I have to sleep with you. If not now, then soon," she said.

"Me? Harold Cohen? The guy who lived with you? And loved you? Who couldn't get near you with a ten foot pole because I became a version of Danny? Me you're hot for? Your brother symbol?"

"It's a whole new ball game," she said, pressing close to me. "Marrying Mom has made you my father." She kissed me again and just before returning to the festivities said, "Don't worry, Dad, there'll be plenty of opportunities."

I sat on the bed and stared out the window into infinite space. I thought of my parents and wondered if I should abandon the theatre and return to rabbinical school. . . . All I could mutter to myself as I remained a limp, hunched figure was an ageold line of my grandfather's which goes "Oy vey."

The episode reeks with incestuous overtones, a persistent fascination of Allen's. There is Cohen's desire for Connie (and her sister) as well as her mother. Then there is Connie's infatuation with Cohen, at first dampened by his resemblance to her brother, and later rekindled in anticipation of his becoming her "father." Connie's desire for Cohen waxes and wanes in accordance with the two images he projects, each having the opposite incestuous effect: the brother-image repelling her, the father-image enticing her. Here we have a snakepit full of incestuous insinuations–much as in the convoluted real-life story of Woody, Soon-Yi, and Dylan. The concluding words of the story, "oy vey," are, of course, not meant to repudiate the perversion–again, much as the real-life Allen never admitted any guilt for his perverse behavior–but rather to elicit the reader's sympathy for his *nebish* hero, the suffering, almost noble, father/husband who anticipates the painful sexual demands that both women will thereafter make upon him (in the same house?).

Reviewing Allen's work over the years, one notices that while in this story, written in his early period, a young man pursues an older woman, in the films of Allen's later years older men pursue younger women. Does this shift reflect the stages of sexual fantasy of the author's life? In any case, it can hardly be denied that among successful writers and film producers none are so consumed with the subjects of incest and cross-generational sexuality as Allen. Woody explores violating societal norms both vertically and horizontally.

In *Hannah and Her Sisters*, Hannah's husband has an affair with her sister. "She came into my empty life and changed it, and I've paid her back by banging her sister in a hotel room." In *Manhattan*, a Hollywood writer has his script curtailed because "child molestation is a touchy subject with the affiliates." He responds, "Read the papers; half the country's doing it." Allen often plays an older man enthralled with young girls. In *Love and Death,* he is advised by a "sage" that the secret of life can be found in a steady diet of "two blond 12-year-old girls whenever possible." In *Manhattan,* he jests about his young conquest, "I'm dating a girl who does her homework." In *Annie Hall,* his friend considers the mathematical possibilities of having an affair with sixteen-year-old twins. And, in the film that opened the very week the scandal broke, *Husband and Wives,* he assumes the role of a college professor who has an affair with a student a third his age (her term paper is "Oral Sex in an Age of Deconstruction"), almost presaging Soon-Yi. "Do you seduce all your students?" professor Allen is asked.

In these scenes, Woody does not use heavy, crashing strokes that might drive the audience off. He prefers, and is master of, the gentle, bantering approach, which innocently evolves into compromising situations, as if nothing is anyone's fault. It just happened! One can hardly help sympathizing with the Chaplinesque, nebish, hero/villain type, usually played by Allen himself. By portraying middle-class morality–family, faith, patriotism–as consistently hypocritical, he opens the way for a portrayal of the wretched back alleys of (usually Jewish) life. "The heart wants what it wants."

As a faithful and paying member of our therapeutic society, Allen has been undergoing psychiatric treatment, we are told, for some thirty years. If his therapy has not been able to turn him into a husband and a responsible father, why has it at least not prevented these aberrations? Could it be because psychotherapy is often "practiced in a moral vacuum" where one is directed to the "health" and "fulfillment" of the patient, where right and wrong become relevant only if the patient himself is concerned with them? But, "if what we all aspire to is health rather than virtue, gratification rather than strength of character, how can we hope to find a foundation for a lasting commitment? If I have 'grown' and my mate hasn't kept up, is even impeding my own 'growth,' what possible reason could I have for remaining faithful? The 'health' choice is clear: find someone better-suited to my current needs." In discussing his behavior lapses, Woody might have been told that he must learn how "to forgive himself." But, the fact is that no one can forgive himself. Only God and those whom we have harmed can.[14]

Woody's adoring audience, stunned by the perverse behavior of the real-life writer-actor, did not flock to his next film as to previous ones and seemed uneasy with the muted enthusiasm that reviewers, normally ardent over an Allen production, were offering. Most upsetting was Allen's repeated denial that his actions created any moral dilemma at all—this from one whose purpose was never just to entertain but to pass judgment, to moralize, to instruct the present angst generation, which has revered him as its guru.

Woody would have fit very well into Paul Johnson's revelatory *The Intellectuals*, which seeks to demonstrate that a number of the most famed modern reformers—Shelley, Marx, Sartre, Brecht, etc.—led such morally outrageous lives as to call into question the validity of their teachings. Political campaigns regularly raise the question of whether one's private life has any bearing on one's public career—the "character thing" as opposed to "keeping to the issues." But, character is an issue of every issue. Well-intentioned advocates of health and welfare policies, whose cost has spiralled out of control, are now being forced to revise their thinking because they failed to take into account the extent of fraud. Some are turning their attention to the formation of character among the very young. "In the long run," writes James Wilson, "the public interest depends on private virtue."[15] The case of Woody Allen makes it more difficult to argue the irrelevancy of personal behavior to public life, between one's character and one's art.

What is Judaism about if not the centrality of virtue? How can a Jew maintain any other position? Nevertheless, some do, just as numerous critics ignored Allen's life in reviewing his latest film. Vincent Canby of the *New York Times*, for example, applauded *Husbands and Wives* as "strong, wise and exhilarating . . . Fact? Fiction? Fantasy? Who cares?" while Gene Siskel (Jewish) expressed delight–"two thumbs up!" But, many in the audience, as well as some of the critics, did care, and those who bought tickets watched uncomfortably, almost with a sense of foreboding, finding allusions everywhere to Woody's tangled biography.

This time Allen had crossed the boundary. Many did what they should have done before and considered the moral consequences played out in real life to what was portrayed on the screen. In the throes of the momentary Allen-stupor, the media even resorted, briefly, to a reconsideration of traditional family values, which some found, despite shortcomings, to have served as the most effective way to keep the sexual impulse within bounds, and even to ennoble it.

God Wants the Heart

"The heart wants what it wants!"

Allen's defense of his personal life is a recurrent message in his dramas. Beneath the pseudosophisticated comedies–decorated with Kafka and Sartre and embroidered with stinging sarcasm against middle-class values–is the infantile line of the screaming child: "The heart wants what it wants." The pulsating amoeba-like human blindly following its tropism, or the blundering man/beast driven by volcanic impulses, is, in a society mired in moral uncertainty, not often diverted from its course by the unaided will alone. Cleverly packaged, Allen appeals to our savage nature. Once the corrupted heart is the sole arbiter, what objection can be raised to adultery or homosexuality or, more to the point, pedophilia or incest? How, in fact, can *any* perverse sexual behavior be denied? The next step would be for Woody to argue, supported by the usual vocal clutch of crazies, that incest, whether by nature or nurture, is a compulsion for which no one is responsible. Ours is an age that too often sees the perpetrator as victim. All are victims–the Los Angeles rioter, the inner-city drug addict, the AIDS carrier, the pedophiliac, and the incest activist. Blame is variously laid upon society, racism, rage, the white man, poverty, or simply genes. Everyone is innocent; no one is responsible. Woody has summed it up: "The heart wants what the heart wants."

How, then, shall we deal with the oft-quoted talmudic dictum, "*God* wants the heart"?

Judaism sees the heart as the seat of desire, both love and lust. (*You shall love the Lord your God with "both your hearts"* is the reading the rabbis give the commandment based upon an unusual vocalization of the Hebrew.) In other words, one must conquer the evil by sublimating and ennobling it so that God can be served with "all" our heart. Judaism does not stifle the heart's desire, but trains the spirit through the will to guide it.

Judaism offers a third option: man is neither deaf nor impotent; he can hear the Voice and do the deed. But, his power to act is not self-generated. Alone, the mind is no match for passion. A central theme of Allen's films is "the titanic, tragic-comic struggle between intellect and lust."[16] What if the intellect is right–

can it alone control lust? A moment of self-scrutiny is sufficient to tell us: not often. The fire of passion can only be controlled by another fire, a greater fire: "Thou shalt not!" And, later, "Thou shalt!" To civilize means to moderate desire into acceptable social patterns: it is the internalization of virtue.

Three existential options are always present: exploitation, escape, and sanctification. The way of exploitation says nature is holy and thereby unleashes the beast within man: the pagan glorification of our basic drives. The way of escape says nature is unholy and thereby frustrates the natural desires of man: the classical Eastern suppression of our basic drives. Judaism says nature is neither holy nor unholy, but is waiting to be made holy, and thereby sublimates the natural desires of man through a system of mitzvot to the service of God.

Judaism has achieved the sublimation of impulse through the continual nourishment of the spirit and the pattern of the law. Training in the demanding regimen of commandments, worship, and the lifelong study of Torah is the Jewish manner of turning "human beings" into "being human" (Heschel). It requires diligence, sacrifice, and constancy, but the result is the rarest of beings: moral man. Uncivilized humans were—and are—wont to act like beasts or amoeba, blindly following their impulses. According to Judaism, however, our sexual nature can be controlled and hallowed by means of marriage, the home, and the family. Thus is the beast tamed and steps taken to establish a virtuous and rational society.

Allen has read his Sartre, Kafka, and Camus, but I wonder if he has ever looked into the books of the great Jewish thinker, Abraham Heschel. In the spirit of Talmud's remark, "God desires the heart," Heschel tells us the following:

> Man lives in three realms: the animal, the rational and the spiritual. The animal realm is spiritually neutral, and neutrality breeds peril. There is dross in the natural state of living and much that is untidy, crude and cruel. Who will tame the brute in us when passion overwhelms the mind? Who will teach us that the good is worth the price of self-denial? . . . The silent atrocities, the secret scandals, which no law can prevent, are the true seat of moral infection. . . . The problem of living begins . . . in the way we deal with envy, greed, and pride. . . . The only safeguard against constant danger is constant vigilance, constant guidance. Such vigilance is given to him who lives by the light of Sinai.[17]

For some, it took the tragedy of Mia and Woody to demonstrate the value of marriage. True, the marriage relationship is filled with pitfalls, but it beats the alternatives. A growing number of moderns balk at the marital contract. They yearn to be free of entanglements, to roam, finding momentary pleasure where they chance, to walk in and out of the mysterious process of conception as they wish. There is a male proclivity to behave like insects who deposit their seed and disappear. Over the millennia, one of the stages in educating men meant compelling, persuading, and enticing him, through law, reason, and feminine charm, until he acknowledged the value of remaining loyal to a single woman–the mother of his children, whom he would protect and support–and made a commitment to do so for life. So the notion of the human couple, and marriage, emerged, of which Adam and Eve serve as the primeval pattern for all human creatures.

Even when born into a society where those supports are in place, however, it has still proven necessary to expose males to regular and intensive guidance. Furthermore, through the miracles of modern science, woman has been freed from excessive childbearing and enabled to enrich her marriage and expand her own life. But, her new independence likewise provides her the option of repudiating marriage altogether and consider returning to the level of the precivilizational predator male.

Consider the incest taboo, which serves to prevent the power relations and emotional ties of the family from being abused. Proper human growth involves gradually separating emotionally from your family so that you can go off and start one of your own. Incest may permanently disrupt that process. In this age of mass abandonment of marriage, the clear lines of familial relations, however, have been blurred with disastrous consequences. Young girls, for example, are most often sexually abused by their stepfathers. But, if it is true that the taboos against incest inhibit exploitation of the power relations and emotional ties of the family, then those emotional connections that bind the new family may be almost as significant as the "bloodline." Only the future can tell just how deeply Mia and the children, who must deal with a confusion of bonding levels, have been scarred psychologically and spiritually. Mia's mother, Maureen O'Sullivan, protested that Woody had violated her daughter's soul and her God.

But, had Woody not violated his own God? Judaism stands as inexorably against the idolatry of the new paganism as it did against the old. And, so should the Jew.

Allen is guilty of "emotional incest and grotesque disregard for the impact of his behavior on others," writes Mona Charen in regard to Soon-Yi. How, she asks, could a man of Woody Allen's obvious intelligence have the "moral obtuseness" to claim, in an interview, that the fact that his nineteen-year-old girlfriend was the daughter of Mia Farrow had "no bearing on the relationship"? The answer, she suggests, is found in our morally polluted environment, on the one hand, and, on the other, in the public acclaim with which Woody's every step has been greeted. Charen suggests that had Mia and Woody met before the sexual revolution, in the forties instead of the eighties, the more traditional mores of the time would have encouraged him to marry Mia, especially if they intended to raise a family. And, if he had married, it would have been far more difficult for Woody to justify to others and to himself his sexual entanglement with Mia's daughter, whom he had known and helped raise since the age of ten. If the virtues of marital bonds need validation, the sad ending of Woody and Mia has provided it for us.

One recent divorcée reminds us that the vast supportive network for marriage and the family, the laws, customs, and restrictions of every society, are in the process of being swept away. Institutions that have traditionally aided and encouraged marriage now function as collaborators, even co-conspirators, in the broken promise. No-fault divorce is readily available, and prenuptial agreements anticipating divorce are all the rage, while religious leaders seem more interested in the fate of the rain forest than in the endangered promises of those in their congregations. The pulpit has replaced "marriage" and "spouse" with "relationships" and "partners." Lacking public support, one is thrown back to one's own private initiative. But, isn't marriage a purely private affair, and, if a marriage does not last, of whose concern is it except to the couple themselves?

> The answer is stunningly simple but it bears repeating. It makes a big difference to the chil-

> dren. While there are any number of alternatives to the nuclear family, all the evidence suggests that nothing else works so well. Children need a father and a mother, male and female. And they need the stability of one set of rules, not two–so it seems eminently more desirable that the parents live together, love one another, and work things out as a family. Hardly foolproof, but surely more likely to produce happy, productive children than any other arrangement. Without children, we have no society. Marriage, then, is the foundation of community, the model for our communal life.[18]

Marriage and family, which Scripture understands as part of the divine plan, might have prevented the Mia-Woody affair by setting boundaries and establishing responsibilities while providing the threshold for love and companionship. Mia's children require a father and a mother who are married and live together in a home. They need one set of rules, not two. They require the security of permanence as they grow to adulthood and are confronted with ever new problems. They need relationships that are clear and easily comprehended. Fragility, uncertainty, confusion, and separation foster instability, inadequacy, and sometimes abuse. Though by no means foolproof, marriage is more likely to produce well-adjusted children than any other method.

Because Allen's work has been couched in clever dialogue, sly humor, appealing artistry, and perverse fantasy, the Jewish public has expressed little dissatisfaction. But, since when did art or wit transcend morality? If *Mein Kampf* had been written in the style of Henry James, would it be a superior book? The people-Israel have been taught to beware of using the measuring rods of art or science alone to judge a nation.

Amos cursed the ivory palaces in Samaria, because they represented an immoral society. Matthew Arnold juxtaposed the Greeks' holiness of beauty to the Jews' beauty of holiness. Heine, who abandoned the faith of Israel and worshipped at the altar of Hellenism, recanted on his syphilitic deathbed.

> Formerly I felt little affection for Moses, probably because the Hellenic spirit was dominant within me, and I could not pardon the Jewish lawgiver for his intolerance of images. I failed to see that despite his hostile attitude toward art, Moses was himself a great artist, gifted with a true artist's spirit. Only in him, as in his Egyptian neighbors, the artistic instinct was exercised solely upon the colossal and the indestructible. But unlike the Egyptians he did not shape his works of art out of brick and granite. His pyramids were built of human material. He transformed a feeble race of shepherds into a people bidding defiance to the centuries—a great eternal, holy people, God's people, an exemplar to all other peoples, the prototype of mankind. He created Israel. . . . Now I understand that the Greeks were only beautiful youths, while the Jews have always been men, powerful, inflexible men.

Another question is why Woody's lifestyle offended the same audience that extolled his art style. For the artist Maplethorpe to insert a whip into his anus or urinate into another's mouth on TV would be repulsive to the viewer. Why then laud his photos of such acts? Is it not the action itself, whether performed or described, which should be judged? Outrage was expressed for Woody's behavior: why not for his films and writings over the years?

Let me suggest several answers. First, there is the tendency to distinguish between the aesthetic and the moral dimensions: modern art's "liberation" from ethics. Then there is the distinction between fantasy and reality: the audience can get its "kicks" by imagining behavior it would not engage in. Further, there is the argument, usually made by producers or writers, that such art has no effect on conduct, and, in fact, mitigates the viewer's potentially outrageous impulses by harmlessly draining his desire in the process of viewing the film. But, if what we see and read has no effect upon our behavior, it is difficult to explain why millions of dollars are yearly spent advertising on TV in the expectation that a mere thirty seconds will send the viewer off to purchase this or that particular item. Censorship is by no means the anathema many claim. On the college campus, for example, there is no hesitancy in giving Political Correctness free reign to dictate proper speech and behavior at the expense of severe punishment. Censorship is a communal constant; the only variable is what we censor and why. The welfare of society requires that limits be set for art and literature.

Let us remember that just as in the American South it was propaganda which defined the black man as subhuman that made it acceptable to treat him as such, and just as in Nazi Germany a step-by-step process of indoctrination desensitized the German people into accepting the propaganda that Jews were vermin, so significant elements of America's cultural elite, by its example, desensitizes this nation morally. At first the public was encouraged to fantasize about premarital sex, until it became so accepted that today talk-show interviewers commonly ask, "When did you first have sex?"; then about adultery, until many have come to believe everybody is doing it (a Hollywood poll gives

55 percent approval!); then about homosexuality, until we are beginning to think that it has nothing to do with AIDS, and that only homophobes object to sodomy. In a memorable but foreboding phrase, Senator Moynahan has described this process as "defining deviancy downward."

Allen is now inviting us to fantasize about the next stages, incest and pedophilia, though he denies having committed either. And, why not? The heart wants what the heart wants. Once we abandon the strictures of marriage, family, and the home, the bulwarks of Jewish and Christian morality, why not approve pedophilia and incest? Meanwhile, around the corner lurks the dark shadow of bestiality, the coupling of animal and human, which we may be told is just another "sexual orientation," more easily available and less expensive. Indeed, in *Everything You Always Wanted to Know About Sex* (released in 1972), Allen tells us that

> [Gene] Wilder and the sheep became a torrid item during the filming and had a highly publicized affair, which culminated in his being caught in a Butte hotel room with the sheep, her mother and a teenager who told the judge she was Little Bopeep.

Allen has contributed mightily to the perverse pursuit of depravity. To civilize, as we have noted, has meant, first, to curb unacceptable behavior, such as robbery, rape or murder; then, to so encourage virtue through cultural affirmation, education, and the example of the family, that even the temptation to perform such acts is muted. Most drivers, for example, automatically stop at a red light and are not prone to shoplift. To the extent that moral teachings are internalized, so will moral behavior and character change. Jews have long been taught to measure a civilization not so much by its power or art as by the extent to which honesty, compassion, and humility have become part of the daily life of its people. Finally, the process of moral education is never-ending, proceeding from everything we see, read, and hear, on film, in magazines, in the classroom, and at the dinner table. What the heart wants is in large measure what it is *taught* to want.[19]

Jewish Response

How could so many American Jewish leaders have been taken in by Allen? If a growing number of these leaders are sympathetic with those who are accepting of premarital sex and even adultery; with those who consider all AIDS carriers as innocent as cancer victims and not willfully guilty of the sexual and drug-abusive behavior which has almost always brought it on; with those who consider homosexuality as just another "lifestyle," like Rabbi Schindler, the president of the Reform movement's congregational arm, who shamefully and with considerable public flourish, installed the woman rabbi of the largest "gay" synagogue by taking the occasion to assail the concept of "family values" advocated by one political party in the 1992 presidential campaign, declaring that "their 'values' have been proffered through American history as coded words for racism, anti-Semitism, misogyny and xenophobia, and this year, a not-so-new twist, homophobia"[20]–if all this is possible, then why should we be surprised at the silence or the occasional applause from Jewish leaders which has greeted the Allen phenomenon all these years?

Jewish community organizations had no response to the Allen scandal. David Pollack of the Jewish Community Relations Council of New York said, "There is no Jewish angle." The Anti-Defamation League, fierce in its opposition to little children having a moment of silent prayer in school and outraged by a Southern governor's referring to the role of a particular religion (Christianity) in American democracy, had no comment. "I don't think we have anything to say about it," said their spokesperson. "It is simply a child-custody dispute. There's nothing Jewish about it." The Jewish Telegraphic Agency daily bulletin, which has recorded every sneeze of Begin and Rabin over the years, carried not a word about Allen.

Worse, much of the Jewish outcry that did surface was not against Allen, but against those who dared attack him! At the 1992 Republican Convention, the quip was heard that the Democratic platform had made no mention of God: they had Woody Allen instead! In the remark of Newt Gingrich, the Republican whip—"I call this the Woody Allen plank. . . . It fits the Democratic Party platform perfectly"—Richard Goldstein of the *Liberal Voice* found undertones of anti-Semitism.

> Sure, it's a code, but so is the Republican attack on Hollywood and the "media elite." These are words that since the '50s connote Jewishness to people. The Republicans can't attack Jews directly so they use codes. The notion of Woody as a kind of Jewish icon lends itself to the ideas of Jews subverting the Christian family, an idea which is very old and very dark.

A columnist in the *Village Voice* wrote,

> There are two kinds of people in the world: those who think Woody Allen is the genius spokesman of our collective angst, and those who think he's a filthy Jewish liberal . . . elitist, Communist madman. Another name for those two groups are Democrats and Republicans.[21]

Do American Jews accept the categorization of themselves as advocates of Woody Allen? That is the way they shall be seen, if those on the Left have their way.

The kind of invective that associates Jews with sexual permissiveness and even perversity has spread far beyond its old lower Manhattan hunting ground. Where it may lead can be seen from a letter to the *California Lawyer*, which reaches the 133,500 practitioners in the state, responding to a cover story in a recent issue entitled "Gays at Law: Life in a Straight-Laced Profession."

> Nothing today is more striking in our culture than the sexual mania of the Jews who edit, write and read current publications. "Our" (!) legal magazine presents a good insight into the Jewish psyche–greed for money, inveterate vulgarity, complete disregard of non-Oriental norms of decency and an insatiable itch for all the uglier aspects of sex. I believe that the progressive deterioration of morality can be directly attributable to the growing predominance of Jews in our national life.[22]

By its silence to the perverse behavior advocated by Allen in his writings and his films, his Jewish audience has betrayed elemental Jewish values: the sanctity of marriage and irreplaceability of the family. Anchored at the very core of Judaism, these teachings have become the bedrock of Western civilization through the book from which the daughter religions draw nourishment, teachings upon which Judaism itself has built a healthy and joyous community strong enough to endure the maelstroms of history without the benefit of land or army, an achievement unique in human annals.

Betrayal of the People

The accepting Jewish audience of Allen's writings and films has not only contributed to a betrayal of Jewish values, but a betrayal of the Jewish people, for no one more than Allen has enabled so many to view the Jew, especially the religious Jew, in so corrupt a manner.

A characteristic of Allen's work is obsession with Jews. He seems a disciple of Isaac Bashevis Singer in delighting to depict snippets of precisely the Orthodox dimension of Jewish life—difficult for Allen to locate in America since their numbers are not large—as, almost exclusively, ugly, foolish, and false. It is one thing to portray disapprovingly Jewish gangsters or charlatans like Lepke Buchalter, Meyer Lansky, or Arnold Rothstein; it is quite another, however, to select the bearded Jew, the yeshiva bokhur, and the Sabbath observer as objects of satire, in the hope that the sheer juxtaposition of piety and perversion will engender humor. To present a Jew as a pimp, Allen will typically prefer him to be a bearded, hatted, Kiddush-chanting pimp.

Just how much humanity, to say nothing of truth, the humorist is willing to sacrifice to gain a guffaw is the question. Humor, altogether pleasant under normal circumstances, can, under abnormal circumstances, become an idol, the standard by which all else is judged. By idolatrous humor, I mean the notion that whatever produces a laugh and sells tickets is good. Idolatry is the alternate faith of the twentieth century. The Communist doctrine argued that whatever benefited Russia, though it meant informing on a friend or crushing a neighboring country's freedom, was good; others may believe that anything that makes money, brings fame, grants power, or gives pleasure is good. National esteem, fame, gold, and, of course, laughter, are all perfectly desirable and proper acquisitions, relative to some higher system of values. They are, in other words, "relative" goods. However, once one turns a relative good into an "absolute," an idol before which we prostrate ourselves and by which we judge all else good or bad, right or wrong, that idol becomes a demon that inevitably destroys us. Allen's belief in "anything for a laugh," even the substance of his people's heritage, even furthering anti-Jewish stereotypes, diminishes him as an artist. Jews have been taught to consider only One as the absolute, to which all else is relative. Humor to rouse the spirits of the downcast, yes; to demean what society holds sacred, or to shame another just to get a laugh, no. Intellect, to ferret out the secrets of nature, yes; to rob the widow or to build crematoria, no. Desire for one's wife, yes; for another's wife, no.

In the story of Harold Cohen mentioned above, notice that his name is not Smith or Jones or even Goldberg, but Cohen, the Hebrew for "priest," which, apart from being distinguishably Jewish, is religiously so. Cohen, ostensibly a descendant of the biblical priests and a past rabbinical student to boot, marries the mother of his former bed-mate on the seder evening, which his parents, along with virtually every other Jew, was attending. ("My folks could not make it, a previous commitment to sacrifice a lamb taking precedence.") It is difficult to imagine any more radical or vulgar denial of one's identity.

Consider another example from the same collection.

> Brooklyn: tree-lined streets . . . A small boy helps a bearded old man across the street and says, "Good Sabbath." The old man smiles and

> empties his pipe on the boy's head. The child runs crying into his house.

Here again is a juxtaposition of opposites: piety and perversion. The first contrasts the proper and expected–an old, bearded man greeted by a child's "Good Sabbath"–with the improper and unexpected: "emptying a pipe" (on the Sabbath?) on the child's head, reducing him to tears. Religious images–Sabbath, bearded, elderly Jew, as with Cohen, rabbinical student, seder evening–are all served up to us, not as a single dish of Jewish piety but tossed by Allen with sadism and incest into one repellent goulash. The concoction is meant to evoke laughter. Tears and rage would be better, for the corruption of the author, and for the obtuseness, and worse, of fawning Jewish critics and patient Jewish admirers who have waited in long lines outside box offices to be entertained at the expense of their souls.

Finally, here are two items from Allen's piece, "Hasidic Tales, With a Guide to Their Interpretation by the Noted Scholar."

> 1. A man journeyed to Chelm in order to seek the advice of Rabbi Ben Kaddish, the holiest of all ninth century rabbis and perhaps the greatest noodge of the medieval era.
>
> "Rabbi," the man asked, "where can I find peace?"
>
> The Hasid surveyed him and said, "Quick look behind you!"
>
> The man turned around, and Rabbi Ben Kaddish smashed him in the back of the head with a candlestick.
>
> "Is that peaceful enough for you?" he chuckled, adjusting his yarmulke.

In this tale [the "noted scholar" explains] a meaningless question is asked. Not only is the question meaningless but so is the man who journeys to Chelm to ask it. Not that he was so far away from Chelm to begin with, but why shouldn't he stay where he is? Why is he bothering Rabbi Ben Kaddish–the Rabbi doesn't have enough trouble? The truth is, the Rabbi's in over his head with gamblers, and he has also been named in a paternity case by a Mrs. Hecht. No, the point of this tale is that this man has nothing better to do with his time than journey around and get on people's nerves. For this, the Rabbi bashes his head in, which, according to the Torah, is one of the most subtle methods of showing concern. In a similar version of this tale, the Rabbi leaps on top of the man in a frenzy and carves the story of Ruth on his nose with a stylus.

2. Rabbi Zwi Chaim Yisroel, an Orthodox scholar of the old school and a man who developed whining to an art unheard of in the West, was unanimously hailed as the wisest man of the Renaissance by his fellow Hebrews, who totalled a sixteenth of one per cent of the population. Once, while he was on his way to synagogue to celebrate the sacred Jewish holiday commemorating God's reneging on every promise, a woman stopped him and asked the following question: Rabbi, why are we not allowed to eat pork?"

"We're not?" the Rev said incredulously. "Uhoh."

This is one of the few stories in all Hasidic literature that deals with Hebrew law. The Rabbi knows he shouldn't eat pork; he doesn't care, though, because he likes pork. Not only does he

> like pork; he gets a kick out of rolling Easter eggs. In short, he cares very little about traditional Orthodoxy and regards God's covenant with Abraham as "just so much chin music." Why pork was proscribed by Hebraic law is still unclear, and some scholars believe that the Torah merely suggested not eating pork in certain restaurants.

Consider the image Allen projects of his so-called Hasidic rabbi: ignorance, fraud, adultery, hypocrisy, and violence.

What is he getting at by all this? Imagine a rabbi, a Hasidic rabbi, no less, with all the visible paraphernalia of intense Orthodoxy, who likes pork, as a Gentile; strikes people, as a savage; gambles, as a desperado; fornicates, as a libertine; mocks God, as a skeptic; and knows nothing, as an ignoramus. Should we snicker with Allen, or cry? His method is to conjure up the image of piety and then portray the perverse.

Are there limits to humor, a point beyond which its glitter dulls and turns ominous; when, instead of inviting joy, it sets loose demons to prance? That turning point is sometimes quite evident. Thus, we stop laughing at one who trips and falls, after he strikes his head and lies unconscious on the ground, or at one who slips on a boat, when he sinks in the water. Or, to take a historical example, when, in one of the more bizarre forms of Chinese torture, a victim is quite literally tickled to death.

The humorist's boundaries are somewhat more complex, though not all that difficult to discern. Comic wit may not amuse those of a different ethnic or cultural disposition. A joke about blacks titillates some whites but not blacks: Amos and Andy humor, offensive to blacks, is no longer acceptable. Similarly, whites found it difficult to join the snickers of the black audience which, a number of years ago, heard Jesse Jackson relate how, when working in a restaurant in the South, he would spit on the food going to white tables.

In Allen's case, however, his own people are often the butt of sneering sarcasm. In his depiction of religious Jews as adulterers, lechers, and hypocrites, the point separating humor from what is less than humor, and more, is long passed. Why does he do it? Out of concern for them? Because he would reform Jews and must first lay open their sins? There is a long and noble tradition of just that, beginning with the Bible. Who more eloquently than the prophets of Israel denounced the shortcomings of that people? But, Allen hardly operates in this tradition. The prophets condemned their people out of love: *Whom God loveth, He chastiseth. . . . You alone [Israel] have I chosen from among all the families of the earth, therefore will I visit all your iniquities upon you.* The prophets, of course, were not humorists, but Sholom Aleichem was. His stories are loving satires of the simple Jews of the East European shtetls. Indeed, Jewish humor is typically self-critical. The Jew has historically had the healthy ability to step back and joke about himself. But, he has done so out of love.

Does one detect a scintilla of love for the people of Israel from Allen's depiction of rabbinic frauds? Yes, there is a certain helplessness, an affectionate nebishkeit, that marks some of his characters. But, this does not justify the unremitting stream of mockery he directs against the Jew. That mockery has a long and tragic history. Allen's depiction of the Jew as a pious, profligate fraud, a threat to the innocent gentile maiden and society at large, seems to have stepped lifelike out of the pages of Fuchs's classic of anti-Semitic satire, the three-volume German work, *The Jew in Caricature.* Fuchs's collection emerged from the convolutions of medieval demonic mythology, which culminated in Streicher's *Der Sturmer.*

Allen's one public foray into contemporary Jewish affairs was his infamous op-ed piece in the *New York Times* in which he castigated the anti-intifada tactics of the Jewish state, claiming that "Israel's policies defy belief." Shortly afterwards (23 June 1988), Eli Wiesel responded with a moving review of the tragic situation in which public opinion has rushed to condemn the Jewish state unfairly, putting Israel in the "place of America during Vietnam, France during Algeria and the Soviet Union during the Gulag.

"Many critics," Wiesel continued, now training his sights upon Allen and his crowd, "were outdone by some Jewish intellectuals who had never done anything for Israel but now shamelessly used their Jewishness to justify their attacks against Israel."

Allen's satires of his own people are marked by a self-hatred that resurfaced among other post-Holocaust American-Jewish writers and has even reached Israel. The precocious and tragic Jewish writer of Prague in the twenties, Otto Weininger, having written a book accusing the Jews of corrupting European culture and committing suicide to conclude his argument, became the subject of a play by an Israeli *Nefesh Yehudi* (*A Jewish Soul*), in which his *Selbst-Hass* is expressed in lines such as "I am a member of a cursed race"; "Judaism is a pollution"; and "The Aryan spirit will vomit out this filth." Translated into English, the play was a hit in Edinburgh (whose University sought to honor Arafat shortly afterwards) and, of course, translated into German to be produced in Germany, where the tiny Jewish community felt compelled to picket the theater in protest.

Allen projects an ugly picture of the Jew, not in some offbeat journal but fleshed out in color and drama on the giant screen for the general public to view. To take but one example, consider the lusting of the Jew for the Gentile woman. This standard anti-Semitic canard was part of the devil mythology of the Jew from the Middle Ages to Hitler's Third Reich, incorporated into centuries of anti-Jewish law. Allen's works are replete with such episodes. Yet, Jewish critics and agencies that spend millions to monitor the barometer of anti-Jewish feeling are silent at Allen's defamations. Of course, it will be countered, why the fuss? Allen is merely poking fun. The average Gentile reader or viewer, however, may be drawing a more ominous lesson. And, now Allen apparently confirms all that in real life, as the Mia Farrow, Soon-Yi, and Dylan incidents make clear.

One need not exhaust Allen's books or films to observe that he is a gifted humorist, whose specialty is juxtaposing opposites. Such unexpected association of opposites is, of course, a commonplace of comedy. But, Allen raises the stakes, widening the poles as far as they will go: the cosmic and the trivial, the solemn and the silly, the eternal and the momentary. Thus, "Not only is there no God but try getting a plumber on a weekend," or "The universe is merely a fleeting idea in God's mind–a pretty uncomfortable thought, particularly if you've just made a down payment on a house."

Christians have been impressed with Allen's divine probings. In 1974, the editor of an offbeat religious publication, *Wittenburg Door*, called attention to them by naming him, on the basis of a survey of seminary students, "theologian of the year." But, it was several years later, in 1977, when a writer for the *Christian Century*, a leading Protestant journal, concurred in raising Woody Allen to the eminence of "theologian," that it was time to become suspicious. That denomination seems to have been meant seriously, for since then Allen's works have been ransacked for deeper "meanings"; a series of interviews found him thoughtful, even profound.[23] Can the Christian elevation of Allen be related to his own demeaning of Jews and Judaism?

Allen, playing theologian, claims that "philosophical and religious issues" have interested him over the years "more than social and topical things." The reader perceives, however, only the clever carping of the cynic. One's response to Allen's humor is not just a matter of taste; it depends on the degree of skepticism in one's soul. We may laugh, but we pay a price. The greatest Jewish comic writer of recent times, Sholom Aleichem, took delicious delight in poking fun at every inch of Jewish life in Eastern Europe, with one exception–the sacred; you will hardly find a single example in all his writings. To belittle the *institution* of religion, its frail human trappings, is a choice subject of the biblical prophets. But, when Amos cursed the priests at Beth El, when Jeremiah excoriated the temple-goers as murderers, or when Moses ground the golden calf into dust, they did so to preserve the sacred, not to mock it.

Now it is in the nature of the sacred that it be set apart (the Hebrew *kadosh* literally means "separate"), always to elude the bounds of human expression. After the mind has mastered all, the numinous still conjures fear and trembling for the unfathomed mystery. To laugh at the sacred is to drive it off. Abraham Heschel, in describing the spiritual conditions that led to World War II, observed, "We ridiculed superstition until we lost the ability to believe." Something of that is reflected in Allen's kind of humor. In the final analysis, it is the attitude toward the sacred that reveals the character of a civilization. When we say that our age is one in which the worst horror is that there is no horror, we mean there are no limits, no restraints, no taboos; it is an age when anything can be laughed at, where nothing is sacred.

There are no surprises, no mysteries. A cosmic numbness envelops us. Immune to wonder, we gaze at the stars–and yawn. Vulgarities that shocked a former generation are taken in stride; sanctities that elicited reverence are met with silent scorn. Allen's gentle bantering about God should not startle us, if He is only an illusion. But, what if He is not make-believe? What if He is real, Presence and Power, the soul of our very life? How can one laugh at that? Yet, for some, Woody Allen is a "theologian."

Zelig

Allen's film, *Zelig*, warmly welcomed by most viewers and reviewers, provides a litmus test of his attitude to the Jewish people. It represents both the author's strength and weakness.

Leonard Zelig, played by Allen himself, is a Brooklyn Jew who, in the 1920s, achieves international notoriety as the human "chameleon," that is, one who, willynilly, takes on the appearance of whomever he is with at the moment. Thus, at an elegant Long Island party, Zelig, in formal attire and manners, walks into the crowded kitchen and, presto, his language and dress turn into that of the help. He becomes black among blacks, obese among the fat, slant-eyed among the Chinese, and Hitler-like among Nazis.

Obviously, Allen is treating conformism in this film, and, of course, conformism is a part of the American character. But, it is as much a part of the German, French, and English character, for to live in any society is to become a part of that society by adopting its mores and habits. One can pursue the universality of

Allen's intent by arguing that he is not a Jewish writer at all but simply an American writer who happens to be a Jew, as Philip Roth, Saul Bellow, and others have claimed about themselves. They argue that they use Jewish characters and situations not in order to say anything "Jewish," but simply because Jews and Jewishness are a part of their particular store of experience. To what extent it is true that these writers are simply American authors who use Jewish material, as Faulkner, for example, used Mississippi memories, is open to question. It is one thing for an author who has grown up in Chicago to use Chicagoans of various kinds in his novels, but if they are all ugly, cheap, and vicious, doesn't this say something not only about Chicagoans but also about the author's perception of Chicagoans? If Allen's (and Roth's) Jews are in good measure lecherous, crude seducers, does this not imply something about the author's view of Jews?

The particular conformism Allen would seem to be portraying is not simply, as has been suggested, an aspect of the American character, but of the Jewish character. Allen is examining Jewish conformism, albeit of those American Jews. Zelig is a Jew. His bearded actor-father appears on the Yiddish stage; Zelig wears a kipah as a child in the Brooklyn streets; he is attacked by anti-Semites (his parents take the side of the anti-Semites!); undergoing analysis he reveals, "I had a dream when I was 12 years old in which I asked a rabbi the meaning of life. He told me the meaning of life–in Hebrew. But I don't understand Hebrew. Then he asked me for $600 for Hebrew lessons!"

Zelig's conformism is Jewish conformism, the central problem and the much examined phenomenon of post-Emancipation Jewry, commonly termed "assimilation." What libraries have been written, what pools of tears shed, what mountains of joy accumulated as a result of that word! Caged within ghetto bars for centuries, the Jews emerged into the freedom of Western society where they drank in its culture, tasted its pleasure, and enjoyed its power. They demanded citizenship and were so eager to be accepted by the majority that they often offered themselves, sacrificed their history, faith, and way of life, their "identity," in order that the stigma of their difference might be obliterated. The roads they traveled, the difficulties they met along the way to achieve this goal have been described in countless records and are embedded in the memory of almost every Jewish family of the twentieth century.

Zelig is a satire on the absurdity of the lengths to which Jews have gone to assimilate. Irving Howe, author of *The World of Our Fathers*, expert on the Jewish immigrant, and one of several Jewish authorities who actually appear in the film to lend the Zelig tale credence, has observed that "Zelig's story reflects the Jewish experience in America: to push in, to find one's place in the culture and to assimilate. He wanted to assimilate like crazy."

Allen's film can be understood, then, as a satire—carried to ridiculous lengths in the person of a human chameleon—of all the adjustments of noses, accents, names, and creeds that Jews have undergone so that they can be accepted into the club, the church, the business, the family. Furthermore, the film provides ample justification for Zelig's repudiation of his own Jewishness because every Jewish experience of his early life seems negative: the dying Yiddish stage; his parents siding with the anti-Semite who beats up the young Zelig; the rabbi who wants six hundred dollars to teach Hebrew to a twelve-year-old. Though bizarre, these examples are not altogether untrue of the inheritance of American Jews and would seem to provide Zelig with justification for fleeing his origins. In view of the absence of any redeeming Jewish experience presented in the film, Zelig is one of many culturally deprived Jews who seek to abandon their Jewishness.

The treatment of Jewish assimilation in *Zelig* seems standard enough both sociologically–problems within and allurements without–and psychologically: Zelig, the human chameleon, suffers from an emotional ailment. His case is understood as an identity loss that puzzles psychiatrists. He finally undergoes treatment by a renowned analyst, who, indeed, cures Zelig by returning his identity to him. He is now no longer the adaptive, elusive chameleon, but Zelig himself. The parallel to modern studies of assimilation, which argue from environmental factors that loss of identity is curable by the restoration of the patient to his real self, is clear. So, we may conclude, in Allen's Zelig we have a clever, comic–indeed, classic–portrayal of assimilation and its cure. Having triumphantly shed his chameleon conformism, and now returned to his true self through the blessings of modern psychiatry, the restored Zelig emerges once again hale and hearty, takes his final bow, and the curtain falls.

Only it does not. The film does not come to an end at that point. It continues, and concludes not with Zelig's regaining his Jewish identity, affirming it, and living with it happily ever after. It concludes, *mirabile dictu,* with Zelig's marrying his analyst, Dr. Eudora Nesbitt Fletcher (played by Mia Farrow, of course), chosen, and meant to be understood, as the "other," a blond Gentile, in stark contrast to darkhaired, sallow-complexioned Zelig, complete with "Jewish" nose and glasses!

This is the film's real joke: Zelig's obliteration of himself as a Jew through the final act of assimilation, intermarriage, entered into not as a sick chameleon but as a cured Jew. In other words, Allen is telling us that the way a healthy, normal Jew behaves, with his identity quite intact and in possession of all of his faculties, is to disappear, to self-destruct, to do exactly what the sick, chameleon Jew had attempted again and again, only now to do it consciously and, above all, lovingly and joyously. All the earlier examples of Zelig's automatic and bizarre conformism to all manner of other persons, irrespective of size, age, color, or station, are considered clinical evidence of severe emotional dislocation, requiring removal from society and lengthy treatment in a mental institution–except for one final act of conformism–intermarriage. This, the truest of all chameleon acts for the emancipated Jew, is not treated as troubling at all, certainly not a subject for psychological analysis. Quite the contrary, marriage to Eudora Fletcher is the act of a healthy, sane Zelig–perhaps the only sensible thing for a healthy Jew to do.

Allen's last laugh–a theological one, if you will–is that the rediscovery of one's Jewish identity leads not to Jewish affirmation but, on the contrary, to total Jewish denial. And why not? One could present a plausible argument for Zelig's decision to opt out on the basis of his one-sided Jewish memories. There is not a single redeeming Jewish experience in the entire film; indeed, there is hardly a redeeming Jewish scene in any of Allen's books or films. Instead, we find sadistic elders, incestuous yeshiva students, Yom Kippur buffoonery, evil and ignorant rabbis. If all religious Jewish encounters are cheap turnoffs, and there are no compensating qualities, then Zelig's self-destruction could be the paradigm for all Jews.

Some argue that the later film *Crimes and Misdemeanors* marked a serious shift in Allen's methods, a more sober approach, a gentler, kinder treatment of Jews, and suggest that he may even have taken to heart what a few critics had been saying. Whatever its virtues, I do not believe that it escapes our criticism. The lesson the Jewish adulterer hero teaches the audience is that there is no God, and religion is just so much guilt-baggage. Allen's naive nihilism triumphs again.

Outraged by the enthusiastic response critics (including Jewish critics) gave the film, Leon Wieseltier of the *New Republic* writes:

> It is a matter of honor to hate this film. . . . As usual, Allen dishonors his Jewishness. Jewish is smart, smart is ugly, Jewish is ugly. He gives a shul and a seder and a wedding peopled with Jewish grotesques. The fathers are weak . . . the mothers are mighty . . . the sons are pale and doomed. . . . There is not a frame of it that fails to degrade, to debase, and to demean something precious. It is the work of a consumer, a tourist, a peacock, a counterfeiter, a voyeur, a coward, a philistine, a creep. It is a stain on the culture that produced it. . . . It is [a Jewish soap opera], a kind of *General Synagogue.* Judah the ophthalmologist is cheating on Miriam with Dolores and comes for counsel to Ben the rabbi, whose brother Lester is a television producer whose brother-in-law Cliff is a documentary filmmaker who is hoping that [blond Gentile] Halley will desire him because he has discovered . . . Louis Levy, a Jewish philosopher . . . played by my old friend, Martin Bergmann, wise and learned psychoanalyst. . . . In the film Louis Levy reflects, and jumps out a window. My friend, in other words, played Primo Levi; and it was Primo Levi's role to help Woody Allen get into a woman's pants.[24]

The Woody Allen craze was, in part, understandable. Gifted, clever, an actor, writer, and director, Allen has a fine eye for the human comedy and the talent to translate it into the contemporary idiom. But, Allen's humor is cause for concern. Willing to do anything for a laugh, Allen uses his people's dignity for amusement. His delight in distorting and defaming religious Jews as a recurrent theme of his work is more than disturbing: it is cause for fear and trembling, for it represents one of the most widely disseminated perverse portrayals of Jews. Never before have so many Americans seen so ugly a depiction of religious Jews as in his oeuvre.

For the Gentile, Allen's depiction of religious Jews as pious frauds, and worse, can only confirm ancient Christian canards of the Jew as hypocrite, devil, despoiler of morality, and corrupter of culture. For Jews, the matter is more complicated: Allen has not only been a favorite, but to many a model of Jewish talent. Almost never has he been a subject of alarm for the Jewish critic or even the Jewish establishment. The silence of Jews to Allen's attack on their most prized possession, family morality; his celebration of death through intermarriage; and his demeaning of those with religious commitment is a betrayal both of Jewish faith and of the Jewish people. Why Jews want to demean themselves is a question that Hollywood "theologians" have yet to address.

We stand tremulously near the edge of the precipice, in an age not of some grand successor faith but of a throwback to a more primitive one: Baghdad's totalitarian beast and New York's trousered ape. Talent such as Allen's is too rare to be squandered–therefore, the lament, not only for what Allen has done, but for where his people stand, and what he could have done.

Endnotes

1. "Woody Allen: Theologian?" *Midstream* (March 1985).

2. Maureen Orth, "Mia's Story," *Vanity Fair* (November 1992).

3. Ibid.

4. *Time*, 31 August 1992.

5. Orth, "Mia's Story."

6. Ibid.

7. Ibid.

8. Phoebe Hoban, "Woody and Mia," *New York Magazine* (21 September 1992): 35.

9. Ibid.

10. Orth, "Mia's Story."

11. Ibid.

12. Ibid.

13. Ibid.

14. Kari Gold, "On Marrying, Again," *First Things* (November 1992): 9, 10.

15. Mark Gerson, "Battler for the Republic," *Public Review* (Fall 1992).

16. *Time*.

17. Heschel, *God in Search of Man* (Philadelphia: JPS, 1956), 382, 3.

18. Gold, "On Marrying."

19. The lesson seems to have been taught quite well. The film *Husbands and Wives* portrays a Barnard College student coming on to her professor, played by Allen. In a follow-up, a random sampling of Barnard coeds were interviewed by a

creative reporter who put the question, "If Woody Allen were your professor, would you have an affair with him?" Here are the answers:

"I probably would. Why not? I've always found him rather charming in sort of a weird way. . . . I mean, maybe if he was just my professor I wouldn't look up to him as much, but maybe, sure." "I don't think so. It depends on what line he used." "It would be tempting, but I wouldn't do it." "I would not have an affair with one of my professors." "Maybe some professors, but not him." "I think he's ugly. He's disgusting." "I don't find him attractive. He's old. He's too hairy." "I've seen some very ugly guys that are very charismatic . . . But he's just too short." "I think it's basically unethical to be involved with your professor." "My mother did when she was in college–[had an affair] with Woody Allen. [I wouldn't have an affair with him] because if my mother did it, it's kind of a mother-daughter thing and that would be bad." (Daniel Radosh, "Reality Check," *Spy*, November 1992)

20. *Jewish Week*, 2 October 1992.

21. *Jerusalem Post*, 4 September 1992.

22. *New York Times*, 10 October 1992.

23. John Dart, "Woody Allen, Theologian," *Christian Century* (June 1977): 585–9.

The well-known Christian writer, Martin Marty, singled Allen out as one to be emulated by young ministers who, he counseled, might try to speak of life as interestingly as Allen did of death: "Death is one of the few things that can be done as easily as lying down" and "I do not believe in an afterlife, although I am bringing a change of underwear."

Allen's pontifications on religion include the following:

"I would define my position somewhere between atheism and agnosticism. I vacillate between the two positions." God "doesn't exist, or if He does, He really can't be trusted." "I don't approve of any of the major religions but religious faith . . . does interest me." "God is silent. Now if we can only get man to shut up." "Raised in the Jewish tradition, [I was] taught never to marry a Gentile woman, shave on Saturday, and most especially, never to shave a Gentile woman on Saturday."

24. Leon Wieseltier, *The New Republic* (27 November 1989): 43.

EIGHT

Heschel

I have written about the need for a living bridge between the generations, between the ancient tradition of Judaism and the modern challenge of a secular society. It may seem to some readers that what I demand is too much, beyond the scope of any individual; that, as in so many other areas of American life, we must give ourselves over not to the individual but to the corporate structure, to some vast complex of compartmentalized functions. But, I believe the key to Jewish renewal is in the hands of its leaders. And, I had the pleasure and the privilege to know one man who was indeed the embodiment of all I speak of. I was a student of Abraham Joshua Heschel. And I had the honor of calling him a friend. The reader will already have encountered many passages in the foregoing chapters quoted in his name. Now there will be an opportunity to learn something about the man himself.

In some ways it would be easier to treat Heschel the philosopher, the biblical scholar, or even the poet, for then an area of investigation would be marked out and the printed word available for all to examine. To discuss Heschel the man, however, is another matter—

perhaps a more difficult matter. Not only his words, but his dreams, his deeds, his entire life now become the subject of inquiry. Inquiries such as this are fraught with danger today, because ours is an age of flaunting irreverence, when debunking has taken on all the trappings of a national sport, and historians revel in revealing the clay feet of the mightiest. Heschel himself once observed that "Suspect thy neighbor as thyself" had become the newly emended version of the commandment. Contemporary biographers, nurtured in this subversive view of humanity, tend to be skeptical of human dignity.

A major theme of Heschel's writings, however, was human grandeur and dignity. For this, we find no argument more compelling than his works. As a youth, he titled his first book of poems, *Der Shem Hameforash: Mentsh*, that is, "Man, the Ineffable Name of God." For our purpose, the question is not so much what he intended by his defense of human grandeur, as how Heschel's views were related to his own life. "My father," his daughter has testified, "was the kind of man he wrote about."[1] Could he have written the following passage, for example, without experiencing something of what he wrote?

> Awareness of God is as close to the pious man as the throbbing of his own heart, often deep and calm but at times overwhelming, intoxicating, setting the soul afire. The momentous reality of God stands there as peace, power, and endless tranquility, as an inexhaustible source of help, as boundless compassion, as an open gate awaiting prayer. It sometimes happens that the life of a pious man becomes so involved in God that his heart overflows as though it were a cup in the hand of God.[2]

One cannot properly understand Heschel the man without studying his thought. The obverse is also true: to properly understand Heschel's thought, one must examine his life.

Nasi: A Prince of His People

Who was Abraham Joshua Heschel?

If the sages of Talmud were correct in saying that Israel's teachers are its royalty, then Heschel, the preeminent Jewish teacher of our generation, was a Nasi, a prince of his people. Indeed, he was elected to high office as much by others as by his own.

The Catholics elected Heschel.

His pervasive influence was felt at Vatican Council II, which was to review Catholic-Jewish relations in the form of a schema on the Jews. Asked by Cardinal Bea to draw up a proposal, Heschel composed a document which has served as a guideline for Catholics. Heschel traveled to Rome several times, where he argued for the church's acceptance of "the permanent preciousness of the Jewish people," which meant the abandonment of its mission to the Jews and the recognition of its role in history. Heschel's efforts at Vatican II were of enormous significance. Moreover, Heschel left a deep impression in Italy. He made a lecture tour there in conjunction with the Vatican; his books were translated into Italian, and he is, I believe, the only Jewish thinker to be quoted by a pope in this century.[3] After Heschel's death, the Catholic publication, *America*, devoted an entire issue to his memory (10 March 1973). A number of major studies on Heschel's thought have been written by Catholics. Surely this unprecedented conference is final testimony of the esteem of Catholics for Heschel.

Perhaps these two personal episodes will help to illustrate Heschel's relationship to the Catholic community:[4]

One afternoon Heschel told me that he had just received a delegation of nuns. Their order was considering whether or not to give up their formal, longer habit for shorter, less cumbersome clothing. "What did you advise?" I asked. "I told them that such a personal matter should be settled by themselves." "But what is your opinion?" I persisted. "I do not believe they should change," he replied.

How unusual that the nuns should have come to him at all with such a request!

Once, while walking past St. Patrick's Cathedral, a Jew (Dr. Shlomo Noble of the YIVO Institute) noticed in progress a protest demonstration against the war in Vietnam, where Cardinal Cooke had gone to support the military mission. While the Jew took a leaflet and put a few coins on the tray, the young boy who had handed him the tract looked at him, and then, trying to make contact, said hesitantly, "I know Rabbi Heschel."[5]

That name bridged the gap between a Catholic boy and the Jewish world.

The Protestants also elected Heschel.

The most influential Protestant thinker in America in this century, Reinhold Niebuhr, placed Heschel for the first time before the American reading public when, on the front page of the Sunday *New York Herald Tribune Book Review* of 1 April 1951, discussing his first major work, *Man Is Not Alone*, he wrote, "Abraham Heschel is one of the treasuries of spirit by which the persecutions, unloosed in Europe, inadvertently enriched our American culture. . . . He will become a commanding and authoritative voice not only in the Jewish community but in the religious life of America."[6]

Years later (1965–1966), Heschel became the first Jewish professor at The Union Theological Seminary in New York.

Shortly after his death, I saw a handwritten letter on Heschel's desk from a noted Protestant, which began with the salutation: "Dear Father Abraham"! And in his column in *The Christian Century*, Martin Marty wrote: "Has the death of anyone since Pope John moved us so much?"[7]

And, the Muslims elected Heschel.

In 1972, some months before his death and against doctor's orders, Abraham Heschel attended a hitherto unpublicized conference in Rome. "It was the first occasion since the establishment of the State of Israel—and the last—that religious and other leaders of the three faiths involved in Jerusalem had met together to define the religious content of their devotion to the Holy City."[8] The conference had been proposed by the Anglican archbishop of Jerusalem and was sponsored by the Center for Mediterranean Studies in Rome, in cooperation with the Friends and the Jerusalem Foundation, "to explore the religious dynamics of the Jerusalem problem by attempting to define the spiritual necessities embedded in each of the three religions involved with the city."[9] It was their hope that political considerations might be influenced by the "devout and profound personalities present."[10]

Archbishop Appleton opened each day's discussion with prayers, and a reading was given by each of the different faiths. Heschel was invited to read for the Jews. Observing that the coming Sabbath immediately preceded Rosh Hashana, the Jewish New Year, he recited the prophetical portion from Isaiah assigned for that Sabbath in the synagogue liturgy:

> For Zion's sake will I not hold my peace,
>
> And for Jerusalem's sake I will not rest . . .
>
> I have set watchmen upon thy walls, O Jerusalem,

They shall never hold their peace day nor night:

Ye that are the Lord's remembrancers,

Take ye no rest, and give Him no rest,

Till He establish, and till He make Jerusalem

A praise in the earth. . . .

For He said: "Surely, they are My people,

Children that will not deal falsely."

In all their affliction He was afflicted, And the angel of His presence saved them;

And He bore them, and carried them all the days of old. (Isa. 62:1, 2, 4, 57; 63:89)

After the ecumenical service had concluded, Heschel visibly moved the Muslims by remarking that "it is important for me to remember now, that while I have prayed from the heart for the Muslims all my life, I have never prayed with them before, or been face-to-face with them to talk about God. This is so important. We must go further."[11]

Heschel believed that seemingly insoluble problems, even one so hoary and complex as Jerusalem, could be resolved if a spiritual understanding were first achieved. He trusted that even during those few meetings a "common language among the religions could be found."[12] Summarizing the conference, the center director, E. A. Bayne, wrote me.

> In such a setting Rabbi Heschel performed superbly as we had hoped. Although fragile in health, his spirit never flagged. . . . Largely because of his presence, I believe, in support of the spiritual dimension of the inquiry, the seminar was rewarding. . . . Had we the funds, however, another session could have been fruitful, if not definitive; but it was not to be.[13]

At the close of the final meeting, Heschel, who moved slowly in those days, shuffled toward the door with only the two Muslim Kahdis apparently remaining behind. One approached him, squeezed his hand and departed. The second took his hand and said: "I have read all that you have written. God bless your work."

The blacks elected Heschel.

A picture which should hang in black and Jewish homes is that of Heschel and Martin Luther King, Jr., marching arm-in-arm in Selma, Alabama, an event Heschel recalled in typically striking summation: "When I marched in Selma, my feet were praying." Heschel and King not only marched together, they had profound respect for each other as well. Shortly before King's assassination, Heschel said of him:

> Martin Luther King is a sign that God has not forsaken the United States of America. God has sent him to us. . . . His mission is sacred. . . . I call upon every Jew to hearken to his voice, to share his vision, to follow in his way. The whole future of America will depend upon the . . . influence of Dr. King.[14]

Describing Heschel as "one of the great men of our age, a truly great prophet," King recognized Heschel's contribution to the civil rights movement:

> He has been with us in many struggles. I remember marching from Selma to Montgomery, how he stood at my side. . . . I remember very well when we were in Chicago for the Conference on Religion and Race. . . . His speech inspired clergymen of all faiths . . . to do something that they had not done before.[15]

In that historic speech to which King referred, given in 1963 at the initial Conference on Religion and Race in Chicago, Heschel's opening words startled his audience and helped to set the stage for the momentous changes that were to come:

> At the first Conference on Religion and Race, the main participants were Pharaoh and Moses. Moses' words were: "Thus says the Lord, the God of Israel, let my people go that they may celebrate a feast to me." While Pharaoh retorted: "Who is the Lord that I should heed His voice and let Israel go?"
>
> The outcome of that summit meeting has not come to an end. Pharaoh is not ready to capitulate. The Exodus began but is far from having been completed.[16]

By 1984, the black-Jewish coalition from the civil rights era, which had been ailing throughout the 1970s, came to an end as the Reverend Jesse Jackson, a Baptist preacher like King, started to preach a very different sermon to the Jewish community. During the warmer days of their relationship, some blacks had believed Jews were not "white," as many Jews had believed that blacks were not "goyim." But, attitudes changed and blacks began to see Jews who had advanced on the ladder of financial success not only as whites but as super-scapegoat-whites. Jews, for their part, saw that some blacks were capable of such anti-Semitism as to be branded supergoyim.

Jews began cooling off to the civil rights movement as discrimination *for* blacks replaced discrimination against them; affirmative action shifted from "equal opportunity," its original intent, into strict "quotas," and honest competition was replaced by a massive government supported spoils system. A black candidate–instead of the Ku Klux Klan–injected anti-Semitism into the 1984 presidential campaign. For both blacks and Jews, the anti-Semitic aspects of the Jackson phenomenon was a danger signal. "For the first time in American history," writes Lucy Davidowicz, historian of the Holocaust, "antisemitism has become a major political issue." As they had refused to disavow the Ku Klux Klan in the 1924 campaign, so in the 1984 campaign, the Democratic party's "failure to repudiate by name, loud and clear, the purveyors of racist antisemitism" showed that anti-Jewish bigotry had "voter appeal." Still, in 1983, when a conference was convened to confront black-Jewish relations, it was structured around the personalities of Heschel and King. By exploring their lives and teachings, it was hoped that a common spiritual ground might be laid, out of which a constructive dialogue on sensitive issues could grow.

The poor and the humiliated elected Heschel.

The eloquence of his voice and the power of his word were heard again and again on behalf of the neglected and the forlorn. He once said he was propelled out of the security of the ivory tower of research into the swirling domain of public issues because of his study of the prophets. "Prophecy," he wrote, "is the voice that God has lent to the silent agony, a voice to the plundered poor. . . . God is raging in the prophet's words." In Heschel's voice, an echo of that rage was heard.

The aged elected Heschel.

He was their most understanding and eloquent spokesman. In 1961, the first White House Conference on Aging found some six thousand delegates in attendance. Hundreds of sessions took place and countless papers from noted authorities were given. However one address–Heschel's–so overwhelmed the assembly that it was selected as the single representative statement for the conference and appeared in the congressional record, as well as on the official recording, whose other side contains the address of President Eisenhower. These are the closing words of Heschel's speech:

> We must seek ways to overcome the traumatic fear of being old, the prejudice, the discrimination against those advanced in years. All men are created equal, including those advanced in years. To be retired does not mean to be retarded. Being old is not necessarily the same as being stale. The effort to restore the dignity of old age will depend upon our ability to revive the equation of old age and wisdom. Wisdom is the substance upon which the inner security of the old will forever depend. But the attainment of wisdom is the work of a lifetime.
>
> Old men need a vision, not only recreation.
>
> Old men need a dream, not only a memory.
>
> It takes three things to attain a sense of significant being:
>
> God
>
> A Soul
>
> And a Moment
>
> And these three are always here.
>
> Just to be is a blessing.
>
> Just to live is holy.[17]

The Russian Jews elected Heschel.

He was among the first to alert us to the calamity in those early years when few were aware of it. He urged Elie Weisel to travel to Russia, the result of which was his book, *The Jews of Silence*–Jews, that is, who speak out of fear, in silence, with their eyes. Heschel's plea on behalf of Russian Jews led to rescue efforts that have brought thousands of them into freedom. Heschel used to remind us that "the Russian Jews will do more for us than we will ever do for them." He was referring to the courageous example of those who persisted as Jews for seventy-five years without synagogues, religious schools, or books, and against the vicious antireligious and anti-Semitic apparatus of the Soviet government. In one of his early addresses, he compared modern Jewry's attitude toward the Russian Jews to the attitude of ancient Jewry toward the Ten Lost Tribes:

> One of the tragic failures of ancient Judaism was the indifference of our people to the Ten Tribes of Israel which were carried away into exile by Assyria after the Northern Kingdom of Samaria was destroyed. Uncared for, unattended to, overlooked, and abandoned, the ten tribes were consigned to oblivion. . . . At the end they vanished. . . . There is a nightmare that terrifies me today: the unawareness of our being involved in a new failure, in a tragic dereliction of duty. East European Jewry vanished. Russian Jewry is the last remnant of a people destroyed in extermination camps, the last remnant of a spiritual glory that is no more. Let the twentieth century not enter the annals of Jewish history as the century of physical and spiritual destruction.[18]

The Jews of Europe, living and dead, had in Heschel a spokesman.

His inaugural address at The Union Theological Seminary before a distinguished body of Christian leaders, began thus:

> I speak as a member of a congregation whose founder was Abraham, and the name of my Rabbi is Moses. I speak as a person who was able to leave Warsaw, the city in which I was

> born, just six weeks before the disaster began. My destination was New York, it would have been Auschwitz or Treblinka. I am a brand plucked from the fire, on which my people was burned to death. I am a brand plucked from the fire of an altar of Satan on which millions of human lives were exterminated to evil's greater glory, and on which so much else was consumed: the divine image of so many human beings, many people's faith in the God of justice and compassion, and much of the secret and power of attachment to the Bible bred and cherished in the hearts of men for nearly 2,000 years.[19]

He delivered their unforgettable eulogy in his book *The Earth Is the Lord's*, in which he sketched the lasting values of East European Jewry, and which he wrote while still in Cincinnati during the war years. I saw him daily at that time, but rarely did he discuss what must have grieved him most, the end of the thousand year period of East European Jewry, which he called "The golden era of Jewish history."[20] Instead of describing the horror–the "Holocaust"–he preferred to write about what was most enduring from that golden era: its beauty, its meaning, its holiness. He referred me to a short story, written by a friend of his, in which a Hasidic Master warned his disciples, in the name of sanity, not to dwell over much upon the horrors that were to come, citing as proof the Book of Exodus, in which only the first few chapters deal with the sufferings of slavery, while the preponderance of the volume dwells upon the "going out from Egypt."[21] Of course, we need both records–the Holocaust and the Holiness. It was the way of Heschel, however, to choose the affirmative portrayal of the noble. Of East European Jewry, he wrote:

> The little Jewish communities in Eastern Europe were like sacred texts opened before the eyes of God, so close were their houses of worship to Mount Sinai. In their humble wooden synagogues, looking as if they were deliberately closing themselves off from the world, the Jews purified the souls that God had given them. They did not write songs. They themselves were songs.[22]

The Catholics, the Protestants, the blacks, among others, all respected Heschel as a Nasi, a prince of his people.

Shalem: A Complete Person

Who was Rabbi Abraham Joshua Heschel? He was shalem, a complete person, a person marvelously whole.

Born in Warsaw, Poland, in 1907, a descendant of an illustrious line of Hasidic rabbis, even from early childhood Heschel was viewed with great expectations. At the age of four or five, scholars would place him on a table and interrogate him for the surprising and amusing answers he would give. When his father died during his tenth year, there were those who wanted the young boy to succeed him almost at once. He had already mastered many of the classical religious texts; he had begun to write; and, the words he spoke were a strange combination of maturity and youth. The sheer joy he felt as a child, so uncontainable at times that he would burst out in laughter when he met a good friend in the street, was later tamed into an easy sense of humor that added to his special personal charm. But, there was also astounding knowledge, keen understanding, and profound feeling: an awareness that human beings dwell on the tangent of the infinite, within the holy dimension; that human life is part of the life of God. Some Hasidic leaders felt that he might bring about a renewal of their movement, which had grown dormant in the twentieth century. Speaking about his early childhood, Heschel wrote in a rare personal note:

> I was born in Warsaw, Poland, but my cradle stood in Mezbizh (a small town in the province of Podolia, Ukraine), where the Baal Shem Tov, founder of the Hasidic movement, lived during the last twenty years of his life. That is where my father came from, and he continued to regard it as his home. . . . I was named after my grandfather, Rabbi Abraham Joshua Heschel, "The Apter Rav," and last great rebbe of Mezbizh. He was marvelous in all his ways, and it was as if the Baal Shem Tov had come to life in him. . . .
>
> Enchanted by a wealth of traditions and tales, I felt truly at home in Mezbizh. That little town so distant from Warsaw and yet so near was the place to which my childish imagination went on many journeys.[23]

It can be said with certainty that the years in Warsaw provided that nourishment of spirit and intellect, that inner dignity and awareness of who he was that gave permanent direction to Heschel's life. It could not, however, prevent him from peering beyond and, in the end, setting out from his home to explore the world of Western civilization, which thundered and glittered about him. Departing from Warsaw in his teens, he traveled first to Vilna, where he pursued his secular education and joined a promising group of young Yiddish poets; then on to Berlin, the metropolis of science and philosophy in the 1920s, where he immersed himself in the culture of the West and began to publish his first books and establish his career.

He claimed he was no longer a Hasid. He had indeed abandoned their style of dress and their restricted social contacts for the larger world, both Jewish and German. But, somehow Hasidism remained within Heschel:

> In my childhood and in my youth, I was the recipient of many blessings. I lived in the presence of quite a number of extraordinary persons I could revere. And just as I lived as a child in their presence, their presence continues to live in me as an adult. And yet I am not just a dwelling place for other people, an echo of the past. . . . I disagree with those who think of the present in the past tense. . . . The greatest danger is to become obsolete. I try not to be stale. I try to remain young. I have one talent and that is the capacity to be tremendously surprised, surprised at life, at ideas. This is to me the supreme Hasidic imperative.[24]

In 1952, he gave a memorable description of the conflict he experienced between Berlin and Warsaw, between the intellectual claim of the university and the way of Torah:

> I came with great hunger to the University of Berlin to study philosophy. I looked for a system of thought, for the depth of the spirit, for the meaning of existence. Erudite and profound scholars gave courses in Logic, Epistemology, Esthetics, Ethics and Metaphysics. . . .
>
> Yet, in spite of the intellectual power and honesty which I was privileged to witness, I became increasingly aware of the gulf that separated my views from those held at the university. To them, religion was a feeling. To me, religion included the insights of the Torah which is a vision of man from the point of view of God. They spoke of God from the point of view of man. To them God was an idea, a postulate of reason. They

granted Him the status of being a logical possibility. But to assume that he had existence would have been a crime against epistemology.

In those months in Berlin I went through moments of profound bitterness. I felt very much alone with my own problems and anxieties. I walked alone in the evenings through the magnificent streets of Berlin. I admired the solidity of its architecture, the overwhelming drive and power of a dynamic civilization. There were concerts, theatres, and lectures by famous scholars about the latest theories and inventions, and I was pondering whether to go to the new Max Reinhardt play or to a lecture about the theory of relativity.

Suddenly I noticed the sun had gone down, evening had arrived. . . .

I had forgotten God. I had forgotten Sinai–I had forgotten that sunset is my business–that my task is "to restore the world to the Kingship of the Lord."

So I began to utter the words of the evening prayer.

"Blessed Art Thou, Lord Our God, King Of The Universe Who By His Word Brings On The Evening."

. . . On that evening in the streets of Berlin, I was not in a mood to pray. My heart was heavy, my soul was sad. It was difficult for the lofty words of prayer to break through the dark clouds of my inner life. But how would I dare not to pray? How would I dare to miss an evening prayer?[25]

Forced to flee the Nazis, Heschel made his way, through Poland and England, to the United States.

After half a decade at The Hebrew Union College in Cincinnati, the rest of his years here were spent in his small, crowded study at the Jewish Theological Seminary in New York from which his works emanated and to which many made pilgrimage.

In Eastern Europe, Heschel acquired his ancestral learning and piety; in Berlin, his philosophy, method, and European culture; in the United States, within the blessing of a free society which he treasured, the full extent of his power was reached.

If the worlds of his environment were universal, so were the worlds of his scholarship. What he wrote of Maimonides–that "his achievement seems so incredible that one is almost inclined to believe that Maimonides is the name for a whole academy of scholars rather than the name of an individual"[26]–could be said of Heschel himself. He contributed major works in fields that required their own separate disciplines–the Bible, rabbinics, philosophy, Hasidism, theology, and ethics, among others. It was this mastery of virtually the entire range of Jewish creative experience, as well as that of Western culture, which contributed to the richness of his thinking. He was equally gifted in four languages: Yiddish, Hebrew, German, and English–and would select the language to write the book he was engaged in according to its subject.

Heschel's immense productivity, despite being uprooted twice from his cultural milieu, was not unrelated to his understanding that, with the ending of East European Jewry, he was one of the few who could leave the record of what had been. He felt a solemn burden: to pass this legacy on to the next generation. How then could one waste valuable time?

> A world has vanished. All that remains is a sanctuary hidden in the realm of the spirit. We of this generation are still holding the key. Unless

> we remember, unless we unlock it, the treasury of the ages will remain a secret of God. . . . We are either the last Jews or those who will hand over the entire past to generations to come.[27]

Heschel, above all, held that key. And, he lived with the knowledge that he held it.

Finally, in addition to the worlds of his environment and his scholarship, the worlds of Heschel's concern were likewise universal, bridging the divisions which tend to divide Jews. He was equally at home with secular Yiddishists, Zionist Hebraists, poets, artists, Hasidim, Reform, Conservative and Orthodox Jews. Heschel reached out a hand to those of other faiths because of the depth, not the shallowness, of his own spiritual life: the deeper the roots, the broader the branches. Or, as one Christian scholar noted, "Heschel was most human as he was most Jewish."[28] His ecumenical call was grounded in his belief that human life partakes in the life of God; that human beings dwell both in the realm of nature and the dimension of the holy, that the divine image, and not only the chromosome and the circulatory system, is the common bond of humankind. Beneath the divisiveness of creeds lie those underpinnings of religion, such as humility, compassion, awe, and faith, which characterize the community of all true persons of spirit. "Different are the languages of prayer," he wrote, "but the tears are the same."[29]

It was this spiritual fraternity of humankind which Heschel acted upon in his ecumenical relations. His effort to nurture this bond was responded to so warmly by others, because their spirits, not only their minds, were engaged. He knew that if the divine fellowship did not enjoin us, a demonic one would. While some are "wary of the ecumenical movement," he wrote, "there is another ecumenical movement, worldwide in influence: nihilism. We must choose between interfaith and inter-nihilism."[30]

An example of how Heschel was perceived by Gentiles comes from the letter of an executive of the Bell System. He told how in the 1960s this corporation had an arrangement with Dartmouth College whereby each summer fifteen of its more promising members of middle management spent eight weeks in Hanover, New Hampshire, studying the humanities and meeting special guests invited for a twenty-four-hour period. In the summer of 1964, Heschel was such a guest. Despite the passage of a decade and a half, Heschel's theme—the dignity, uniqueness, and sacredness of being human—was still fresh in his mind. Of his encounter with Heschel, the executive wrote:

> You must understand that the Bell System group was made up of middle-aged, gentile business executives, whose normal concerns were those of the corporation, and yet each member of the group was, I remember, struck by the aura of reverence, wisdom, and concern for mankind which seemed to emanate from Rabbi Heschel. In my own case, I felt that his thoughts were communicated to me through a medium far beyond his words. If, when he had finished, he had risen and beckoned me to follow, I would have done so without questions. Even after 15 years, I am convinced that, on that day, I sat with a Biblical prophet.[31]

Heschel's environment, his scholarship, and his concern were each characterized by an unusually broad range. This contributed to the wholeness of his person: the breadth of his understanding as well as its depth.

Zaddik of the Generation

We have said that Heschel was a Nasi, a prince of his people, and Shalem, a whole person. Let us pose the question a final time. Who was Heschel?

He was a zaddik. The zaddik of his generation.

Behind his public face as thinker, writer, and advocate, was a private undisclosed frame–the zaddik, the Hasidic master, that remarkable new leader who emerged from the movement of Hasidism, and who renewed the life of eighteenth and nineteenth century East European Jewry. Heschel must be understood, in good measure, against the pattern of those masters. Since succession in Hasidic leadership was dynastic, Heschel, as a member of that royalty, had been raised to sit upon the zaddik's throne, as his father and his father's father had done before. Indeed, of him even more was expected. And yet, though he abdicated his destined role by departing for the West, that is what he ultimately became: a zaddik–the zaddik of his generation.[32]

The zaddik was both scholar and pietist, master of prayer and teacher of Torah, bound up with God and the center of the community, wielder of power yet humble, a teacher by example as well as by word, one who affirmed life by celebrating it in joy, whose every act was meant to glorify God. When we consider Heschel's life and work against this description, we see how he approximated it.

Heschel's rich inner life was sustained primarily by prayer, about which he has given us as profound an analysis as we possess. That analysis–descriptive, analytical, poetic, suggestive–is surely, in part, personal. For example:

> Prayer is spiritual ecstasy. It is as if all our vital thoughts in fierce ardor would burst the mind to stream toward God. A keen single force draws

> our yearning for the utmost out of the seclusion of the soul. We try to see our visions in His light, to feel our life as His affair. We begin by letting the thought of Him engage our minds, by realizing His name and entering into a reverie which leads through beauty and stillness, from feeling to thought, and from understanding to devotion.[33]

In the midforties, Heschel initiated me into the regimen of daily worship. I would join him in his room at dawn to pray the morning service. Those were unforgettable hours. With his large prayer shawl about him and his tefilin on his head and arm, he paced the room reciting the long pages by heart, at first slowly and softly but then more quickly and loudly, the words flowing as a torrent from him, at times roaring like a lion, rising at last to a culmination of motionless silence, all within. Time opened to eternity.

The task of the zaddik was to seek out the sparks of holiness everywhere, even amidst evil. This too was true of Heschel. He often restrained himself from unnecessary criticism, even when under attack, preferring to dwell upon the virtues of others. How sad, I once observed, that a forthcoming wedding consisted of two orphans who would be bereft of family at the festivities. How wonderful, Heschel corrected me, that two orphans, each with no one else, had found each other!

Isolation was anathema to the zaddik. Indeed, to the classic Hasidic writers Noah was decried as the symbol of the unconcerned leader, because he "walked *with* God," that is, in such selfish seclusion that he, in effect, caused the Flood; conversely, Abraham was acclaimed as the symbol of the zaddik, because he walked *before* God "in the midst of the city," and would have prevented the Deluge had he lived earlier.[34] So it was with Heschel. His door was open to all. And, they came, not only with problems of the intellect, but with problems of life. Other scholars protected their privacy and were unavailable. Not so Heschel.

The zaddik stood for exalted leadership, believing that all could be changed by a true master. In class each year, Heschel would recall the answer that the German poet, Rainer Maria Rilke, gave to the young man who wrote, asking whether he should become a poet: Only if you cannot live without being a poet! That was Heschel's advice to incipient rabbis (or ministers): become a rabbi only if your life depends upon it. Before his death, Moses prayed for a worthy successor–"Let the Lord set a man over the congregation, who will go out before them and will come in before them . . . that the congregation of the Lord be not as sheep which have no shepherd" (Num. 27:18). To which Heschel would quote the interpretation of the Hasidic master of Kotzk: To "go out before them" can be translated in Yiddish as "*ois-gehen far zey*," which means, one who is willing to die for them!

For the zaddik, the task of creating a righteous people was a divine command. Hasidic society, which was marked by a community of Hasidim around their particular zaddik, strove to achieve a fellowship of love, responsibility, and justice. It represented, in microcosm, a model pattern of community. The struggle for righteousness includes a concomitant struggle against evil; to despair, or to withdraw from that ongoing effort, is tantamount to denial. Heschel was discouraged by the failure of European theologians to adequately contend with the oncoming horror of nazism, a failure which he ascribed, in part, to the prevailing belief in human worthlessness and helplessness. He told me how, shortly before the war, in 1938, he visited Switzerland and was impressed with the work of

Ragatz, a theologian who, with a number of followers, had turned against theology, was deep into the Hebrew Bible, and was devoting himself to social institutions and politics in the belief that the only hope at that moment was to come to the aid of fellow human beings. He also went to Basel, then under the influence of Karl Barth. "When I asserted that in this time of the rise of totalitarianism the single most important task for religious persons is to understand and work for a just state," Heschel said, "I was met with rejection. Even accused of being an atheist. After all, I did not talk theology. What could one expect of man, they argued, was he not depraved and beyond the hope of history?"

The zaddik not only taught Torah, he was Torah, a living Torah. His disciples learned from his life, not only his words. On the anniversary of the death of Albert Schweitzer, Heschel would recount the latter's life in class: how he forsook glory as a famed philosopher, organist, and musicologist, to become a common doctor in a clinic in deepest Africa as atonement for the sins of the white race. In the last chapter of his book on Maimonides, Heschel proposed a solution to a paradox that has long puzzled scholars. Toward the end of his life, Maimonides, a giant in philosophy, law, and science, advised his translator, Ibn Tibbon, by letter, not to take the long journey from Europe to visit him in Egypt, because he could spend little time with him even were he to come. There follows an exhausting itinerary of Maimonides' schedule of daily medical work from early dawn to late evening with time only for a single meal. Why? Why did he forsake his momentous unfinished scholarly works to heal the sick, which any doctor could have done? Heschel suggests an answer:

> This is Maimonides' last metamorphosis: From metaphysics to medicine, from contemplation to practice, from speculation to the imitation of God. Preoccupation with the concrete man and the effort to aid him in his suffering is now the form of religious devotion. . . . Personal achievement is abandoned for enhancing God's presence in human deeds.[35]

What Heschel said of Maimonides, could be said of himself. Despite the frailty of his health, the preciousness of each hour of his life, the books yet to be written that were laid out so clearly in his mind, he spent more and more time in the last years of his life on the social issues: civil rights, the Vietnam war, the plight of Russian Jewry. Prayer had become deed.

According to his own testimony, two opposite Hasidic masters served as models to Heschel: the Baal Shem Tov, the founder of Hasidism, and his counterpart, Rabbi Mendl of Kotzk. About their influence on him he wrote:

> The earliest fascination I can recall is associated with the Baal Shem, whose parables disclosed some of the first insights I gained as a child. He remained a model too sublime to follow, yet too overwhelming to ignore.
>
> It was in my ninth year that the presence of Reb Menahem Mendl of Kotzk, known as the Kotzker, entered my life. Since then he has remained a steady companion and a haunting challenge. Although he often stunted me, he also urged me to confront perplexities that I might have preferred to evade.
>
> Years later I realized that, in being guided by both the Baal Shem Tov and the Kotzker, I had allowed two forces to carry on a struggle within me. . . . The one reminded me that there could

> be a Heaven on earth, the other shocked me into discovering Hell in the alleged heavenly places in our world. . . . The Baal Shem dwelled in my life like a lamp while the Kotzker struck like lightning.[36]

In his philosophy, as in his life, a polarity of ways prevailed: the love, forgiveness, beauty, and gentleness of the Baal Shem and the contempt for fraud, the fearless pursuit of truth of the Kotzker.

As a master in the tradition of the Kotzker, Heschel spoke out boldly. His words were like a hammer upon a rock. Sparks lit up the darkness of apathy.

"Emblazoned over the gates of the world in which we live," Heschel warned German Quakers in the late thirties, "is the escutcheon of the demons. The mark of Cain in the face of man has come to overshadow the likeness of God. Fellowmen turned out to be evil ghosts, monstrous and weird."

At a conference of American religious leaders, he lamented,

> This is a time to cry out. One is ashamed to be human. One is embarrassed to be called religious in the face of religion's failures to keep alive the image of God in the face of man. . . . Religion has declined not because it was refuted, but because it became irrelevant, dull, oppressive, insipid. . . . We have imprisoned God in our sanctuaries and slogans, and now the word of God is dying on our lips. . . . There is darkness in the East, and smugness in the West. What of the night? What of the night?

He admonished theologians that "one can only speak of God in the presence of God . . . that a theory of God can easily become a substitute for God, impressive to the mind when God as a living reality is absent from the soul."[37]

Heschel chided Jewish religious leaders that there seemed to be two kinds of rabbis: those who are willing to kill every Jew for a din (a law), and those who are willing to kill every din for a Jew. Reform rabbis were reproached for their prejudice against the Law: "Let us beware lest we reduce the Bible to literature, Jewish observance to good manners, the Talmud to Emily Post." The Orthodox were cautioned for an "all or nothing" approach: "The intransigent refuse to surrender a single iota, yet are ready to surrender the multitudes of Israel";[38] while Conservatives were stunned to be asked whether "the synagogue has become a graveyard where prayer is buried? Many labor in the vineyard of oratory, but who knows how to inspire others to pray? . . . The modern synagogue suffers from a severe cold. . . . Our motto is monotony. The fire has gone out of our worship. It is cold, stiff, and dead. . . . Rabbis have become masters of ceremonies, but Judaism does not stand on ceremonies."[39]

Heschel attacked the popular notion of self-expression before Jewish educators. "The supreme goal (for the child) is self-attachment to what is greater than the self, rather than self-expression. First there must be something to be expressed, an emotion, a vision, an end. . . . Everything," he added, "depends on the person who stands in front of the classroom. To guide a pupil into the promised land, the teacher must have been there himself. . . . What we need more than text books are textpeople [*sic*]."

At a American Medical Association convention, he warned that medicine itself was in need of therapy, that while "medicine is a sacred art," too many doctors had become plumbers, and that sickness was not only a physical disorder but a "crisis of the total person." He spoke of the "nightmare of medical bills," and berated them for creating a "sisyphus complex," curing the patient physically while destroying him economically.[40] (The San Francisco paper the following day ran a headline: "Dr. Heschel's Bitter Pill"!)

Few were to depart from such lectures unchanged. The searing words were in the spirit of the master of Kotzk.

But, even more than a cry for justice, one heard from Heschel a call to grandeur, to compassion, to hope, a song of celebration and exaltation. It was the voice of the other, still greater master: the Baal Shem Tov.

"The universe is not a waif and life is not a derelict. Man is neither the Lord of the universe nor even the master of his own destiny. Our life is not our own property but a possession of God. And it is this divine ownership that makes life a sacred thing."

"Over all the darkness of experience hovers the vision of a different day."

Or—"We live by the conviction that acts of goodness reflect the hidden light of his holiness. His light is above our minds but not beyond our will. It is within our power to mirror His unending love in deeds of kindness, like brooks that hold the sky."

Again—"The world of things we perceive is but a veil. Its flutter is music, its ornament science, but what it conceals is inscrutable. Its silence remains unbroken; no words can carry it away. Sometimes we wish that the world could cry out and tell us about that which made it pregnant with fear-filling grandeur. Sometimes we wish our own heart would speak of that which made it heavy with wonder."

"God's dream is not to be alone, but to have mankind as a partner."

"To pray is to dream in league with God, to envision his holy visions."

"The word of God never comes to an end. No word is God's last word."

For Jews, hearing and reading Heschel meant understanding, often for the first time, the message, and the glory, of their destiny.

"Judaism is the track of God in the wilderness of oblivion. By being what we are, namely Jews, by attuning our own yearning to the lonely holiness in this world, we will aid humanity more than by any particular service we may render." For "what we do as individuals is a trivial episode; what we attain as Israel causes us to become a part of eternity. . . . The people-Israel is the tree, we are the leaves. It is the belonging to the stem that keeps us alive."

"There has perhaps never been more need of Judaism than in our time, a time in which many cherished hopes of humanity lie crushed. We should be pioneers as were our fathers three thousand years ago. The future of all men depends upon their realizing that the sense of holiness is as vital as health. By following the Jewish way of life we maintain that sense and preserve the light for mankind's future visions."

"We are God's stake in human history. We are the dawn and the dusk, the challenge and the test. How strange to be a Jew and go astray on God's perilous errands. We have been offered as a pattern of worship and as a prey for scorn, but there is more still in our destiny. We carry the gold of God in our souls to forge the gate of the kingdom. The time for the kingdom may be far off, but the task is plain: to retain our share in God in spite of peril and contempt. . . . Loyal to the presence of the ultimate in the common, we may be able to make it clear that man is more than man, that in doing the finite he may perceive the infinite."

How could one hear such words and not listen to their echo, and re-echo, not ponder them, and be changed by them?

Who was Rabbi Abraham Joshua Heschel? He was Nasi, a prince of his people. He was shalem, marvelously whole. He was zaddik hador, a master for our age.

Endnotes

1. Susannah Heschel, in an address at a conference on A. J. Heschel sponsored by the Chicago Board of Jewish Education, 20–21 February 1983.

2. Abraham Joshua Heschel, *Man Is Not Alone: A Philosophy of Religion* (New York: Farrar, Straus, and Young, 1951), 282.

3. Cf. "Editorial: Contemporary Judaism and the Christian," *America*, 128 (10 March 1973), 202.

4. Some of my remarks are in the first person; I knew Heschel intimately from 1942, two years after his arrival in America, and much is drawn from a diary of conversations with him which I kept from 1949 to 1953.

5. Personal communication, S. Noble.

6. Reinhold Niebuhr, "Masterful Analysis of Faith," *New York Herald Tribune Book Review*, 118 (1 April 1951), 12.

7. Martin Marty, *The Christian Century* 19 (17 January 1973), 87.

8. E. A. Bayne, pamphlet published by the Center for Mediterranean Studies in Rome, 1973.

9. Letter from E. A. Bayne to Samuel H. Dresner, 29 December 1982.

10. Ibid.

11. Bayne, pamphlet, op. cit.

12. Ibid.

13. Bayne, correspondence, op. cit.

14. Abraham Joshua Heschel, quoted in *Conservative Judaism* 22 (Spring 1968): 1.

15. Martin Luther King, quoted in *Conservative Judaism* 22 (Spring 1968): 1.

16. Abraham Joshua Heschel, *The Insecurity of Freedom: Essays on Human Existence* (New York: Farrar, Straus and Giroux, 1966), 85.

17. Heschel, *Freedom*, 84.

18. Heschel, *Freedom*, 271, 273.

19. Abraham Joshua Heschel, "No Religion Is an Island," *Union Seminary Quarterly Review* 21 (January 1966): 117.

20. Abraham Joshua Heschel, *The Earth Is the Lords's: The Inner World of the Jew in Eastern Europe* (New York: Henry Schuman, Inc., 1950), 10.

21. Cf. Fischel Schneirson, "Ani Maamin" ("I Believe"); English translation by S. Dresner, *Conservative Judaism* 22 (Spring 1968): 20–30.

22. Heschel, *The Earth Is the Lord's*, 92–93.

23. Abraham Joshua Heschel, *A Passion for Truth* (New York: Farrar, Straus, and Giroux, 1973), p. xiii.

24. Abraham Joshua Heschel, "In Search of Exaltation," *Jewish Heritage* 13 (Fall 1971): 29, 30, 35.

25. Abraham Joshua Heschel, *Man's Quest for God: Studies in Prayer and Symbolism* (New York: Charles Scribners and Sons, 1954), 94–98.

26. Heschel, *Freedom*, 285.

27. Heschel, *The Earth Is the Lord's*, 107.

28. W. D. Davies, "Conscience, Scholar, Witness," *America* 128 (10 March 1973): 215.

29. Heschel, *Freedom*, 180.

30. Heschel, "No Religion Is an Island," 119.

31. Letter from S. H. Washburn to Samuel H. Dresner, 20 March 1979.

32. Cf. Samuel H. Dresner, *The Zaddik* (New York: Abelard-Schuman, 1960; Schocken, 1974).

33. Heschel, *Man's Quest*, 18–19.

34. Cf. Dresner, *The Zaddik*, chapters 4 and 7.

35. Heschel, *Freedom*, 290.

36. Heschel, *A Passion for Truth*, pp. xiv-xv.

37. Abraham Joshua Heschel, "The Jewish Notion of God and Christian Renewal," *Theology of Renewal*, ed. L. K. Shook, vol. 1 (New York: Herder & Herder, 1968), 106; from an address to a congress of Catholic theologians in Toronto, 1967.

38. Heschel, *Freedom*, 205; from an address entitled "The Individual Jew and His Obligations," delivered in 1957 at the Jerusalem Ideological Conference, convened at the Hebrew University.

39. Heschel, *Man's Quest*, 149; from an address originally entitled "The Spirit of Prayer," delivered in 1953 at the annual convention of The Rabbinical Assembly of America, in Atlantic City, N.J.

40. Ibid., 33, 35, 34.

NINE

The Bomb

Glancing through the Sunday *New York Times* literary, art, and music sections, it is almost embarrassing to note the plethora of Jewish names. The central role played by Jews in the arts, both as creative artists and as critics, novelists, poets, and thinkers, as university academicians, editors and publishers, musicians, conductors, and composers is nothing less than astounding. One is reminded of prewar Budapest or Vienna.

Twenty years ago *Time* magazine ran an article claiming that "the United States is becoming more Jewish. . . . Among American intellectuals the Jew has even become a culture hero." It went on to quote poet Robert Lowell, who declared that "Jewishness is the center of today's literature much as the West was in the 30s." Twenty years later (26 February 1990), *Time* repeated the same theme, informing us that "Jews are news. It is an axiom of journalism. An indispensable one, too, because it is otherwise impossible to explain why the deeds and misdeeds of a dot-on-the-map Israel get an absurdly disproportionate amount of news coverage around the world."

Nothing seems to have changed.

For centuries, the Jews were locked up in ghettos, silent, shut off from the outside world that passed them by, an anachronism in the course of history, a fossil that seemed long ago to have outlived its usefulness. With the fall of the ghetto walls, not only has the Jew emerged into the life stream of the nations, but seems today to have become a symbol, for some the savior, of modern man. For example, as mentioned above, the little state of Israel, no larger than Rhode Island, and with a comparable population, draws more permanent reporters–some three hundred–than any other city, apart from Washington and Brussels, the European center. It draws more than London, Paris, Berlin, or Moscow. Whatever transpires there has the world's attention, as the close scrutiny of the Lebanon War, the West Bank uprising, and the peace negotiations testify.

Thrust front and center upon the world's stage, attracting all the spotlights of history, the question arises: Why the fascination? Why the consuming curiosity with a people whose numbers are so ridiculously small that they should have been swallowed up long ago by the glittering new life outside the ghetto. Why the interest in books and plays that are, in many cases, quite mediocre?

The Miracle of Survival

I would like to suggest a reason why the world finds the Jews fascinating, reads books, and attends plays by and about them. It is because, to the Gentile, the people-Israel are a mystery. It is the mystery of a people that have faced death and lived, that have confronted the devil and salvaged their soul.

For Israel has survived. It has known physical evil and conquered it, defying all the pronouncements of doom by history's mightiest rulers, and each time rising Phoenix-like from the graves that were dug for it. More than three thousand years ago, Pharaoh Merneptah of Egypt exultingly proclaimed the words he had inscribed in his Temple of the Dead: "Israel's . . . seed exists no more." Two thousand years ago, the Emperor Titus returned triumphantly to Rome in the flush of his conquest over the Jews, whose cities he had leveled and whose God he believed he had cremated in the holocaust of the temple. To suspend the moment eternally in history, he erected a massive arch on which there was inscribed in bas-relief, for all to gaze upon in future centuries, the record of Roman victory and Jewish degradation. With masterful artistry, that relief contrasts the grand entry of Titus into Rome riding upon his chariot of triumph, against the straggling remnants of the Jewish captives who hauled the precious spoils of the temple, even the great golden seven-branched menorah. To commemorate the finality of the conquest, Roman coins were stamped "*Judea est perdita*" (Judea is destroyed!).

Even when he knew he could no longer win the war in 1944, Hitler never lost his determination to achieve one obsessive goal, to make the world Judenrein! So, he pressed on with maniacal fury during those final months, shipping huge carloads of human cattle to Auschwitz, refusing to the very end to divert desperately needed equipment, men, and funds from his insane war on the Jews.

But, the people-Israel survived.

Not only did they survive physical evil again and again, but, what is equally remarkable, they prevailed spiritually. They remained sane. Before Rome drove them into exile, they had already prepared that amazing world of a book, the Talmud, which became their portable homeland, the source of their wisdom, and the blueprint for the fortresses of holiness they built wherever they dwelt. So when, at last, the Jews crept forth from the cages of Auschwitz, they did not ravage Europe, thirsting for revenge, seeking to cut down the "blue-eyed, blond haired Aryan devils" who had permitted and perpetrated the Holocaust. Instead, they quietly went about the excruciatingly difficult task of rebuilding their broken lives, learning new languages, finding new wives and husbands, raising new families, acquiring new trades, and, miracle of miracles, reestablishing the old-new land of their fathers, the land of Israel. On 30 November 1947, the sovereignty of the Jewish State–which Titus thought he had destroyed forever in 70 C.E. and under whose arch no Jew had walked, out of shame–was celebrated by a parade of the Jews of Rome which led for the first time in two millennia beneath that same hated arch.

The people-Israel are a mystery because today the whole world stands in the very place where Israel has always stood–on the brink of annihilation! The growing danger of nuclear war has made of our earth a vast time bomb waiting to explode.

In the past, we were horrified by the taking of a single life, more so at the taking of groups of lives and still more so at the attempted decimation of entire nations. But, the destruction of humankind itself was never a possibility, never even conceivable. Even the bloodiest battles of the past–the wars of Ghengis Kahn, the Thirty Years' War, the Civil War, World Wars I and II–affected only a small part of the human race. There was always "mankind." Now, it is both conceivable and possible that there may be no mankind at all. For the first time, destructive power has reached the point of "overkill," that is, to kill many times over, the entire human population on our planet. This is what makes our age radically different from all the ages that have gone before. Nuclear war today may mean the "end." Nor is the making of the bomb any longer a dark secret shared by only two great powers that have reached an understanding. Any nation, given the resources, can produce it, and, as more nations obtain it, the possibility of controlling it grows less and less.

Fallibility and Design

Scientists tell us that under the present conditions it is statistically almost certain that one or more bombs will go off–

(1) because of *mechanical failure*. Some machine or instrument of critical significance is bound eventually to break down. Let one spine-tingling example suffice. Some years ago at the Colorado Springs nerve center of the North American Defense System (NORAD), which was manned by both United States and Canadian personnel, the newly installed Ballistic Missile Early Warning System (BMEWS), which has immense radar installations in Greenland and elsewhere along our northern coast, suddenly began flashing signals of a missile attack coming from Russia. The Canadian officer in charge gave the dreaded signal for war-alert but withheld the release signal while frantic telephone calls to the Joint Chiefs were held.

Why? Because despite evidence of missiles en route, there was no substantiating evidence of ground-firing. Furthermore, NORAD in Colorado could not reach the Greenland radar center by phone. It was later learned that an iceberg had severed the cable. For almost half an hour no action was taken, which, had there really been an attack, would have been disastrous. Why? Because they knew that Kruschev was at the very moment in New York at the United Nations, and it seemed a strange time for an attack (though it was also argued that a Russian takeover had planned an attack at just this time when we would be least likely to retaliate). Finally, the truth became known. The rising moon had bounced signals off the powerful Greenland radar installation–a possibility no one had considered before! But, what if another officer had been in control? Or, what if Kruschev had not been in New York?

One or more bombs will go off–

(2) because of *human fallibility*. Despite all our precautions, thousands of men are in a position to trigger the bomb. What happens if one has a mental breakdown or a seizure? Or, more probably, what happens if, under the tension of battle, mistakes are made in an area where no mistakes can be made? Two cases in the Persian Gulf demonstrate the point. In 1987, when the American frigate Stark was struck by two Iraqi missiles at a loss of thirty-seven lives, American failure to defend itself was not laid to mechanical causes but to "human error." Far more serious was the 1988 disastrous shooting down of an Iranian civilian plane by an American naval vessel with the loss of 290 lives. At first, blame was levelled at the plane having been off course and failing to identify itself, then, as conflicting information on the plane came in, guilt was shifted in part to the malfunction of the super sophisticated Aegis radar system, until the official naval board of inquiry brought in a report that found both the plane and the equipment blameless. Once again, it was human error. In the stress of battle, radar operators on the Vincennes mistakenly convinced themselves that the aircraft they had spotted taking off from the airport in Iran was hostile and intended to attack them. "You see what you want to see and hear what you want to hear," observed one officer. Another, who had served in an Aegis ship, said crews train constantly with tapes that simulate every conceivable battle situation. But, "the excitement factor is missing." Military psychologists

say that "immense stress is suffered during the first battle and perceptions are confused with reality. Soldiers often shoot at shadows or at each other in their first night of combat, and pilots misread their instruments and fly in the wrong direction."

(3) Because of *human design.* As the proliferation of atomic weapons spreads to other nations, increased apprehension escalates the possibility that one of them will decide for apparently compelling reasons on an atomic strike. Who knows but that the chaotic conditions accompanying the breakup of the Soviet empire may not lead to a military takeover in which the awareness of Russia's fading nuclear superiority will suggest a last ditch attempt to fulfill the Communist dream of world conquest by making a first strike, with or without provocation, intended to destroy our capacity to retaliate and render us helpless. Or, to take a different scenario, the old Union of Soviet Socialist Republics possesses fifteen thousand nuclear weapons, each capable of turning Indiana into a series of craters, and forty thousand devices, each able to incinerate New York City and small enough to be stored in the back of a small truck. Further, some 20 percent of the Soviet Union's gross national product went into a nuclear weapon network that employed thousands of first-rate scientists. Is it not reasonable to assume that, on the one hand, with such an overabundance of weapons and experts in a situation of chaos and poverty, and, on the other hand, with countries, both scrupulous and unscrupulous, eager to develop a nuclear strike capability and offering limitless rewards to possess the means, that, despite every effort to prevent it, some of these instruments and humans will, in fact, find their way to these lands?

As the bomb becomes more readily available to the nonsuperpowers, can an Assad, a Kaddafi, a

Hussein, or some future South American, Asian, or African dictator, be relied upon never to act out of hysterics? For that matter, can we? Iraq's Saddam Hussein, who was not averse to using poison gas in the war with Iran or on his own Kurdish citizens, and who threatened to exterminate half of Israel with it, may produce the bomb, despite all efforts to prevent him. "Put yourself in the Oval Office," according to the scenario suggested by William Saffire. "Saddam moves on Saudi Arabia. The United States warns him that means war. Saddam says fine, the first city he will take out is New York. You know he has the means and the will."[1]

As sober and informed an authority as Les Aspins, chairman of the Senate Armed Services Committee, responded in much the same way on an August 1991 television interview in which he was queried on the possible need for American reintervention in Iraq. He said that the single most important factor was the new knowledge that Hussein possessed a far more advanced capacity to produce the bomb than we had anticipated (as the Israelis had constantly warned). Had we known this before, he added, it would have catapulted our nation into an overwhelming early support of the Persian Gulf war. It became apparent, he went on, that Hussein had followed a double-pronged program to manufacture the bomb, one of which had totally escaped American detection. Consequently, the policy of sanctions alone might very well have given him time to produce the bomb, thus altering the nature of the hazard dramatically. Aspin proceeded to caution that the ending of the Cold War was no reason for relaxing our nuclear concern, for while that welcome event surely eased the danger of a Soviet threat, fifteen Third World countries were now on the verge of becoming just such a threat. Further, the Soviet menace, though formidable, was, after all, believed to be amenable to deterrence, because it assumed a prevalent rationality which would deter a first strike, lest Russia be destroyed through an automatic American counterstrike. These Third World countries, however, may be less constrained by reason! This requires, he concluded, *(a)* prevention: an embargo of nuclear material to such countries *(b)* preemption: should embargo fail and bombs be developed, air strikes against specific sites, and *(c)* defense: should both embargo and preemption fail, the development of a system that can protect America from nuclear attack.

What the congressman was, in fact, describing was the raising of the curtain on a new and chilling chapter in human history.

A single atomic murderer can assassinate our world.

There are no easy answers. No escape. No foolproof defense. No vast impenetrable dome that will slide over our cities at the press of a button. And slowly, but inevitably, we seem to be drifting toward total catastrophe. That is why "limited" wars, such as Vietnam, Korea, or Iran-Iraq are so dangerous. How can one be sure that they will remain "limited"? How could we know that a war which quickly moves from the involvement of one thousand to one hundred thousand men would not move from standard to nuclear weapons just as suddenly and unpredictably? We suffered defeat in Vietnam rather than fight a nuclear war because of the tremendous pressure at home, but, if the military had had their way, when all else had failed and rather than face defeat, nuclear weapons would certainly have been used. Can we be so sure that they will not be used in some future limited war? Can we be sure that limited wars will remain limited?

When one of the early astronauts was walking out in space, he disobeyed orders to return to the capsule.

The official reason given was because he was overcome with excitement at the magnificent view and the novel experience. But, one reporter who talked to him at length gave a different reason privately. He said the astronaut disobeyed orders to return because his deepest self did not want to go back to a planet that had been cursed by Hiroshima and Auschwitz and would one day explode. Something within him rebelled at the thought of living on the earth once again after having come so close to a new start elsewhere.

Most people, of course, prefer not to dwell upon such eventualities. They go about their customary ways, nonchalantly pursuing business as usual. But, there are thousands, even millions, who *do* think about such things. And, in the back of our minds all of us think about them.

The dread of our time pervades the subconscious of man.

There is a frantic search for a way out. But, all of the old paths are sealed. At such a moment in history, when hopelessness envelopes humanity, it is not strange that some have found a new appreciation of the people-Israel. For example, Harvard's theologian, Harvey Cox, wrote that

> Christians are really honorary Jews. All Jesus does for Israel's hope is to universalize it, to make it available even to us *Goyim.* But the church has betrayed this gift. Instead of universalizing this hope; we have etherealized it. . . . We need as our theological starting point a Jesus who is neither the ecclesiastical nor the existentialist Jesus, but the Jewish Jesus.

The Protestant biblical scholar, Robert Grant, wrote, "I wish we might give up all 'missions to Jews' and begin to understand one another; . . . though I would gladly see far more men and women converted to the imperishable heart of the Jewish faith, its utter trust in God, its utter devotion to his revealed will." When Gentiles devour Jewish books and flock to Jewish plays and read about Jewish history and explore the faith of Israel, some seem to be saying:

You, people of Israel, you almost alone have stood where all the world now stands. You have tottered on the brink of total annihilation, again and again, and have survived–and remained sane. Therefore you must have something to say to us. Tell us your secret that we too might live. You, Israel, who have gone through one Auschwitz, the Auschwitz of Hitler, have a message for us who stand before another, the universal nuclear Auschwitz.

Madness

The first answer the people-Israel have to these demands is contained in a parable first told by Rabbi Nahman of Bratzlav 150 years ago:

Long ago in a land beyond the seas, a terrible prophecy was revealed to the king one night through the magic of the stars.

"The crops of the next harvest will be cursed, and whoever eats of them will go mad!"

At once the king gathered together from near and far his wisest advisors to take counsel as to how they might meet the approaching calamity. Many proposals were made by the nobles but all were rejected, for the alternatives were equally and terribly clear: if they ate the food they would go mad; if they refused to eat they would die of starvation. Madness or death; which should the choice be?

In despair, they turned to the king, and he spoke: "Since there will be no food other than that which is cursed, we have no course but to eat and remain alive."

"But," he added, addressing his most faithful counselor, "I have still enough provisions to save one man.

I shall put them in your house so that you may escape the common fate. This will be your duty: when we have all lost our senses, you will ride through the kingdom, and in all the streets of the cities, in the shops, the squares, the markets, in the fields before the cottages, you will cry out: 'My Brothers, my brothers. Remember that you are mad!' "

This is the first thing the people-Israel have to say to the world–that it is mad. And, the world needs to hear it. It may even want to hear it–and from Israel.

Man, put on earth with a mind and a soul and the ability to fashion a paradise, instead prefers to turn the powers of his genius into kindling a blazing hell. Man, given a heart to love his neighbor and to serve his God, instead pursues power and passion, until he is ready to destroy himself as well as his fellow man.

Robert Jay Lifton studied the dual personalities of the Nazi doctors who conducted their sinister experiments and fateful examinations in Hitler's concentration camps. These doctors were, in many instances, genuine healers, peaceful men of science who, for love of their country, descended into an abyss of evil. They enacted what Lifton calls "doubling," a mental disguise which allowed them to separate their role as doctor for the Reich from their role as doctor for humanity.

Lifton has since turned his attention to scientists and researchers in the nuclear field, where he sees the same "doubling" affecting them as well. These scientists must convince themselves that they are preventing war, that they are developing weapons in the name of deterrence. And yet, deterrence only has meaning if both sides are willing to use their weapons. This formula is, of course, a maddening paradox, since it argues that peace is only possible when war is intended.

We know the dark results of the "doubling" that affected the Nazi doctors. What can be the results of this present madness?

If an individual commits suicide, it often implies insanity; what shall we say of the deliberate self-immolation of all men?

Upsetting the Balance

The second thing Israel has to say is that man is upsetting the balance.

There was once a town in the heart of America where all life seemed to be in harmony with its surroundings. It had fertile farms, prosperous farmers, birds in the trees, fish in the streams, and flowers blooming gaily along the roadside. Then, a white powder fell from the sky like snow and a fearful blight crept over the land. Cattle and sheep sickened. Hens could not hatch eggs. Strange illnesses appeared among people. Children were stricken at play and died within a few hours, and roadsides were lined with browned vegetation, as if swept by fire.

Such is the picture drawn of the future by Rachel Carson, writing about our ecological dilemma. Her thesis was that indiscriminate use of insecticides, such as DDT, threatened to let loose upon man and the countryside a flood of dangerous chemicals which would in time, and already has to some extent, upset the natural harmony throughout nature with the most serious consequences to human society. She called her book *Silent Spring.*

Our worst fears about the ecological state are presently being realized and are guiding governments into slow but definite steps of cooperation. Whether it is too late to regain the balance we have lost in nature only time will tell.

Now, if there is danger in "upsetting the balance" in the world of nature, what of the world of man? If the natural realm can tolerate only so much foreign substance, what of the human realm? In scanning the pages of history, we learn that spiritually man has been able to contend with the evils of moral waste much as the kidneys rid the body of physical waste. Enormous as infamy may have appeared in the past, man has always possessed sufficient resources to emerge from darkness into light, to rise up from defeat after defeat and struggle onward. But, just as there comes a time when the intake of alcohol, for example, rises beyond the capacity point for the kidneys to function, when excessive insecticide overpowers the cleansing powers of nature, so there is a point when man's malevolence grows so enormous as to render inoperable the spiritual dynamics of former ages. So, what we always knew could happen within the body of a single person–that his protective resources might under certain circumstances no longer be able to maintain life–and now know can happen for parts of nature, we are compelled to admit is possible for the entire human race.

The prophets warned that humans cannot lay sin upon sin without consequence–that there might come a time when the amount of evil man does becomes so monstrous that it can be borne no more. Then not only the birds will be silenced, but humanity itself.

This is precisely the situation we face. The toleration point of evil in history *has* been reached. We are now on the verge of "upsetting the balance" of man himself and, because of man, not just a few million acres, but all of nature as well–all creation. Greater damage will be done to those robins and salmon by nuclear radiation than by any other method. We dare not continue to pollute the stream of human life.

It is not enough to say, not precise enough to say—as is said again and again—that our spiritual progress has not kept up with our technological progress. It is, rather, that our *technological advance has finally reached such a point of absolute power that a moral revolution is demanded to harness it to good purposes and prevent its being used for evil purposes.*

Dreadful though this prospect is, it defines our position. Scientific progress has brought us to the spiritual saturation point.

And, we are not ready.

Ultimate concerns are now *immediate* concerns. They are now, perhaps, for the first time in the history of mankind, seen in a new light and from the most practical vantage point—not just from the mountain retreat, but from the scientist's lecture and the weekly magazine as well.

In 1952, Albert Schweitzer wrote in a letter to a Swedish newspaper that

> the idea of a kingdom of peace has been known to mankind for centuries. People did not believe they could make it come true. It was viewed as something purely religious that could not be applied to reality, but actually it is something that *must* be realized. This insight is urged upon us by the times in which we live. If mankind is not to perish, then we have no choice but to place our hope in the spirit, which is different from the spirit of the world.[2]

The inescapable facts of our situation are forcing us with merciless pressure to penetrate to the very meaning of life itself. Now, thinking about the meaning of life is not something the man on the street could be expected to be concerned with down through the ages, despite the influence of philosophy, poetry, and religion. But, in the atomic age all of us must entertain the possibility that man may be called to account for his actions by overwhelming disaster, that life as we know it may cease to exist–that humanity itself is only an experiment.

An Experiment

The third thing that Israel can say is that man is only an experiment. From the very beginning, the creation of humanity was a doubtful venture. This is the verdict of more than a few of the ancient sages of Israel.

In the first chapter of Genesis we read: *In the beginning* God *created the heavens and the earth;* while in the second chapter, *the* Lord God *created the heavens and the earth.* To the question why we are told "God" is the creator in the first chapter and the "Lord God" in the second, the rabbis gave this explanation. There are two Hebrew names for the Divinity: *Elohim*, God; and *Adonoy*, Lord. The Bible uses the name Elohim (God) to represent the quality of divine *justice*, and *Adonoy* (Lord) to stand for the quality of divine *mercy*. Originally the world was to have been created on the basis of justice. Therefore, in Genesis, chapter 1, it is written, *In the beginning* God (Elohim = divine justice) *created the heavens and the earth.* But, when He saw that the world could not so survive, the quality of mercy was added to enable humanity to exist. Therefore, in Genesis, chapter 2, it is written: *the* Lord (*Adonoy* = divine mercy) God *created the heavens and the earth.*

Likewise in the creation of man: in the first chapter of Genesis, we read, *And* God *created man;* while in the second, *Then the* Lord God *formed man.* Again, the creator of man in chapter 1 is "God," but "the Lord God" in chapter 2. Notice that both in this example and the one above, divine mercy was not only added but made to precede divine justice, as if to tell us: The

Almighty wanted to found His world on absolute justice, and even commenced to do so, but He soon perceived that this could not be. Mercy must not only be joined to justice, but take precedence, otherwise humanity cannot survive.

According to another rabbinic version of creation, God made and destroyed many worlds before He made ours. When it was time for man to be created, consternation arose in heaven. Truth and justice argued against his creation, for it was foreseen that he would be neither truthful nor just, but lie and pervert righteousness. Therefore, according to the rabbis, God cast truth and justice aside, brought forth mercy, and, while the angels were weighing the merits of the case (whether or not man should be created), God made him, a fait accompli!–and then confronted heaven with this creature.

Has man been able to justify God's hope? We are told that the schools of Hillel and Shammai disputed two and a half years whether it would have been better if man had or had not been created. Finally, they agreed that it would have been better had he not been created, but since he is already here let him examine his deeds and repent.

What the rabbis are saying, and drawing their understanding from the Bible, is that man exists through God's grace and not by His justice, and, therefore, that humanity's continual existence hangs in the balance. Though truth and justice opposed man's creation–nor did the angels agree to it, because of the evil he would do–man was, nevertheless, created in the hope that he would choose the blessing over the curse, life over death.

History has been a record of God's disappointment with man. The Bible may be described as God's search for the righteous man, and His repeated failure.

Adam disappointed God. Adam's first act was an act of rebellion. *Where art thou?* God cried. What has happened to this creature I made to rule My earth, to dwell in a garden paradise and to serve Me? *Therefore the Lord God sent him forth from the Garden of Eden, to till the ground from whence he was taken. So He drove out the man.* Next, the child of Adam, Cain, disappointed God. He slew his brother, Abel. *And the Lord said unto Cain: "Where is Abel thy brother?" And he said: "I know not; am I my brother's keeper?"* God called out to both Adam and Cain. Both denied their guilt. *And the Lord saw that the wickedness of man was great in the earth, and that every imagination of the thoughts of his heart was evil continually. And it repented the Lord that He had made man on earth, and it grieved Him at His heart. And the Lord said: "I will blot out man whom I have created from the face of the earth; both man and beast, and creeping things, and the fowl of the air; for it repenteth Me that I have made them."* Noah alone survived the Flood, a second Adam in a clean new world. But, Noah's drunkenness too disappointed God. And, his descendants in their rebellious pride built a great tower reaching up to the heavens, that they themselves might become gods. Again God punished them, this time by confounding their language and scattering them abroad upon the face of all the earth.

Then the Almighty offered mankind another hope, perhaps its last. Not a single person, like Adam or Noah, but a family, Abraham, Isaac, Jacob, and the people that would come from them, the children of Israel, a small people crushed by slavery, and open, perhaps, to His Word. To this people, He revealed His will at Sinai, that through them the world might come to know the Lord and follow His ways. If humankind will accept the Torah, the rabbis warned, the world will survive; but if not, it will return to chaos.

Adam failed, Cain failed, Noah failed, the generations of the tower of Babel failed. Is it so inconceivable that man's final chance was given with the covenant at Sinai? Ludicrous as this may have sounded a century ago, it does not today. Perhaps our earth will take its place among the others which were said to have been created and destroyed. Perhaps we are being abandoned today–to ourselves.

Mitzvah

Judaism claims to possess an answer to this grim prospect.

The fourth thing that Israel can say to a crazed world is that there is a way of sanity. That way is the way of holy deeds, the way of *mitzvah*. It is remarkable that that way, the Jewish way of life, requires no essential change in the face of present unprecedented conditions. The Jew has always acknowledged the persistence of evil and known that the world was unredeemed. He took quite literally the teaching that the fate of the world hangs upon whether men love God and do His will. He looked at life not as an exercise in pleasure, but as an opportunity to raise all things to God through deeds of daily service. Hence the great emphasis on the right deed–as if life could be violated or hallowed by the power of person; as if each human act either hindered or furthered the divine redemption.

Creation is not complete, the sages teach. God has left it unfinished in order to invite us into partnership with Him to complete it. Judaism is a reminder of the grandeur and the earnestness of that task. The Talmud says that before a man performs each act he must consider that upon it alone may depend the fate of the world. Therefore, the vast discipline of the Law wherein the *mitzvot* train a man how to hallow the everyday.

The sanctification of all of life is the goal of Judaism, and it is achieved through the regimen of the *mitzvot.*

> The world [Heschel wrote] is not a derelict which the Creator had abandoned to chance. Life is not an opportunity for indulgence, but a mission entrusted to every individual, an enterprise at least as responsible, for example, as the management of a factory. Every man constantly produces thoughts, deeds, words, committing them either to the power of holiness or the power of impunity. He is constantly engaged in building, or destroying. His task is to restore, by fulfilling the Torah, what has been impaired in the cosmos, to labor in the service of the cosmos for the sake of God. . . . Scientists dedicate their lives to the study of the habitats of insects. To them every trifle is important. The Jewish sages investigated just as passionately the laws that ought to govern human conduct. Wishing to banish the chaos of human existence and civilize the life of man according to the Torah, they trembled over every move, every breath; no detail was treated lightly. . . . Man has not advanced very far from the coast of chaos. A frantic call to disorder shrieks in the world. Where is the power that can offset that alluring call? The world cannot remain a vacuum. We are either ministers of the sacred or seekers of evil. The only safeguard against constant danger is constant vigilance, constant guidance. *(The Earth Is the Lord's)*

Rabbi Nahman of Bratslav grimly etched the insane condition of our world. But, that did not mean he believed it was forsaken. So long as there were those who remained sane by remaining loyal to the divine task, then hope was possible. Because Rabbi

Nahman understood the perilous state of humanity, he urged that we not forget our unique power to change and serve and repair, and never, never to give way to hopelessness.

"Gevalt, kinder. Zayt zikh nit meyeiush?" (Beware, my children, from falling into despair!)

These words of Rabbi Nahman are inscribed in the folk language of the people upon the walls of every Bratslaver *Shtibl* (prayer room), that each Jew might read them every time he entered to pray or study, words that remained even during those final days of horror and death.

Hope

Karl Jaspers touched the heart of the message of the people-Israel when he wrote:

> Malice and stupidity, hitherto limited to their consequences, are today dragging all mankind to its destruction. Unless we henceforward live all for one and each for all, we shall perish together. This unprecedented situation requires a response to scale. The response was given long ago. It looks beyond politics, and it has often been repeated since the prophets of the Old Testament first daringly uttered it and passed it on to all future ages. Because it has often been repeated in vain, sometimes seriously and sometimes unseriously over the centuries, many have become weary of it. Now, however, we must face the extraordinary situation urgently imposed: we must transform our outlook and our ways of thinking, our moral-political will. An idea that has long been present in individuals but has so far remained powerless, has become the condition of the survival of mankind. I believe I am not exaggerating. Those

who go on living just as they lived before have not grasped the danger. Merely to conceive it intellectually does not mean that it has been absorbed into the reality of one's life. Without a change of heart the life of mankind is lost forever. To survive, man must change. If he thinks only of the moment everything will come to an end, almost certainly the day the atomic war breaks out.

The change can only be brought about by each and every man in his own conduct of life: first within himself, and then in the realization that he is not alone. Every tiniest deed, every smallest word, every nuance of behavior among the millions and billions who are alive, is important. What takes place on the large and public scale is merely a symptom of that which is done in private by the many. The statesman who makes a highly moral appeal at the conference table and then behaves disloyally at home shares in the responsibility for continuation of the evil he warns against. Total destruction was often mentioned by the ancient prophets. The "Day of Yahweh" will come when everything will be destroyed. The early Christians spoke of an impending end of the world. Today, such perspectives have once again become unavoidable, this time in consequence of technological developments. Except for those who live thoughtlessly from day to day, they must once again become the central preoccupation of our life. Even though we cannot safely rely on reason in men, is there nonetheless some basis left for confidence? When despair says: Nothing avails–let us not think about it–let us live for the present–what lies in store for us is death in any case–is this really the last word, is there really nothing

> after that? No, was Jeremiah's reply to his despairing disciple Baruch, when the state and the nation and even the religion of the Jews, become worshippers of Isis, lay in ruins: *Thus saith the Lord: Behold, that which I have built will I break down, and that which I have planted I will pluck up . . . And seekest thou great things for thyself? Seek them not: For, behold, I will bring evil upon all flesh.*
>
> What Jeremiah meant was: God is enough.
>
> This, and this only, is the ultimate horizon, in the perspective of which everything falls into its right place. It is here that courage grows out of confidence in the ultimate ground of Being, which no worldly shipwreck can destroy, not even the shipwreck of reason. Then wings are given to the will, our will to achieve, to venture, to see purpose in the process of building within human existence so long as human existence lasts, even if we do not know how long our achievements will endure.[3]

A Time for Truth

The world has questions to ask. And, the faith of the people-Israel has answers to give. But, what will happen if the world, in fear and trembling, puts its terrible questions to Jews and finds that they have nothing to say? What if they stutter and stammer, with the shame of ignorance written on their faces? If it is true that the United States is becoming more Jewish, it is likewise true, as that same *Time* article noted, that "American Jews are becoming *less* Jewish."

It is time the truth were told.

After Auschwitz, Christian writers dealt with the Jew with a new sense of respect. To find a recurrence of anti-Semitic themes in contemporary fiction after the war, one must go to the Jewish writers! The Jew as pervert, criminal, scoundrel, resister of family ties, repudiator of national loyalties, debunker of the sacred–these are themes that Jewish writers, playwrights, and producers introduced into literature once again. The reprieve was over. Once again Jews became fair game for vilification.

Some Christian churches have from time to time called for a dialogue with the Jews. Both Catholics and Protestants seem in earnest about coming to a better understanding with Jews and Judaism. Nor is this concern limited to theologians. Laymen are willing to participate, too. But, what will happen at such ecumenical meetings if they are between knowledgeable, committed Christians who have read their Niebuhr and Neuhaus (perhaps Wiesel and Heschel too), attend church on Sunday, and contribute their tithe regularly–and Jews who lack knowledge of their own rich legacy and barely practice it?

What if the world looks into their minds and asks who Isaiah was, or how the Psalmist prayed, or what the Baal Shem Tov taught, or how Rabbi Akiva remained serene as the Romans burned him, in an attempt to explore the palaces of wisdom, compassion, and justice they have been told these men built, so that their own poverty might be enriched–and Jews are unable to answer?

Or, what if they open the doors to the Jewish community, searching for that devotion in worship, commitment to principle, concern for self-discipline, and passion for justice which they seek for themselves–and find instead that it is as bigoted, pleasure-centered, and racked with petty bickering as their own?

When the people-Israel was locked in its ghettos and the Torah was its life and holiness its way, they had something to say to the world. But the world did not ask them. Now the world is asking. And the question is: Does Israel still have the power to speak?

The haunting words of the prophet ring in our ears.

You are my witnesses, saith the Lord (Isa. 43:12).

Is this not what the people-Israel are being told by all the terrors of history and all the follies of man? Does this proclamation not sweep aside all the fumbling attempts to define the Jew–nation, race, or religion–and hold before us that divine demand which alone determines our being? The words of the prophet have not lost their meaning for our day: You, Israel, have witnessed the holiness of this world at Sinai.

And, you have witnessed the horror of this world at Auschwitz.

You have witnessed the grandeur and the glory of man.

And, you have seen the horror and the evil of man.

You have witnessed what no other people has.

Therefore, you must be My witnesses.

Israel's task is to fulfill its destiny, to be loyal to the covenant, to testify in this world on His behalf by proclaiming the truth amidst all the idolatries of man, to reveal the madness of our age and point the way toward sanity.

"Judaism is the track of God in the wilderness of oblivion," writes Heschel. "By being what we are, namely Jews; by attuning our own yearning to the lonely holiness in this world, we will aid humanity more than by any particular service we may render."[4]

Elie Wiesel has told us that when the pitiful remnant of haggard Jews emerged from the forests and the concentration camps in 1945, the world, stunned by the realization of what it had done or had permitted to be done, was in a mood of expectation. They were open to a message from a people that had endured the unendurable and returned from the gates of hell. They were waiting for a word from this people, a word that might destroy or create or transform. There was an atmosphere of trembling expectation. It was a timeless moment.

But, Wiesel laments, they said nothing. They did nothing. They demanded nothing for the world. And, that priceless moment passed.

Has it passed? Perhaps not. Perhaps that moment still endures, even today. Perhaps the mood of expectation still persists. Perhaps the tragedy is so immense that it has taken decades for it slowly to unfold in the records, trials, histories, poems, plays, and novels of a hundred languages, and only now has the full impact of the miracle of the people-Israel's existence sunk into the minds of man. Plus, the realization that, barring a miracle, the bomb will explode.

Perhaps it is all this that has brought about the strange turning to the Jew, waiting for word from those who have emerged from Hitler's Auschwitz which might prevent the approaching nuclear Auschwitz.

Endnotes

1. *New York Times*, 7 July 1990.

2. Cited in *The American Spectator* (December 1992): 63. One feels obligated, when citing Schweitzer–among the noblest figures of the twentieth century, who has, alas, almost been forgotten–to point briefly to the beauty of his character. Here are two of his letters.

Responding to a French Catholic Boy Scout whose troop had been named for Schweitzer, he wrote,

> Don't choose to make your life into something great. Make your life good and true. Maintain your simplicity. Stick to the idea of always doing whatever is consistent with the spirit of children of

> God. I don't see why your goal should disappear as you grow older. Staying young doesn't mean having the soul of a child, it means having the soul of a child of God, the soul of a man trying to be a child of God, animated by the spirit of God. Seek simplicity.

To a handicapped woman, he wrote,

> Do not quarrel with God, do not quarrel with man: leave all incomprehensible things alone, seek only one thing: the growth of the spiritual person, so that you may achieve peace of mind, which is higher than all reason, and so that you may give people something of the spirit of peace. (Op. Cit.)

3. Karl Jaspers, "The Atom Bomb and the Future," *The Evergreen Review* (Summer, 1958): 37–57.

4. A.J. Heschel, *The Earth Is the Lord's* (New York: Schuman, 1950), 108.

TEN

Modernity Exhausted

A Parable of Alienation

Once a father and child were traveling together by wagon, when they reached a glen with an abundance of delicious berries. Attracted by the fruit, the child asked the father to stop so he could pick some. The father agreed but reminded his child to be quick, for the journey was long and time was short. The child, however, delighting in the sweet taste of the berries, wandered further into the forest.

"We must be on our way, for the moments are fleeting and the road still lies before us," called the father, to no avail. The child's desire overcame him.

"Were he not my only child whom I love, I would punish him," thought the father. He gave him one final warning. "Wherever you are, my child, hearken to these words of mine, lest, in your search for the berries, you lose yourself in the forest:

> "When you cry out, 'My father, my father,' I shall answer, 'My child, my child.' So long as you hear my voice, you can safely return to me. But, beware! Should you no longer hear my voice, know that you are lost in the thickets of the forest. Then you must run to me with all the speed at your command, until you find me."

Though first told in far-off Eastern Europe some two hundred years ago by one of the most remarkable men of the age, Rabbi Elimelekh of Lizhensk, the parable rings true for modern man and, particularly, for the modern Jew. It is a parable of alienation, a parable for those who no longer hear the "voice."

The incredible opportunities for power, pleasure, and fortune which our age affords has led to a frantic search to drain every pleasure to the dregs, to exploit all the instruments of power and to collect an endless array of glittering gadgets. In the process, the faith of many has been eroded. We have abandoned the kingdom of God for the kingdom of Caesar. Our inner life has turned sour. Sated with sensuality, drugged with success, we continue to wander ever deeper into this fabled jungle of delights, oblivious of the warning. Master over all save ourselves, prober of the mysteries of the universe yet confounded by the agony of our own hearts, we cry out at last—"My Father, My Father!"—but, alas, are too distant and too dulled to hear the response, "My child, My child!"

The hour is late.

All that is left to do is to turn and run in headlong flight, until we find our Father in heaven.

The Decline of Religion

Daniel Bell, a profound student of American culture, has written in the introduction to the last collection of his essays, *Winding Passage,*

> These are the words of a prodigal son. They are essays written in my middle years, midway in the journey of our life, in that dark wood, seeking a return to the straight way of my ancestors. I know that the world I live in is vastly different from theirs, yet the duplex nature of man remains largely the same, now as then.[1]

Former fellow-traveler and secularist, Bell now chooses a different path, one that leads into an inquiry into the transcendent. Thus, the volume concludes with an essay entitled "The Return of the Sacred?" which, though suggesting a tentative and probationary position, nevertheless, as we shall see, provides the key to his thinking and is the point of departure for the present inquiry.

> At the end of the 18th century and into the middle of the 19th century almost every enlightened thinker expected religion to disappear in the 20th century. That belief was based on the power of *reason*. Religion was associated with superstition, fetishism, and unprovable beliefs, a form of fear used as protection against other fears, a form of security one associated with children and which they believed had arisen in the "childhood" of the human race.[2]

One of the signs of modernity is the commonality of this argument. It was heard during, and before, one's college years, pronounced by sages and popularizers with such dogmatic gravity that it became an unshakable catechism, at the very least for the social sciences. Religion was tantamount to magic, superstition, fear of the unknown, emerging during the childhood of man, acceptable to the uncultured, a crutch for the ignorant, a sop to the bewildered, an "opiate for the masses." Maturity and reason would cure us of the affliction. A more rational answer coming from the Greeks was philosophy, whose task it was to uncover the *physis*, or the hidden order of nature. The determining phrase which occurs in Aristotle and later in Hegel and Marx is "the realization of philosophy."[3] In other words, while the infant crawls with religion, the adult walks with reason, which, when "realized," will clear up all those puzzles and mysteries which confounded us since the primary years of our civilization. Appropriating the language of faith, both Hegel and Marx project the perfect society at the end of time when man–not God–would be fulfilled.

Thus, in the nineteenth century when Swinburne writes:

> Glory to man in the highest,
> The maker and master of things . . .

he applies to man what formerly was said of God. And Shelley, in his "Prometheus Unbound," invokes a similar theme:

> The painted veil . . . is torn aside;
> The loathsome mask has fallen, the man remains,
> Scepterless, free, uncircumscribed, but man,
> Equal, unclassed, tribeless, and nationless,
> Exempt from awe, worship, decree, the king
> Over himself. . . .

With the "realization" of philosophy, or the victory of reason, man will be "exempt from awe," and "worship," because there is nothing of which to be in awe, nothing to worship–except, of course, man himself, who, complete, fulfilled, "a king over himself," becomes God. "The criticism of religion," Marx said, "ends with the precept that the supreme being for man, is man."

From the nineteenth century on, reason, through which the natural order is revealed, is replaced by *rationalization*, whereby the technical order is established by means of bureaucracy and efficiency. The network of family bonds, for example, gives way to the "efficient" welfare state. Such a society is transformed into what Max Weber called "an iron cage." "With the progress of science and technology," he wrote, "man has lost his sense . . . of the sacred. Reality has become flat and utilitarian, leaving a great void in the souls of men, which they seek to fill by furious activity and through various devices and substitutes."[4]

Modernism, according to Bell, can be characterized by several factors:

(a) Secularization, which is the withdrawal of religion from politics and aesthetics to ritual and leisure time. No longer coterminus with life itself, religion is but a single option among others. As aesthetics is separated from religion, releasing art from moral bounds, so government is no longer censored by ethical requirements. A "disenchantment," or *entzauberung*, takes place. Religious acts themselves become secularized. Homilies substitute politics for Scripture, Latin is replaced by the vernacular, ancient chants are supplanted by young men with guitars, priests shed their distinctive garb.

(b) The authority and influence of tradition diminishes.

(c) Classical faith is replaced by the religions of politics, impulse, and culture.

It is this last characteristic of modernism–the new idolatries–upon which I should like to dwell.

In examining the idolatry of *politics*, one naturally begins with the phenomenon of totalitarianism. It is both an economic system and a social theory, but neither the one nor the other–nor both together–can adequately explain a child's reporting his father to the state as a traitor, knowing the severity of punishment that may be meted out. Only fealty to the state in such measure that it transcends loyalty to parents can explain it. And, that ultimate fealty–namely, the standard which determines what is good or bad for us–that is our god. Totalitarianism does, indeed, possess all the trappings of religion. Its divinity is the state; its prophet, Marx or Hitler; its holy scripture, *Mein Kampf* or *Das Kapital*; its ritual, the phantasmagorias of Munich or Lenin Square (Hitler used a three foot by two foot white vellum bound copy of *Mein Kampf* resting on a podium during the Munich rallies much as a missal or the Holy Scriptures at St. Peters); and its paradise, the Aryan world reich or that egalitarian Shangri-la ushered in with the withering away of the state.

Two of the key theoreticians who formulated the Communist creed of "purification by terror" by which the party would achieve the messianic fulfillment of history, were the Jew, Georg Lukacs, and the playwright, Berthold Brecht. In his "Praise of the Party," Brecht argued that it is correct to put a comrade to death, if it is in the interest of the party:

> A single man has two eyes.
> The Party has a thousand eyes.
> A single man can be annihilated.
> But the Party cannot be annihilated.[5]

Lukacs justified evil in the name of a higher good, proposing the infamous "double theory of truth . . . or the noble lie," which justified evil in the name of the higher good.

> Murder is not permitted; murder is unconditional sin. Nevertheless, murder is inescapably necessary; it is not permitted, but it must be done. . . . Man must choose between the purposeful violence of the revolution and the meaningless violence of the old corrupt world. . . . One had to enslave the world in order to heal it. . . . One signed the devil's pact. *(Winding Passage,* 342)

Here we see the gnostic element in communism, the demonic dialectics that sanctified thievery, torture, murder, and war. To bring about the new society, the Communist may rob, cheat, enslave, even blow up the world–all with a good conscience. This is the "devil's pact," the "double theory of evil," the "noble lie" of which Lukacs speaks. "Communist ethics," wrote another revolutionary in the twenties, "makes it the highest duty to accept the necessity of acting wickedly. This is the greatest sacrifice that the Revolution asks of us. The conviction of the communist is that evil transforms itself into bliss through the dialectics of historical revolution."[6]

In the old capitalism, the legitimate drive for economic success was modified by religion, popularly labeled the "Protestant ethic." It meant pride in one's work, frugality, honesty, a day's work for a day's pay. With the removal of the force of religion and the so-called Protestant ethic from economic society, capitalism, as we know it today, has turned into pure hedonism–the hot pursuit of pleasure and power. The purpose of work in our time is not so much pride in what one makes as the sheer enjoyment of what derives from it–houses, food, clothes, cars, vacations–usable "things," momentary impulses. As one result, Detroit cars are less acceptable because they simply do not match the Japanese car produced by the work ethic we abandoned. Quite simply, the engine of capitalism is impulse.

The religion of impulse is all around us, in literature, fashion, photography, advertising, television, and travel. Morality is replaced by psychology, guilt by anxiety. One hears less about what is "good or bad" and more about whether we feel "comfortable" with this or that. Indeed, "to feel comfortable" is one of those expressions that has come to symbolize the new age, pointing to the ever-widening dimension of modernity "beyond good and evil." During the period around the first world war, psychoanalysis developed and was directed toward the individual who was thought to have gained such insight into his life as might enable him to helpfully alter it. The moral frame gave way in the "hedonistic" age to the newer sensitivity training, encounter groups, and joy therapy, which has been directed to groups and sought to unblock one's inhibitions through touching and fondling. No wonder recent surveys estimate that a growing percentage of psychiatrists have sexual relations with their patients and almost 50 percent would like to. (Practitioners have been known to appear on TV to defend such behavior.) The newer nonmoral therapy seeks to free the individual from moral restraint so that he can the "more easily express his impulses." In the old days, we felt guilty if we committed adultery; today, quite the reverse–we are taught to feel guilt if we fail to follow the demands of our impulses.[7]

The cult of mammon has been joined by the cult of orgasm. "Sex," says Max Lerner, "is the last frontier of American life." The most popular magazine articles these days are surveys on intimate sexual feelings. Liberation, once a noble word, has taken on a new meaning: release for repressed sexual impulses. Thus, the astronomical rise in the number of unmarried couples living together, or the abandonment of the norm of heterosexuality altogether. But, impulse, particularly sexual impulse, provides more than the revival of the old/new morality of pleasure versus its inhibition: with the decline of religious ecstasy, impulse affords that momentary intoxication of Dionysian frenzy in which we lose all sense of self.

The third substitution for religion which Bell describes, and in some ways the most insidious, is the worship of *culture*. More than a century ago, Saint

Simon proclaimed, "Christianity is worn out: a new culture is needed to inspire us–art"; and Nietzsche announced that man's true destiny is not immortality but art. The modernist movement in art and literature released a burst of energy that produced an enormous amount of high-level work. But, there was a price to be paid, the sundering of aesthetics from morality. Modernism began by lampooning the duplicity and hypocrisy of the Victorian age, and ended by deriding itself. It sought to remove the false veils, revealing man as he truly was–beast, god, or both. "Man's true metaphysical destiny," Nietzsche declared, "lay not in morality (a paltry, dispirited ethic of slaves) but in art." "Aestheticism became the belief that the task of art is to gratify the subterranean demands of human impulse which religion had not been able to wholly exorcise." It taught that man can "reach the sublime through the debauched." In the imagination of the modernist, "all is permitted–murder, lust, sodomy, incest–in order to nourish the rich fantasies of the unconscious." A shocking transformation took place. Passion, which had been identified with religious suffering and sacrifice, now became

> carnal sensuality which carries one beyond the self. Murder is no longer the mark of Cain but man's uncontrollable excitement with his secret impulses. . . . If God no longer bars the way, then man can pursue the infinite along the paths of eroticism and cruelty and terror. . . . The foundation of aestheticism . . . was the freeing of the erotic from the religious . . . or, making a religion of the erotic, free from all norms of morality and rational conduct.[8]

In literature, it was no longer religion but poetry that was sacred, and no longer the priest but the poet who was holy. In Baudelaire's *The Flowers of Evil*, perhaps the best example of the time, the poet "invokes

God and embraces the devil." Inexorably driven to taste the vices of sin, he explores all its avenues. Indeed, there is in this book "the rigorous logic of an eroticism, which . . . reaches the extremes of bestiality. . . . The poem is lascivious and blasphemous, and extraordinarily beautiful." But, impulse is not sustained. In the morning, after the night's delights, there is only the "cold mask." The end is not in heaven but with Satan, only "the furious and desperate appetite for death, the final darkness."[9]

In the new theater, the most unspeakable became acceptable. Indeed, it argued that whatever was orderly was arbitrary. Madness rather than sanity became, for some, "the touchstone of reality." Plays were no longer "written"; they simply "happen." They were meant to evoke some kind of primitive ritual on the part of the audience. The script is passé. Instead of thinking, planning, and writing–the old way–one "does." For example, in the play *Paradise Now*, the audience is asked to come on stage, while members of the cast wander through the audience puffing marijuana, some of whom then return to the stage, strip their clothes off, imploring the audience to do likewise, for a mass saturnalia. The play "ends" with the audience being called on to vacate the theater, convert the police to anarchism, storm the jails, free those incarcerated, and take over the cities in the name of "the people."[10]

The theater of cruelty gave us, for example, the play *In Destruction of Art* (1961), in which a live chicken is hung on the stage, and, as it is swung back and forth, its head is snipped off with a pair of hedge-clippers. One actor proceeds to seize the severed head, places it between his legs within his unzippered fly, while beating the bird's carcass on the inside of the open piano. In 1968, Hermann Nitsch enlightened his audience with the disemboweling of a sheep on stage, during which the entrails and blood are emptied out upon a young girl, and the actors nail the animal's body to a cross. In the Orgy Mystery Theater, the actors sought to reenact the taurobolium rite of Rome, in which a bull is slaughtered over the head of a man in initiating him into the frygian mysteries, by having actors pour blood and animal intestines upon each other. These "productions" were, of course, dutifully reported, including pictures, in the prestigious *Art in America*, as well as the *Village Voice.*[11]

In such plays we find a return to primitive impulse in which the play itself serves a therapeutic function, whereby actors seek to exorcise the audience with feeling and action rather than thought.

These productions of the sixties were set in the dank cellars of Greenwich Village cellar theaters. In 1992, however, one could enter prestigious Lincoln Center to see "performance artist" Karen Finley shrieking obscenities, while she exposed her breasts to smear them with chocolate sauce that was meant to represent the feces with which men, she cried out, smear all women. Finley's work was, of course, subsidized by John Frohnmayer's National Endowment for the Arts. As was Annie Sprinkle, who beckoned the audience up to the stage to examine at close range a certain part of her anatomy. All in the name of "art."

In the same year, *Baltimore Waltz* by Paula Vogel opened. It is about a trip to Europe by Anna, a grade-school teacher dying of ATD (Acquired Toilet Disease), and her brother, Carl, dismissed for teaching homosexual songs to his young students. Seeking a cure for Anna, they travel to Vienna's Dr. Todesrocheln (deathrattle), famed for his studies in uriosa. "He doesn't write poems about urine," Carl explains, "he drinks it" and prescribes it to his patients. In the time she has left, Anna intends to "f—— her brains out" and proceeds to do so on stage in a vertical bed with every man she can find. Carl, for his part, is avidly pursuing his homosexual liaisons. Meanwhile, the siblings are drawing ever closer. While Dr. T. and Anna toast each other with urine, it is revealed that Carl and not Anna is the one who is dying. When he does, Anna engages in the ultimate debauchery, performing incestuous necrophilia on the corpse. The play is dedicated to the author's brother, Carl, who was in fact fired as an elementary school teacher for his flagrant homosexuality and did invite his sister to Europe. Unaware of his suffering from AIDS, she declined. He died in Baltimore. The play received most favorable reviews and an award from AT&T.[12]

It is against this raging outburst of feeling in modern art, drama, and literature that one better understands the great historic religions of Judaism, Christianity, and Islam, which are all religions of restraint. They knew that beneath normal behavior boils a network of underground impulses, which each age described in its own fashion–the Dionysian frenzies of the Hellenistic world, the Manichaean rumblings of Rome, the holiness of sin in the Sabbatean and Frankist heresies of the Jews–and that these subterranean forces continue to beat against the mighty walls of religious restraints. With the substitution of culture–by which we mean the expressive arts–for religion, man not only abandoned moderation, but these demonic impulses, once sublimated by religion, gradually embraced and pervaded all aspects of modern culture. The consequence is that nothing is now unutterable or untouchable. There is no longer any sacred grove that cannot be trespassed.

The Exhaustion of Modernism

Bell believes "that the 'ground impulses' behind aestheticism and political religions are exhausted. These were the impulses to abolish God and assume that man could take over the powers he had ascribed to God and now sought to claim for himself. This is the common bond between Marx and Nietzsche and the link between the aesthetic and political movements of modernity."[13]

Modernism–the modernism of the idolatries of politics, culture, and impulse–is exhausted. In the area of *culture*, some artists, writers, and thinkers are turning their backs on what formerly bewitched them, for the simple reason that they have tasted the fullness of its fruit. They have succeeded beyond the wildest reaches of their imagination in promoting their wares and found that what they often played with had taken on a life of its own. No longer were they a bizarre underground movement for the select few; rather, they romped under the banners of all the Broadways of pop- and even high-culture of these United States, portrayed in film and on TV, reported on regularly in the daily paper, and held out as a model for children, as American as apple pie. When, however, this apple pie became part of a staple diet, it proved indigestible. What kind of stomach, after all, could assimilate the acids of teen-age pregnancy, child abuse, single-parent families, valueless sex education from infancy (including lessons at age five on how to distinguish between daddy's good "hug" and bad "touch," and at thirteen or so on how to use contraceptives dispensed without knowledge of parents), violent crime (blamed on society), slums which encompass huge areas of major cities unto which certain races dare not enter, loneliness amidst the crowd, and the calamitous social diseases of narcotics, herpes, and AIDS.

Society has always included an avant-garde, an outlandish Bohemian element, a West Bank or a Greenwich village, centers of the so-called counterculture. There were underground magazines, off-beat theaters, borderline poetry and art. The difference today is that the avant-garde has become the man-on-the-street. Bohemia is Broadway. The filthy jokes formerly restricted to burlesque houses and certain nightclubs now exude from films and TV for the millions. Las Vegas is no longer a city but a condition. Books formerly kept apart but available upon special request now flood the shelves of our libraries. One librarian reports that she has become so disgusted with reading the new novels that she has turned to the Bible and finds it fascinating.

Traditional middle-class values have suffered a lethal assault. One advocate of the counterculture described these outmoded values. "The middle-class is obsessed by greed" (which means holding a job and working for a living); "its sex life is prudish" (which means monogamy and fidelity); "its family patterns are debased" (which means they have children); "its slavish conformity to dress and grooming are degrading" (which means that one wears a dress or a shirt, tie and suit, gets a haircut regularly, and bathes regularly); "its mercenary routinization of life is intolerable" (which means that one carries a watch, tries to be on time, goes to sleep at night, and follows some rational pattern of behavior). The counterculture contributed to the "me" generation, the narcissistic society. The arch-image of the middle-class, according to counterculturists, was "The American Gothic," a painting that features the gaunt, dazed figures of a farmer and his wife who, with a pitchfork at their side and wearing an expression of total defeat, stand in front of an austere Kansas farmhouse, as if to say, "Would you want to be like that?"

We live, to use a yiddishism, in an upside-down world. Once there were middle-class values—patriotism, church, family—supported by the popular culture of literature and drama, while the underground promoted antisocial values for the radical enclave. In our age, the roles have been reversed: the underground has taken over. Its values dominate the new pop-culture from the double-entendre lyrics and hot-rock songs which corrode the air-waves to the X-rated videos which comprise 40 percent of the market. The TV soap opera today can hardly be recognized from its parent of thirty years ago. A family TV script under consideration was returned to its author with the following suggestions: one male should be a homosexual; the love scene should lead to rape; the forty-five-year-old female should fall in love with the teen-ager, not the older man; substitute a shotgun blast for the punch; and find a way to introduce a scene that may later turn into incest. Indeed, for every child born in wedlock on a soap opera, five are born out of wedlock, and for every married couple viewed in bed, ten unmarried couples are so filmed. More scenes are shot in bordellos than churches; the prostitute has replaced the nun as the model of compassion, while serious religion is taboo. For the ten- or twelve-year-old, who by that age may already have been instructed in such run-of-the-mill activities as anal and oral sex in his latest AIDS prevention class, all of the above have become part and parcel of the American scene, much as Tarzan or the Bobbsey Twins were in what seems like another age.

American attitudes and behavior are profoundly shaped in a school from which one neither graduates nor needs to leave home to attend—the Hollywood film. A study of several thousand representative films from 1945 to 1985 revealed a radical shift in values over that time span. Not only did the portrayal of nonmarital sex increase considerably, but while 80 percent of the early accounts treated it negatively, this was true for only 9 percent of the later ones. (Even the advent of AIDS did not move Hollywood to depict nonmarital sex as morally wrong, only, at times, unhealthy.) The same pattern was found regarding divorce. While the portrayal of divorce in films increased, the attitude toward it shifted significantly: 40 percent of such films made during the years 1945 to 1955 found divorce unacceptable, but only 9 percent between 1975 and 1985. Prostitution, rarely treated in the early period, was a common feature in the later one, occurring in about 20 percent of the sample films. Once more, initial disapproval gave way to acceptance. Thus, in regard to nonmarital sex, divorce, and prostitution, Hollywood came to adopt a permissive, value-free attitude in the course of a few decades. (Other studies reveal the rise of similar negative portrayals of religion, patriotism, and the traditional family.) Since 1985, all these tendencies have accelerated.[14]

Within his blistering attack on the film industry as destructive of American values by its "glorification of ugliness, [its] assault on the family, and [its] attempt to undermine organized religion," Michael Medved, co-host of "Sneak Previews," described the highly acclaimed 1990 film, *The Cook, the Thief, His Wife and Her Lover*, as a sample of his concern:

> This is not a film for the faint-of-heart–or the delicate of stomach. It begins with the brutal beating of a naked man, while the main character gleefully urinates all over him, and ends with that same character slicing off a piece of a carefully cooked and elegantly prepared human corpse in the most vivid and horrifying scene of cannibalism ever portrayed in motion pictures.

> In between, we are shown necrophilia, sex in a toilet, the unspeakably bloody and sadistic mutilation of a nine-year-old boy, another victim smeared with feces, a woman whose cheek is pierced with a fork, and an edifying scene with two naked bodies writhing together ecstatically in the back of a truck filled with rotting, maggot-infested garbage. There is, in short, unrelieved ugliness, horror, and depravity at every turn. Naturally, the critics loved it.[15]

The public is no longer willing to accept the television networks' hypocritical claim that their programming has no effect on human behavior, when in selling advertising to customers they argue the opposite: that viewing an ad for a car, a perfume, or a bottle of Coke leads to buying it. The 44 percent of the students interviewed at the University of Florida who replied that they would force a woman into a sexual act if it could be done without being discovered or punished is not unrelated to sociologist Scot Boeringer's findings that "books, videos, and magazines had a significant effect in encouraging male sexual aggression."[16]

No longer enticed into the scented gardens of the new paradise, practitioners of the counterculture are fleeing the raging fires of the old hell. Plato's admonition to "seek artists whose instincts guide them to what is lovely and gracious, so that our young people may drink in from their noble work," is once again being heard in the land.

Modernism is exhausted because it has been realized *politically*. Sixty years of communism did not bring the millennium. *Das Kapital* was not the road to heaven but the blueprint for the Gulag. The promise of the classless society was confounded by the high walls of the Lubianka and the vast cemeteries of the Siberian tundras. We know all about the daily terror, the torture chambers, the death camps, the KGB, the tens of millions who were sacrificed in the name of the New Society. The dialectic did not work. The pact with the devil brought the devil, not Elysium. The state did not wither away as predicted, justifying evil means for noble ends. The means became the end, permanent and monstrous—not joy but sullen submission; not utopia but terror; not freedom but entombment in the psychiatric prison. In the name of liberation, suffering peoples seeking freedom were cynically manipulated into Communist police-states in Eastern Europe, Africa, Asia, and even at our back door in Central America. Now, as chaos and hunger rule, the Russians themselves admit that the Communist dream was a nightmare and are taking the first halting, difficult, but momentous, steps toward democracy.

Finally, modernism is exhausted because the religion of *impulse* has been realized. Drugs, originally perceived as the refuge of marginal figures, have in our time been transformed into a "drug culture," which, while delivering its promise of momentary "highs," has unloosed such an onslaught of horrors as to call forth a "War" to exterminate it. Those who early argued the positive powers of narcotics for the masses now behold the holocaust. The new sexual freedom, touted to remove every neurosis, soothe every pain, calm every itch, provide every delight, has turned out no better. It has cursed us with twelve-year-old mothers who drop their newborns into incinerators on the way to school, with thirty-year-old grandmothers married to the welfare state, with anal intercourse specialists who are represented by one of the most powerful political action committees in the nation, with college presidents who serve as the grand pimps of America, with therapeutic adultery, proincest advocates, and with diseases that rival the black death in terror. Pornography has not sublimated the sexual impulse, contrary to the claims of X-rated magazine publishers (naturally) and assorted social-scientists (not so naturally), but inflamed it. Nor has rape been diminished thereby—that was the argument—but exacerbated. The new nakedness in clothes, best described as the prostitute look, or how to reveal the body while feigning to cover it, speaks the language of style in unmistakable tones. The social diseases of family collapse, massive illiteracy, and now AIDS are the harvest we reap for the new "freedom." Sexual liberation has not been the high road to mental health but, rather, to the Russian roulette of unwanted pregnancy and/or unwanted disease. Making random "love" today is like walking by Chicago's infamous Cabrini-Green at night in the knowledge that at any time you can get a bullet in the head.

A young husband and wife saw an attractive silver and black Corvette on a car lot. The price was twenty thousand dollars. They did not have twenty thousand dollars, but they really wanted the car. So, they proposed a swap—their eleven-month-old baby! Surprised? Don't be. If marriage is casual, sex is casual, abortion is casual, and divorce is casual, then why should parenting not be casual? The life of impulse cancels out the life of responsibility. Consequences are irrelevant. Ours is a disposable society. Nothing is meant to be permanent: neither marriage nor children. Like diapers, children are throwaways: one waitress, after serving at a party, gave birth and left the infant in a bag by the door.

In addition to Homecoming and Alumni Weeks, Northern Illinois University added "erotic week," featuring nonstop X-rated films. Princeton went a step further, inviting on 7 March 1991, former porn star Candida Royalle, who presented video clips from her "The Femme" collection and delivered a lecture on

"Women's Pleasure and Images of Desire" in the university film theater. "We really need pleasure," she told the *Daily Princetonian*, "and anything that brings pleasure is really good." A week later Barbara Hammer, who has produced *Superdyke Meets Madam X* and *Dyketactics*, was featured. Turnaway crowds attended the programs which were funded by, among others, the Office of Dean of Students, The Woodrow Wilson School for Public Affairs, the Council for the Humanities, etc.[17]

The exhaustion of sex is captured in Carol Shields' novel *The Republic of Love*, in which she provides a vignette of a romantic(?) encounter in the current world of infant sex education, feminism, AIDS, condoms, and intercourse-as-recreation, where the new woman, having disposed of modesty, displays her up-front approach:

> Quality orgasms were the only kind worth having, she told him. She said this sitting on the edge of Tom's new bed. . . .
>
> They had been to a movie, a German softporn piece with the kind of subtitles that give him headaches. He had a headache now, looking into Charlotte's wide open face.
>
> "We'd better talk about the matter of precautions first," she said. She showed him her condoms and he showed her his. "I hope you don't mind if we use mine," she said. "I'd feel better."
>
> "You don't mind if I ask if you're a complete hetero," she said. She was beginning to sound not tough, but toughened, which was something different. "I mean, I assume you're a hetero, but I need your assurance, if I'm going to relax."

> "Do you by any chance," she asked, "have a herpes history? . . ."
>
> "This may sound kind of weird," she said, "but could you start by rubbing the instep of my feet. Both feet. My feet have always been erogenous. Only about one percent of people have erogenous feet, at least that's what my therapist says. . . ."
>
> After a while she said, "That's good, that feels so good, but your elbow is putting just a bit too much pressure—there, that's better. Yes, that's a lot better. Would you mind reaching over and turning on the light. On. Thanks."
>
> "I don't mind if you talk," she said later. "Just say anything that comes into your head. Any words you like."
>
> "I'm starting to get there," she said. "I'll be another few minutes, though. . . ."
>
> Finally:
>
> "Let's just talk now. Let's just hang on to each other and talk. Let's be, you know, spontaneous. Oh, you don't know how I've needed this. Next time we can try something else if you want. You plan the menu next time."
>
> Never again, he said to himself. Never again.

With politics, culture, and impulse, modernist pretensions have led us to the abyss. We face absurdity and despair. Modern man, so expert at caricaturing others, has himself become a caricature. The difference between the Victorian age and ours is neither their purity versus our sinfulness nor their hypocrisy versus our honesty, but, quite simply, the fact that they possessed something we do not—a sense of guilt. To accuse them of hypocrisy, then, is also to praise them, for hypocrisy, let us remember, is the tribute vice pays to virtue. Today vice, having itself become virtue, needs pay no tribute at all.

In the belief that "faith is no longer possible," writes Bell, fascinating and tragic substitutes were proposed which sought to reach the heights of religious experience. They learned, alas, that

> art or impulse can erase the self only momentarily in the . . . frenzy of the Dionysian act. . . . But intoxication always passes, and there is the cold morning after, which arrives inexorably with the break of day. This inescapable awareness of the future, this eschatological anxiety, leads inevitably to the feeling, the black thread of modernist thought, that each person's own life is at the end of time.[18]

The Role of the Jew

In fashioning modern man's society, where the idols of politics, culture, and impulse are worshiped, Jews have played a major role. This is so, in part, because in the world's largest Jewish community of Eastern Europe, the Middle Ages did not gradually give way, as in the West, to the influences of the Enlightenment's gifts of science and reason. For most of East European Jewry, the Middle Ages extended down to the nineteenth century and even beyond. Many of the grandparents of present-day American Jews emerged overnight, it seemed, from benighted, poverty-stricken villages, little touched by the secular worlds of culture, into the bright lights of modernity with its abundance of new knowledge and undreamt-of opportunity. It should occasion no surprise, then, that Jews, mesmerized as they must have been by what they saw and read and heard, should have been among the chief advocates of modernity, as Bell has defined it.

They became, for example, disciples of the new politics of communism. Some 30 percent of the early leaders of the revolution are estimated to have been Jewish. Emancipated from their ancient faith by the onslaught of modern thought, which the antiquated Judaism of the time was ill-prepared to refute, they transferred their yet unexpended messianic fervor into the new religion of Marx. Such sacrifice, intelligence, and idealism as theirs was hard to duplicate and catapulted many to the very highest offices of the new regime. Out of idealism, there were Jews who signed "a pact with the devil" and who believed in the double theory of truth. In America, the Rosenbergs could steal atomic secrets for the noblest of motives and still believe themselves martyrs to the very moment they faced the electric chair. During the dark years of the depression, many Jews, ignorant of or alienated from Judaism, became radical intelligentsia who fought the bourgeois middle-class values of home, faith, and nation.

Historian Jacob Talmon cites one case that provides a special insight into the Jewish condition of the time. Rosa Luxembourg was a Polish Jewess whose fiery devotion brought her to the leadership of German communism during World War I, until she was murdered by rightist hooligans. While imprisoned, she wrote to a Zionist friend, "Why do you pester me with your Jewish sorrow? There is no room in my heart for the Jewish troubles." Her single-minded efforts for universal peace permitted no pause for particular sympathies. (The same letter, nonetheless, expresses concern for "the South African Bantus and the Chinese coolies.") Talmon makes the telling observation that "twenty-five years later, after the Germans had occupied it, there was not a single Jew left alive in Rosa's native Zamosc."[19]

The religion of impulse likewise found significant Jewish involvement. An unusually high percentage of the material on sexual liberation was written by Jews, as well as significant representation among its advocates. On a more commercial level, for example, Jews have been strongly represented in the *Playboy* enterprises. B'nai Brith's Anti-Defamation League had no problem, for example, when some years back they presented their American Freedom Award at a fashionable black-tie dinner-dance to Hugh Hefner. Both the Jewish establishment and nonestablishment observers took it in stride, raising not a finger of protest. It was Catholic William Buckley of *National Review* who pointed to the Jewish issue:

> About the honoree, the ADL says, with an apparent straight face, that the empire he founded has had a far-reaching impact, not only on the publishing industry, but on the mores of American society as well. "He began with little more than a unique idea for a magazine" (nude women, jokes about copulation and how to seduce girls) "and a philosophy of social change" (the philosophy, quite simply, that the gratification of the male sexual impulse is to be achieved without any second thought of the possible effect upon (a) the girl, (b) the family, (c) your family, (d) and the moral code of self-restraint. (*National Review* 9:3, 1980, 122)

Buckley argued that if the ADL is concerned with discrimination, and that if racial toleration rests upon the belief in "the sanctity of the individual" and the conviction that we are brothers created equal by God, then how can it applaud the creator of the *Playboy* philosophy, which mocks all of this when it "measures human energy by the bustline and by genital energy?"

Jews have been loyal supporters of the new aesthetics. Literature, art, and music are fields in which Jewish influence is significant. While one cannot avoid the conclusion that, while they were leaders in advancing high culture–contributing talent galore, as well as remarkably generous support–they were likewise among those who transformed what were formerly avant-garde enclaves into the mass-media of TV and Hollywood and into cheap literature.

When Andy Warhol, pioneer pornographic filmmaker, drug consumer, and confessed sodomist, had his display of *Ten Portraits of Jews in the Twentieth Century* shown at, of all places, New York's prestigious Jewish Museum, noted critic Hilton Kramer, observed,

> To the many afflictions suffered by the Jewish people in the course of their long history, the new Andy Warhol show at the Jewish Museum cannot be said to make a significant addition. True, the show is vulgar. It reeks of commercialism, and its contribution to art is nil. The way it exploits Jewish subjects without showing the slightest grasp of their significance is offensive–or should be, anyway, if the artist had not already treated so many Jewish subjects in the same tawdry manner. No, the Jews will survive this caper unscathed. So, very likely, will everyone else. But what it may do to the reputation of the Jewish Museum is, as they say, something else.[20]

Panned for hosting a program during AIDS Awareness Week which promoted homosexuality, neither the New York nor any other Jewish museum expressed outrage during the extended debate on the Maplethorpe or Serrano exhibits or to the National Endowment for the Arts' policy of affording grants for works such as these. They preferred to remain silent to the age-old Jewish judgment that art must serve morality.

We have seen that modernism has been realized by Jews, and others, not only along the open by-ways of low-culture but also on high-culture's more restricted avenues. These cases, however, rather than serving as signs of future movement would seem to represent the end of the line. Do Jews really want goddess-feminists or homosexuals as their rabbis, and do they prefer that our most distinguished museum be a meeting place for sexual malcontents or a showplace for the Warhols?[21]

The Parable Today

Alas, many modern Jews, in their search for passion and pleasure and power, have lost themselves in the kingdom of Caesar. Is it not ironic that the descendents of those who wrote the Psalms and offered prayer to the world became, according to all accountings, the least worshipful; those whose ancestors gave themselves to the mastery of the Law were among the most anarchical; those who taught "Thou shalt not" were more alert to the dangers than the benefits of tradition's restraints; and those who revered the sacred became architects of the secular? The chosen people seemed to flatten into normality, becoming what the prophets had warned against: "like all the nations." Perhaps that is why so many young Jews, raised in a society where the profundities and the restraints of Judaism were abandoned, sought the strong communal bonds and the rigid norms that they found in the cults.

A young man once came to a rabbi, complaining, "Rabbi, I have so many worries, my wife, my job, my health. I am terribly worried. What should I do?" "Pray," advised the rabbi. "But I don't know how to pray," answered the young man. "Ah," said the rabbi, "then you really have something to worry about."

Is that not the predicament of the modern Jew?

And, does it not explain the new seriousness about Jewishness, especially among the young? Having explored the kingdom of Caesar to its full and found it wanting, many Jews are inquiring into the kingdom their ancestors once inhabited, the kingdom of God. The postmodern mind is no longer satisfied with the answers of the philosophers or with what the poets, the painters, and even the musicians can offer. The secular divinities they knelt before do not nourish the innermost spirit. They never did. Solutions believed to have resolved all problems proved to be no solutions at all, or, at best, only to lead to further problems; towers built so painstakingly turned to dust; delights that crammed our stomachs can no longer be kept down. And, we are hungry once again for the dry wheat of the spirit.

Many postmodern Jews have discovered a puzzling truth. No license has replaced the Law; no symphony, the Psalms; no chandelier, the Sabbath candles; no opera, Yom Kippur; no country club, the synagogue; no mansion, the home; no Jaguar, a child; no mistress, a wife; no banquet, the Passover seder; no towering metropolis, Jerusalem; no impulse, the joy of doing a mitzvah; no man, God.

Nietzsche said, "God is dead," and Dosteovsky, "If there is no God, all things are possible." Jews have tried all things.

For some time now, those who worshiped the idols in Moscow, Paris, and New York—both the older generation who witness the debris of their youthful fantasies and the younger generation who never knew the fantasy but only see the debris—have begun to wonder if God is truly dead. There is a yearning which will not be silenced by any of the old songs or stilled by any of the old potions.

"What holds one to reality if one's secular system

of meanings prove to be an illusion?" asks former secularist, Daniel Bell.

> I will risk an unfashionable answer–the return of Western society to some conception of religion. . . .
>
> What religion can restore is the continuity of generations, returning us to the existential predicaments which are the ground of humility and care for others.[22]

Religion is not simply magic or illusion. It speaks to the human condition. Religion provides "a set of coherent answers to the core existential questions"–birth, death, success, failure, illness, health, temptation, happiness. It codifies its answers in a creed that has meaning for those who believe in it; it celebrates them in rites that provide an emotional bond for those who participate; and it establishes congregations for those who share this creed and celebration.[23]

This is the terrible dilemma of those who are lost in the wilderness of delight. The fabled supports are gone; dreams have become nightmares, while liberation from restraint and guidance, breaking loose from the yoke of heaven, has made of many, "messengers who have forgotten the message" (Heschel). That is the meaning of the parable with which we began. We have exhausted modernity. We have eaten all the berries we can. We are surfeited. Our souls are sated, and our minds are exploding with passion, power, and pleasure. Now, we seek the recovery of the sacred, the renewal of the transcendent and even the Law.

So we cry, "My Father, My Father!"

Some are fortunate to hear His answer.

But, those who do not may be too distant from His House, too far from His Book, too blinded by prejudice against faith in Him. Then, we can only do what Rabbi Elimelekh warned us to do some two centuries ago: abandon our exploits in the thickets of Caesar's kingdom and run with all our strength, until we find Him Who calls:

"My Child! My Child!"

Endnotes

1. Daniel Bell, *The Winding Passage* (New York: Basic Books, 1976), XI.

2. Ibid., 326.

3. Ibid.

4. Ibid., 327.

5. Ibid., 341

6. Ibid., 343.

7. Daniel Bell, *Cultural Contradictions of Capitalism* (New York: Basic Books, 1976), 72.

8. Bell, *Winding*, 336–38.

9. Ibid., 339–40.

10. Bell, *Cultural*, 140–41.

11. Ibid., 142.

12. *New York Magazine* (2 March 1992): 57.

13. Bell, *Winding*, 344.

14. S. Powers, D. Rothman, and S. Rothman, "Hollywood Movies, Society, and Political Criticism," *The World and I* (April 1991): 563–591.

15. Michael Medved, "Popular Culture and the War Against Standards," *Imprimis* (February 1991): vol. 20, no.2.

16. Cal Thomas, "No Excuse for Sexual Harassment," *Los Angeles Times* Syndicate (11 October 1991).

17. William Rusher, "Princeton Moves on to Ugliness," Newspaper Enterprise Association (28 March 1991).

18. Bell, *Winding*, 287.

19. J. Talmon, "The Jewish Intellectual in Politics," *Midstream* (January 1966): 10.

20. *New York Times*, 19 September 1980.

21. It is of some interest to ponder what form or forms the Jewish reaction against modernism, which has already begun, will take. The eighteenth century heresies of Shabbetai Tzvi and Jacob Frank, for example, were followed by a violent backlash against the Kabbalah, which was viewed by some as the chief culprit, proscribing its dissemination and study and, in some places, pruning the liturgy of its influences.

22. Bell, *Cultural*, 29.

23. Bell, *Winding*, 333–34.

More Good Books from Huntington House

The Best of Human Events
Fifty Years of Conservative Thought and Action

Edited by James C. Roberts

Before Ronald Reagan, before Barry Goldwater, since the closing days of World War II, Human Events stood against the prevailing winds of the liberal political Zeitgeist. Human Events has published the best of three generations of conservative writers—academics, journalists, philosophers, politicians: Frank Chodorov and Richard Weaver, Henry Hazlitt and Hans Sennholz, William F. Buckley and M. Stanton Evans, Jack Kemp and Dan Quayle. A representative sample of their work, marking fifty years of American political and social history, is here collected in a single volume.

ISBN 1-56384-018-9 $34.95 Hardback

Combat Ready
How to Fight the Culture War

by Lynn Stanley

The culture war between traditional values and secular humanism is escalating. At stake are our children. The schools, the liberal media, and even the government, through Outcome Based Education, are indoctrinating our children with moral relativism, instead of moral principles. *Combat Ready* not only discloses the extent to which our society has been influenced by this "anything goes" mentality. It offers sound advice about how parents can protect their children and restore our culture to its biblical foundation.

ISBN 1-56384-074-X $9.99

High on Adventure Stories of Good, Clean, Spine-Tingling Fun

by Stephen Arrington

From meeting a seventeen-and-a-half-foot great white shark face to face, to diving from an airplane toward the earth's surface at 140 MPH, to exploring a sunken battle cruiser from World War II in the dark depths of the South Pacific Ocean, author and adventurer Stephen Arrington retells many exciting tales from his life as a navy frogman and chief diver for the Cousteau Society. Each story is laced with Arrington's Christian belief and outlook that life is an adventure waiting to be had.

ISBN 1-56384-082-0 $7.99

The Media Hates Conservatives: How It Controls the Flow of Information

by Dale A. Berryhill

Here is clear and powerful evidence that the liberal leaning news media brazenly attempted to influence the outcome of the election between President George Bush and Candidate Bill Clinton. Through a careful analysis of television and newspaper coverage, this book confirms a consistent pattern of liberal bias (even to the point of assisting the Clinton campaign). The major media outlets have taken sides in the culture war. Through bias, distortion, and the violation of professional standards, they have opposed the traditional values embraced by conservatives and most Americans, to the detriment of our country.

ISBN 1-56384-060-X $9.99

The Assault: Liberalism's Attack on Religion, Freedom, and Democracy

by Dale A. Berryhill

In *The Liberal Contradiction,* Berryhill showed just how ludicrous it is when civil rights advocates are racists and feminists are sexists. Now he turns to much more disturbing phenomena, revisiting such issues as censorship, civil rights, gay rights, and political correctness in education and offering commentary and punishment, civil liberties, multiculturalism, and religious freedom. Fortunately, the American people are catching on to the hypocrisy. Still, the culture war is far from over.

ISBN 1-56384-077-4 $9.99

Please Tell Me . . . Questions People Ask about Freemasonry—and the Answers

by Tom C. McKenney

Since the publication of his first book, *The Deadly Deception*, Tom McKenney has appeared on over 200 talk shows, answering tough questions about Freemasonry from viewers and audiences throughout the USA and Canada. Now, in his latest book, McKenney has compiled the questions most often asked by the public concerning the cult-like nature and anti-Christian activities of the Masonic movement. McKenney tackles topics, such as; Masonry's occult roots; Death Oaths and Masonic Execution; Masonry and the Illuminati; and Masonry's opposition to Christian schools. Tom McKenney warns Christians of all denominations to extricate themselves from Masonic movements.

ISBN 1-56384-013-8 $9.99

One Man, One Woman, One Lifetime
An Argument for Moral Tradition

by Reuven Bulka

Lifestyles that have been recognized since antiquity as destructive and immoral are promoted today as acceptable choices. Rabbi Reuven Bulka challenges the notion that contemporary society has outgrown the need for moral guidelines. Using both scientific research and classical biblical precepts, he examines changing sexual mores and debunks the arguments offered by activists and the liberal media.

ISBN 1-56384-079-0 $7.99

Hungry for God
Are the Poor Really Unspiritual?

by Larry E. Myers

Inspired by the conviction that the blood of Jesus is the great equalizer, Larry Myers set out to bring much-needed hope and relief to the desperately poor of Mexico. You will be deeply moved by these people, who have so little yet worship their Lord and Savior, even in the midst of their need. You will be inspired by Larry Myers's determination to bring not only medical supplies and food, but light and life to those hungry for God.

ISBN 1056384-075-8 $9.99

How to Homeschool (Yes, You!)

by Julia Toto

Have you considered homeschooling for your children, but you just don't know where to begin? This book is the answer to your prayer. It will cover topics, such as; what's the best curriculum for your children; where to find the right books; if certified teachers teach better than stay-at-home moms; and what to tell your mother-in-law.

ISBN 1-56384-059-6 $4.99

The Dark Side of Freemasonry

by Ed Decker

This book is probably the most significant document ever prepared on the subject of the dark side of the Masonic Lodge. In June 1993, a group of Christian researchers, teachers, and ministry leaders met in Knoxville, Tennessee, to gather together all available information on the subject of Freemasonry and its relationship to the Christian world. Ed Decker brought this explosive material back from Knoxville and here presents it as a warning to those who are unaware of the danger of the Masonic movement.

ISBN 1-56384-061-8 $9.99

Conservative, American & Jewish— I Wouldn't Have It Any Other Way

by Jacob Neusner

Neusner has fought on the front lines of the culture war and here writes reports about sectors of the battles. He has taken a consistent, conservative position in the academy, federal agencies in the humanities and the arts, and in the world of religion in general and Judaism in particular. Engaging, persuasive, controversial in the best sense, these essays set out to change minds and end up touching the hearts and souls of their readers.

ISBN 1-56384-048-0 $9.99

America Betrayed

by Marlin Maddoux

This hard-hitting book exposes the forces in our country which seek to destroy the family, the schools, our culture, and our values. The author details exactly how the news media manipulates your mind. Maddoux is the host of the popular national radio talk show "Point of View."

Gays & Guns
The Case against Homosexuals in the Military

by John Eidsmoe, Ph.D.

The homosexual revolution seeks to overthrow the Laws of Nature. A Lieutenant Colonel in the United States Air Force Reserve, Dr. John Eidsmoe eloquently contends that admitting gays into the military would weaken the combat effectiveness of our armed forces. This cataclysmic step would also legitimize homosexuality, a lifestyle that most Americans know is wrong. While echoing Cicero's assertion that "a sense of what is right is common to all mankind," Eidsmoe rationally defends his belief. There are laws that govern the universe, he reminds us. Laws that compel the earth to rotate on its axis, laws that govern the economy; and so there is also a moral law that governs man's nature. The violation of this moral law is physically, emotionally and spiritually destructive. It is destructive to both the individual and to the community of which he is a member.

ISBN Trade Paper 1-56384-043-X $7.99
ISBN Hardcover 1-56384-046-4 $14.99

The Parched Soul of America: A Poet's View on Our National Decay

by Leslie Kay Hedger with David Reagan

With breathtaking eloquence and astonishing accuracy, modern-day Isaiah and poet Leslie Kay Hedger demonstrates the stagnancy of America's once-majestic image. Using her pen as a weapon, the poet exposes and attacks the forces undermining our culture: Political decadence; the disintegration of the family; and materialism, hedonism, and religious apostasy. America is a nation in rebellion against God. The writer's heartfelt message: **"Turn from your wicked ways and live!"**

ISBN 1-56384-078-2 $10.99

Political Correctness: The Cloning of the American Mind

by David Thibodaux, Ph.D.

The author, a professor of literature at the University of Southwestern Louisiana, confronts head on the movement that is now being called Political Correctness. Political correctness, says Thibodaux, "is an umbrella under which advocates of civil rights, gay and lesbian rights, feminism, and environmental causes have gathered." To incur the wrath of these groups, one only has to disagree with them on political, moral, or social issues. To express traditionally Western concepts in universities today can result in not only ostracism, but even suspension. (According to a recent "McNeil-Lehrer News Hour" report, one student was suspended for discussing the reality of the moral law with an avowed homosexual. He was reinstated only after he apologized.)

ISBN 1-56384-026-X Trade Paper $9.99

Kinsey, Sex and Fraud: The Indoctrination of a People

by Dr. Judith A. Reisman and Edward Eichel

Kinsey, Sex and Fraud describes the research of Alfred Kinsey which shaped Western society's beliefs and understanding of the nature of human sexuality. His unchallenged conclusions are taught at every level of education—elementary, high school, and college—and quoted in textbooks as undisputed truth. The authors clearly demonstrate that Kinsey's research involved illegal experimentations on several hundred children. The survey was carried out on a non-representative group of Americans, including disproportionately large numbers of sex offenders, prostitutes, prison inmates, and exhibitionists.

ISBN 0-910311-20-X $10.99

I Shot an Elephant in My Pajamas—The Morrie Ryskind Story

by Morrie Ryskind with John H. M. Roberts

The Morrie Ryskind story is a classic American success story. The son of Russian Jewish immigrants, Ryskind went on to attend Columbia University and achieve legendary fame on Broadway and in Hollywood, win the Pulitzer Prize, and become a noted nationally syndicated columnist. Writing with his legendary theatrical collaborators George S. Kaufman and George and Ira Gershwin, their political satires had an enormous impact on the development of the musical comedy. In Hollywood, many classic films and four of the Marx Brothers' sublime romps also bear the signatory stamp of genius—Morrie Ryskind. Forced by his increasingly conservative views to abandon script-writing in Hollywood, Ryskind had the satisfaction near the end of his life to welcome into his home his old friend, the newly elected President of the United States, Ronald Reagan.

ISBN 1-56384-000-6 $12.99

Homeless in America: The Solution

by Jeremy Reynalds

Author Jeremy Reynalds' current shelter, Joy Junction, located in Albuquerque, New Mexico, has become the state's largest homeless shelter. Beginning with fifty dollars in his pocket and a lot of compassion, Jeremy Reynalds now runs a shelter that has a yearly budget of over $600,000. He receives no government or United Way funding. Anyone who desires to help can, says Reynalds. If you feel a burden to help those less fortunate than you, read this book.

ISBN 1-56384-063-4 $9.99

Don't Touch That Dial: The Impact of the Media on Children and the Family

by Barbara Hattemer & Robert Showers

Men and women without any stake in the outcome of the war between the pornographers and our families have come to the qualified, professional agreement that media does have an effect on our children—an effect that is devastatingly significant. Highly respected researchers, psychologists, and sociologists join the realm of pediatricians, district attorneys, parents, teachers, pastors, and community leaders—who have diligently remained true to the fight against filthy media—in their latest comprehensive critique of the modern media establishment (i.e., film, television, print, art, curriculum).

ISBN Trade Paper 1-56384-032-4 $9.99
ISBN Hardcover 1-56384-035-9 $19.99

The Extermination of Christianity-A Tyranny of Consensus

by Paul Schenck with Robert L. Schenck

If you are a Christian, you might be shocked to discover that: Popular music, television, and motion pictures are consistently depicting you as a stooge, a hypocrite, a charlatan, a racist, an anti-Semite, or a con artist; you could be expelled from a public high school for giving Christian literature to a classmate; and you could be arrested and jailed for praying on school grounds. This book is a catalogue of anti-Christian propaganda—a record of persecution before it happens!

ISBN 1-56384-051-0 $9.99

Journey into Darkness: Nowhere to Land

by Stephen L. Arrington

This story begins on Hawaii's glistening sands and ends in the mysterious deep with the Great White Shark. In between, he found himself trapped in the drug smuggling trade—unwittingly becoming the "Fall Guy" in the highly publicized John Z. DeLorean drug case. Naval career shattered, his youthful innocence tested, and friends and family put to the test of loyalty, Arrington locked on one truth during his savage stay in prison and endeavors to share that critical truth now. Focusing on a single important message to young people—to stay away from drugs—the author recounts his horrifying prison experience and allows the reader to take a peek at the source of hope and courage that helped him survive.

ISBN 1-56384-003-3 $9.99

New Gods for a New Age

by Richmond Odom

There is a new state religion in this country. The gods of this new religion are Man, Animals, and Earth. Its roots are deeply embedded in Hinduism and other Eastern religions. The author of *New Gods for a New Age* contends that this new religion has become entrenched in our public and political institutions and is being aggressively imposed on all of us. This humanistic-evolutionary world view has carried great destruction in its path which can be seen in college classrooms where Christianity is belittled, in the courtroom where good is called evil and evil is called good, and in government where the self-interest of those who wield political power is served as opposed to the common good.

ISBN 1-56384-062-6 $9.99

When the Wicked Seize a City

by Chuck & Donna McIlhenny with Frank York

A highly publicized lawsuit . . . a house fire-bombed in the night . . . the shatter of windows smashed by politically (and wickedly) motivated vandals cuts into the night . . . All because Chuck McIlhenny voiced God's condemnation of a behavior and life-style and protested the destruction of society that results from its practice. That behavior is homosexuality, and that life-style is the gay culture. This book explores: the rise of gay power and what it will mean if Christians do not organize and prepare for the battle, and homosexual attempts to have the American Psychiatric Association remove pedophilia from the list of mental illnesses (now they want homophobia declared a disorder).

ISBN 1-56384-024-3 $9.99

Heresy Hunters: Character Assassination in the Church

James R. Spencer

An alarming error is sweeping the Christian Church. A small, self-appointed band is confusing Bible-scholarship with character assassination. These *Heresy Hunters* fail to distinguish between genuine error and Christian diversity and turn on their brothers in an ungodly feeding frenzy. Jim Spencer suggests that the heresy hunters themselves might be the real heretics, because their misguided zeal risks splitting the church. He calls upon them to abandon their inquisition.

ISBN 1-56384-042-1 $8.99

Hitler and the New Age

by Bob Rosio

Hail Caesar! Heil Hitler! Hail—who? Who will be next? Many recognize Caesar and Nero and Hitler as forerunners of the future, when one leader, backed by one government and religious church, will lead one worldwide system. The question is, Were they all tools to prepare the way for the very old and evil world order? Bob Rosio believes that studying an extreme type of historical figure, such as Hitler, will help Christians better understand and better prepare a battle plan to stand against the New Age movement and this emerging world order. He describes this book as "a study in the mechanics of evil."

ISBN 1-56384-009-X $9.99

Dinosaurs and the Bible

by David W. Unfred

Every reader, young and old, will be fascinated by this ever-mysterious topic—exactly what happened to the dinosaurs? Author David Unfred draws a very descriptive picture of the history and fate of the dinosaurs, using the Bible as a reference guide. Did dinosaurs really exist? Does the Bible mention dinosaurs? What happened to dinosaurs, or are there some still living, awaiting discovery?

ISBN Hardcover 0-910311-70-6 $12.99

Exposing the AIDS Scandal

by Dr. Paul Cameron

Where do you turn when those who control the flow of information in this country withhold the truth? Why is the national media hiding facts from the public? Can AIDS be spread in ways we're not being told? Finally, a book that gives you a total account for the AIDS epidemic, and what steps can be taken to protect yourself. What you don't know can kill you!

ISBN 0-910311-52-8 $7.99

God's Rebels

by Henry Lee Curry III

From his unique perspective, Dr. Henry Lee Curry III offers a fascinating look at the lives of some of our greatest Southern religious leaders during the Civil War. The rampant Evangelical Christianity prominent at the outbreak of the Civil War, asserts Dr. Curry, is directly traceable to the 2nd Great Awakening of the early 1800s. The evangelical tradition, with its emphasis on strict morality, individual salvation, and emotional worship, had influenced most of Southern Protestantism by this time. Southerners unquestionably believed the voice of the ministers to be the "voice of God"; consequently, the church became one of the most powerful forces influencing Confederate life and morale. Inclined toward a Calvinistic emphasis on predestination, the South was confident that God would sustain its way of life.

ISBN: Trade Paper 0-910311-67-6 $12.99
ISBN: Hardcover 0-910311-68-4 $21.99

Goddess Earth— Exposing the Pagan Agenda of the Environmental Movement

by Samantha Smith

There's a new powerhouse in Washington, wielding ominous influence in Congress—it's called the Environmental movement. Its roots are pagan and its agenda is conspicuously anti—Christian. We should be concerned that the recurring theme of Earth Day and Earth Summit was World Government and a New World Order. The Environmental movement, says Samantha Smith, is a very powerful force attempting to implement World Government.

ISBN 1-56384-064-2 $9.99

America: Awaiting the Verdict

by Mike Fuselier

We are a nation stricken with an infectious disease. The disease is called betrayal—we are a nation that has denied, rejected, and betrayed our Christian past. The symptoms of the disease are many and multiplying daily. Mike Fuselier, thus, encourages Americans to return to the faith of their founding fathers—the faith upon which our law and government rests—or suffer the consequences. To prove that our forebearers were in no way attempting to establish a secular state, as contended by secular humanists, the author presents oft-forgotten but crucial evidence to fortify his—and all Christians'—case.

ISBN 1-56384-034-0 $5.99

The Liberal Contradiction

by Dale A. Berryhill

Why are liberals who took part in student demonstrations in the 1960s now trying to stop Operation Rescue from using the very same tactics? Liberalism claims to advocate some definite moral positions: racism and sexism are wrong; tolerance is right; harming the environment is wrong; protecting it is right. But, contemporary liberalism is undermining its own moral foundation. It contends that its positions are morally right and the opposites are wrong, while at the same time, it denies that a moral law (right and wrong) exists. This is the **Liberal Contradiction** and it leads to many ludicrous (and laughable) inconsistencies.

ISBN 1-56384-055-3 $9.99

Out of Control— Who's Watching Our Child Protection Agencies?

by Brenda Scott

This book of horror stories is true. The deplorable and unauthorized might of Child Protection Services is capable of reaching into and destroying any home in America. No matter how innocent and happy your family may be, you are one accusation away from disaster. Social workers are allowed to violate constitutional rights and often become judge, jury, and executioner. Innocent parents may appear on computer registers and be branded "child abuser" for life. Every year, it is estimated that over 1 million people are falsely accused of child abuse in this country. You could be next, says author and speaker Brenda Scott.

ISBN 1-56384-069-3 $9.99

Subtle Serpent: New Age in the Classroom

by Darylann Whitemarsh & Bill Reisman

There is a new morality being taught to our children in public schools. Without the consent or even awareness of parents—educators and social engineers are aggressively introducing new moral codes to our children. In most instances, these new moral codes contradict traditional values. Darylann Whitemarsh (a 1989 Teacher of the Year recipient) and Bill Reisman (educator and expert on the occult) combine their knowledge to expose the deliberate madness occurring in our public schools.

ISBN 1-56384-016-2 $9.99

Beyond Political Correctness: Are There Limits to This Lunacy?

by David Thibodaux, Ph.D.

Author of the best-selling *Political Correctness: The Cloning of the American Mind,* Dr. David Thibodaux now presents his long awaited sequel—*Beyond Political Correctness: Are There Limits to This Lunacy?* The politically correct movement has now moved beyond college campuses. The movement has succeeded in turning the educational system of this country into a system of indoctrination. Its effect on education was predictable: steadily declining scores on every conceivable test which measures student performance; and, increasing numbers of college freshmen who know a great deal about condoms, homosexuality, and abortion, but whose basic skills in language, math, and science are alarmingly deficient.

ISBN 1-56384-066-9 $9.99

"Soft Porn" Plays Hardball

by Dr. Judith A. Reisman

With amazing clarity, the author demonstrates that pornography imposes on society a view of women and children that encourages violence and sexual abuse. As crimes against women and children increase to alarming proportions, it's of paramount importance that we recognize the cause of this violence. Pornography should be held accountable for the havoc it has wreaked in our homes and our country.

ISBN Trade Paper 0-910311-65-X $8.99
ISBN Hardcover 0-910311-92-7 $16.99

A Jewish Conservative Looks at Pagan America

by Don Feder

With eloquence and insight that rival contemporary commentators and essayists of antiquity, Don Feder's pen finds his targets in the enemies of God, family, and American tradition and morality. Deftly . . . delightfully . . . the master allegorist and Titian with a typewriter brings clarity to the most complex sociological issues and invokes giggles and wry smiles from both followers and foes. Feder is Jewish to the core, and he finds in his Judaism no inconsistency with an American Judeo-Christian ethic. Questions of morality plague school administrators, district court judges, senators, congressmen, parents, and employers; they are wrestling for answers in a "changing world." Feder challenges this generation and directs inquirers to the original books of wisdom: the Torah and the Bible.

ISBN 1-56384-036-7 Trade Paper $9.99
ISBN 1-56384-037-5 Hardcover $19.99

A Call to Manhood: In a Fatherless Society

by David E. Long

Western society is crumbling—from the collapse of the family...to our ailing economic system, from the scandals in the church...to the corruptions in the Halls of Congress, from the decline of business...to the pollution of Hollywood, everywhere, we see moral and societal decay. The reason, says author David Long, is that the vast majority of men in America have received tragically inadequate fathering, ranging from an ineffective father to no father at all. This book presents a refreshing vision and a realistic strategy for men to recapture their biblical masculinity.

ISBN 1-56384-047-2 $9.99

Delicate Balance

by John Zajac

Find out what forces in the universe are at work and why the earth is in a very delicate balance. The author displays his research to present the overall picture at hand that packages and interconnects economics, prophecy, ecology, militarism, and theology. Can modern science unlock the mysteries of the future? Can we determine our own fate—or are we part of a larger scheme beyond our control?

ISBN 0-910311-57-9 $8.99

Hidden Dangers of the Rainbow

by Constance Cumbey

The first book to uncover and expose the New Age movement, this national #1 best-seller paved the way for all other books on the subject. It has become a giant in its category. This book provides the vivid expose of the New Age movement, which the author contends is dedicated to wiping out Christianity and establishing a one world order. This movement, a vast network of occult and pagan organizations, meets the tests of prophecy concerning the Antichrist.

ISBN 0-910311-03-X $9.99

New World Order: The Ancient Plan of Secret Societies

by William T. Still

For thousands of years, secret societies have cultivated an ancient plan which has powerfully influenced world events. Until now, this secret plan has remained hidden from view. This book presents new evidence that a military take-over of the U.S. was considered by some in the administration of one of our recent presidents. Although averted, the forces behind it remain in secretive positions of power.

ISBN 0-910311-64-1 $8.99

The Salt Series

To Moroni With Love

by Ed Decker

Readers are led through the deepest of the Mormon church doctrines and encouraged to honestly determine whether the words can be construed as heresy in light of the true, or as unadulterated language of the Bible. Decker reveals shocking material that has caused countless Mormons to question the church leaders and abandon Mormonism's false teachings.

ISBN 1-56384-021-9 $2.99

Exposing the AIDS Scandal

by Paul Cameron, M.D.

AIDS is 100 percent fatal all of the time. There are believed to be over 1,500,000 people in the United States carrying the AIDS virus. The ever-growing number of cases compels us to question whether there will be a civilization in twenty years.

ISBN 1-56384-023-5 $2.99

Inside the New Age Nightmare

by Randall Baer

Are your children safe from the New Age movement? This former New Age leader, one of the world's foremost experts in crystals, brings to light the darkest of the darkness that surrounds the New Age movement. The week that Randall Baer's original book was released, he met with a puzzling and untimely death—his car ran off a mountain pass. His death is still regarded as suspicious.

ISBN 1-56384-022-7 $2.99

The Question of Freemasonry

by Ed Decker

Blood oaths, blasphemy, and illegal activity—in this day and age it's hard to believe these aberrations still exist; this booklet demonstrates that the Freemasons are not simply a "goodwill," community-oriented organization.

ISBN 1-56384-020-0 $2.99